THE WAY OF THE SPIRIT

A Bible Reading Guide and Commentary

THE WAY OF THE SPIRIT

A Bible Reading Guide and Commentary

Vol. 3

HEIRS OF THE PROPHETS

**The Prophets
(1 Samuel – 2 Kings and Isaiah – Malachi)
Luke's Gospel
Selections from Acts and the Epistles
Revelation**

JOHN McKAY

Collins

Marshall Pickering

William Collins Sons & Co. Ltd
London · Glasgow · Sydney · Auckland
Toronto · Johannesburg

First published in Great Britain in 1990 by
Marshall Pickering

Marshall Pickering is an imprint of
Collins Religious Division,
part of the Collins Publishing Group
8 Grafton Street, London W1X 3LA

British Library Cataloguing in Publication Data
McKay, John
   The way of the spirit
   Vol 3: Heirs of the prophets
   1. Bible
   I. Title

   ISBN 0–551–01944–1

Phototypeset in Linotron Times by
Input Typesetting Ltd, London

Printed and bound in Great Britain by
Billings & Sons Ltd, Worcester

With gratitude to God for all who have
taught me the ways of the Spirit,
encouraged me in his gifts,
and sustained me with prophetic words.

*I wish all the LORD's people were prophets and that the
LORD would put his Spirit on them!*

(Num. 11.29)

*All the prophets from Samuel on, as many as have spoken,
have foretold these days. And you are heirs of the prophets.*

(Acts 3.24f)

Contents

Contents

List of Maps, Charts and Diagrams

List of Maps, Charts and Diagrams

Acknowledgements

Christianity is at heart a charismatic faith continuous with the faith and experience of the Old Testament prophets. That in a nutshell was what I began to appreciate after coming into contact with the work of the Holy Spirit through charismatic renewal in the 1970's. I tried then to write a book like this, but never seemed able to express with satisfaction what I wanted to say. When I complained about that to my wife, Marguerite, she simply said, "You won't be able to write about it until you have lived in the experience of it in a prophetic community yourself." And that is precisely what the Lord has graciously allowed us to do over the past seven years, both in St. Ninian's Scottish Episcopal Church in Prestwick and here at Roffey Place. These have been invaluable times, because in them I have witnessed elements from the whole spectrum of prophetic/charismatic life as described in the pages of both Testaments. Much of the renewal that is occurring in our churches today has a similar feel about it. My thanks therefore to all who have enabled me to enjoy the richness of such living experience.

Thanks also to Pete Goddard once more for the cover design, with its illustration this time symbolising the wind of God's Spirit turning and bringing alive the pages of the Bible. And my thanks again to Marguerite for her work on the manuscript and proofs, but more than that, to both her and my sons for their enthusiasm that sustains me so well.

John McKay
6th May 1989.

Preface

The secret of the Lord *is with them that fear him.*
(Ps. 25.14, AV)

The secret things belong to the Lord *our God, but the things revealed belong to us and to our children for ever.*
(Deut. 29.29)

Surely the Sovereign Lord *does nothing without revealing his plan (secret) to his servants the prophets.* (Amos 3.7)

We speak of God's secret wisdom, a wisdom that has been hidden and that God destined for our glory before time began. God has revealed it to us by his Spirit.
(1 Cor. 2.7,10)

This book is about a secret, the secret of the Lord, lost to men because of sin, but revealed now in Christ. Searching for the meaning of the Bible, of life, of God, of Christ is always more than a matter of academic research. It is a deep longing of heart. And so it will be until the Lord graciously unveils his secret to us by his Spirit.

Baptism in the Spirit causes us to know God as a loving Father, and to see Jesus step out of history and draw close in a strongly personal way. It also introduced me to a company of believers I had formerly found totally enigmatic, Christians who understood the things of God with an assurance I wanted to dismiss as arrogant. But it was not arrogance. It was that they too had learned the secret of the Lord.

I was now reading my Bible with fresh liveliness and clarity and soon realised that that was largely because my new circle of friends included men like the patriarchs, prophets and apostles. They too had been taught the secret. They were kindred spirits. We spoke the same language, shared the same experiences and hopes, understood the same vision. I had linked hands across the centuries with men who had seen all the LORD was now showing me, and a lot more besides. They were not just ancients groping after truths that we understand better today, but men I could learn from, to whom God had also revealed his secret.

Then I saw it was God's desire that all his people should receive this same revelation from the Spirit, and that I should become a witness of the things he had shown me. That is why I have written this book. It does not purport to give all the answers, nor to say anything new. It is only written to share the secret I have learned from God. Please read it as such and be encouraged. We are still heirs of the prophets. The secret they learned remains our inheritance.

The Overall Plan of Study

This volume is the third in a series of four covering the whole Bible. Each deals with a successive period of Old Testament history, concentrates on the books of the Old Testament associated with that period and examines particular aspects of faith related to it. Each volume then traces the sequel to the story told in the Old Testament section through books of the New Testament that seem to provide an appropriate follow up, and in doing so separately examines one of the four well-known portraits of Jesus as Priest, King, Prophet and Lord.

The Purpose of the Series

The purpose is to provide a commentary-guide to the Way of the Spirit through the Bible. Christians who have been influenced over the past 20–30 years by the Charismatic Movement have often spoken to me of a need for some such guide, one that would help them to understand their Bibles better in the light of their experience of the Spirit, and one that would help them to relate their Bible-reading to such matters as the Spirit's ways, the power of faith, the dynamic of the word, revival, healing, and so forth – in fact

		VOL. 1 THE CALL AND THE CROSS	VOL. 2 TIMES OF REFRESHING	VOL. 3 HEIRS OF THE PROPHETS	VOL. 4 MY LORD AND MY GOD
O L D	T E S T A M E N T	2000–1230 BC The Pentateuch Faith, obedience and sacrifice	1230–500 BC The Histories The Kingdom, revival and Messianic hope	1050–400 BC The Prophets Prophecy, revival and charismatic faith	600–0 BC The Writings The Lordship of God in history, worship and belief
N E W	T E S T A M E N T	Mark Romans and Hebrews Jesus as Priest	Matthew Acts and Paul's mission letters Jesus as King	Luke Selection from Acts & various epistles, Revelation Jesus as Prophet	John 1–3 John, Paul's captivity & pastoral letters, James, Peter & Jude Jesus as Lord

everything that relates to personal experience of God in the life of the believer. We shall therefore be endeavouring, as we trace the Bible stories, to lay bare the heart that pulsates within giving them life, to tap their dynamic source – which is, of course, the Spirit of God himself.

As we study the history of Israel, we shall see how, unlike secular history, it is very much a story about God's dealings with men. When we trace the accounts of individual lives, we shall find they too are stories about the working of God's Spirit in transforming men. And throughout we shall also discover just how much the Bible does delight in the very things many Christians love to hear about in the Church today: the miraculous, the prophetic, the visionary, the love and fellowship of Spirit-filled believers, and so forth.

Our aim is therefore to examine the foundations of Christian faith, vision and experience in Scripture. Hence, alongside the chronological and topical arrangement of each volume outlined above, there is another more embracing pattern relating to our overall purpose:
– Vol. 1 outlines the basic principles on which all Christian life and experience need to be founded: faith in God's promises, obedience to his call and acknowledgment of the saving power of Christ's sacrifice.

– Vol. 2 traces the main movements of revival in Biblical history, thus highlighting the principles by which God's kingdom operates and outlining the challenges and vision that inspire all men of the Spirit.

– Vol. 3 examines the experiences and teachings of prophets and other men of the Spirit in both Testaments more directly, demonstrating how their faith and vision are of the very essence of Biblical hope.

– Vol. 4 looks at the common approaches of Spirit-filled Christians and the Bible to worship, service, pastoral matters, the challenges of daily living, and the like.

How to approach the Way of the Spirit in the Bible

These books are written as Bible-reading guides, hence for use in conjunction with the Bible. (A simple reading scheme is provided on pp. 263–9.) As you read the Scriptures, besides looking to the notes for guidance, expect the Holy Spirit himself to interpret what you read and more than that, to lead you to the very source of his truth in the life of God himself. Remember the words of our Lord Jesus: 'You diligently study the Scriptures because you think that by them you possess eternal life. These are the Scriptures that testify about me, yet you refuse to come to me to have life.' (John 5.39f)

The Bible can be read both for its information about the things of God and also for the enjoyment of its life. The first is theology, but on its own that can become the letter that kills, and so it needs to be coupled with the second, for 'the word of God is living and active . . . it penetrates even to dividing soul and spirit . . . it judges the thoughts and attitudes of the heart.' (Heb. 4.12) Our theology has to be living, and it is only the Spirit that gives life.

Paul speaks about the difference between reading Scripture with and without the illumination of the Holy Spirit in 2 Cor. 3.14–18, where he says that those who read without the Spirit do so with a veil over the eyes. 'But,' he continues, 'whenever anyone turns to the Lord, the veil is taken away.' Then he adds, 'Now the Lord is the Spirit . . .' and this 'comes from the Lord, who is the Spirit'. This removal of a veil is something Christians commonly experience after baptism with the Holy Spirit, and so my prayer is that you, the reader, will also know it being lifted as the Spirit enlightens God's Word for you.

Don't allow yourself to become too preoccupied with small details, the precise interpretation of individual passages, words or phrases, complex historical or theological issues, and the like, but rather see yourself walking on the stage of the ancient world, first with the men of Old Testament times, and then with Jesus and his disciples. Go with Jesus around Galilee, listen to him speaking, participate in the astonishment and excitement of the crowd, share in the puzzlement and the illumination of his disciples, get the feel of what you read. The information given in these pages is mainly intended to help you lay hold of that 'feel' for yourself, particularly as it relates to the vision, the power and the life of God these men of old knew.

Read your Bible in something like the way you would read a novel or watch a play. Take yourself into the life of its drama and let the feel of that life flow through your life as you walk and talk with the ancient men of God and with Jesus. Lay hold of their vision and let it become yours as well. Let their longings be your longings and their joys your joys, for therein lies the life God wants you to know in Christ.

All Biblical quotations are taken from the New International Version of the Bible. To avoid confusion, the conventions of the NIV translators have also been adhered to beyond the quotations, e.g., 'he' rather than 'He' for God, 'the Most Holy Place' rather than 'the Holy of Holies', 'Spirit' (of God) rather than 'spirit' in the Old Testament (contrast RSV).

PART ONE

INTRODUCTION

1

The Spirit and the Word

The Spirit and the Word are like two hands God uses to perform all he has to do in relation to mankind and his world. Both were operative in creation (Gen. 1.2–3; Ps. 33.6) and have been active in all history ever since. There have, however, been times when they have been more noticeably at work among God's people than at others, and particularly when the LORD has raised up prophets, people he has empowered with his Spirit to speak his word. Our purpose is to trace their history and see how it relates to Christian living today.

In Num. 11.29 we find Moses saying to Joshua, 'I wish all the LORD's people were prophets and that the LORD would put his Spirit on them!' Our story will take us from that primitive longing, through the birth of prophecy in Samuel's day, down the centuries of Israel's kings to the time of the great writing prophets, on into the prophetic ministry of Jesus and the New Testament Church, ending finally with a glance at the early post-Biblical period. And our primary purpose in tracing this story will be to show how fully we as Christians are 'heirs of the prophets' of old and how akin our faith and our experience is, or should be, to theirs.

Altogether we shall be spanning about 1,500 years, and so it is important right from the start that we have some simplified, overall perspective on the history of these centuries – that is as the Bible views them, since it is the Biblical story we are following here.

1. THE DRAMA OF SALVATION

*All the prophets from Samuel on, as many as have spoken,
have foretold these days. And you are heirs of the prophets
and of the covenant God made with your fathers. He said
to Abraham, 'Through your offspring all peoples on earth
will be blessed.'*

(Acts 3.24f)

What follows here is neither intended to be comprehensive
(for example, it says nothing about worship in Israel), nor
to imply that the Bible is merely a fictitious play. It is simply
an attempt, through a schematic overview, to show the
prophets' place in the history and development of God's
purposes.

Imagine you are at the theatre. Before the curtain rises
a narrator appears on stage to explain the background to
the play you are going to see. He does so by reciting Gen.
1–11.

Prologue: 'Paradise Lost' (Gen. 1–11)

When God first made the earth, 'he saw that it was good,'
indeed 'very good' (1.4,10,12,18,21,25,31). The goodness of
his purpose is clearly illustrated in the description of the
Garden of Eden, a place of rustic idyll and harmony, a kind
of everyman's Paradise. But man chose other ways than
God's and lost it all. Sin, suffering and death multiplied,
until 'God saw how corrupt the earth had become' and 'his
heart was filled with pain' (6.12,6). He showed his judgment
by sending the Flood, but sin continued to multiply, culminating in the Babel disaster which has resulted in total alien-
ation of man from both God and his fellow men.

Can God rescue his world? And if so, how? Or will sin
continue to thwart his original good purposes? Such are the
dramatic questions our play will seek to answer.

ACT 1: The Covenant with Abraham – God's Call and Promise (Gen. 12–50; c. 2000–1300 BC)

Gen. 12: God calls Abraham and promises him land, descendants and through them restoration of blessing to 'all the families of the earth.' Abraham follows the LORD and comes to Canaan.

But – He and his descendants have to learn, often through hard trials and even failures, to trust these promises. They are partially fulfilled at first when children are born in Canaan, but faith remains a problem and Act 1 ends with them in Egypt, out of the land of promise and in slavery.

Q. Is God's will to go on being thwarted by man's unfaithfulness?

A. Perhaps not. The curtain descends on Joseph, now an old man on his death-bed, looking forward in hope as he reminds his brothers of the promises God gave Abraham (Gen. 50.24). But it is now clear that they also need more help from God.

ACT 2: The Covenant with Moses – God's Word is revealed (Exodus – 1 Samuel; c. 1300–1000 BC)

Exod. 3 & 20: God calls Moses, through whom he leads the Israelites out of Egypt. At Sinai he gives the Law, his word by which they may live in continued blessing through obedience. After much rebellion and a disciplinary forty years in the wilderness, Joshua successfully leads them into their promised inheritance in Canaan.

But – In the period of the judges Israel goes after other gods and is consequently oppressed by enemies, finally ending up enslaved again, this time by the Philistines.

Q. Is God's will still to be thwarted by man's failure?

A. As the curtain goes down this time we again see signs of hope as God's Spirit begins to stir in men raising up prophets (Samuel and others) and even a king (Saul).

ACT 3: The Covenant with David – God's Spirit is revealed (1 Samuel – 2 Kings; c. 1000–540 BC)

2 Sam. 7: The Israelites thought a king would solve their problems, but Saul's reign ended in disaster. God then called David and promised him peace, greatness and eternal rule for his descendants. Initially there was evidence of success when he established an empire and when the reign of his son, Solomon, recaptured many of the glories of Eden (1 Kings 4.20f).

But – Solomon and his successors repeatedly turned to other gods. The kingdom split and gradually disintegrated, until the Northern Kingdom (Israel/Ephraim) fell to the Assyrians in 722 and the Southern (Judah) to the Babylonians in 597. Jerusalem was destroyed in 587 and Act 3 ends with Israel in exile in Babylonia, back in bondage again.

Q. Has God's will been finally brought to nothing?

A. Towards the end of this act we begin to hear again a growing voice of hope as the prophets speak about another covenant, a 'New Covenant', by which man's heart will be changed through the working of God's Spirit. The new age of this covenant is to be inaugurated by a Spirit-bearing man, who will later be known as Messiah (cp. Hos. 2; Isa. 9–12; 60–62; Jer. 31,33; Ezek. 36–37).

ACT 4: The Close of the Old Age – a Time of Waiting (Ezra, Nehemiah, etc.; 540–5 BC)

When the Persians overthrew the Babylonian Empire in 539, Jews began returning to Israel and a community was restored around Jerusalem. Its initial enthusiasm was greatly encouraged by the prophets Haggai, Zechariah and others.

But – There was no real evidence of the Old Covenant promises coming to fulfilment. The voice of prophecy fell silent in the fourth century and Jewish religion became increasingly legalistic and ritualistic. After the Persians, the Greeks ruled Palestine, and then, after a brief spell of independence in the second century, the Romans took over.

Q. Had the great purpose of God finally come to stagnation? Had it even fizzled out altogether?

A. The Jews never believed so. At first their prophets maintained them in hope and, when the prophetic voice died, they simply settled down quietly to wait for Messiah and the new age of the Spirit. Also, thanks to their exile Jews were now strategically placed in all major centres of civilization, preparing the world for the coming of Christianity.

ACT 5: The New Covenant – The Dawn of the Age of the Spirit (The New Testament; 5 BC – today)

Jesus comes, born of the Spirit, filled with the Spirit, teaching and performing wonders in the anointing of the Spirit, like one of the prophets of old, yet with a power and authority hitherto unknown to men. He gathers disciples, trains them in his gospel-message and prepares them for the moment when they will themselves be endued with the Spirit, that is, for the long awaited time of the fulfilling of the New Covenant promise proclaimed by the prophets of the Old.

After Pentecost, the disciples, now prophets themselves, filled with the Spirit and armed with God's word, carry Jesus' message and ministry through the ancient world.

But – Almost 2,000 years have passed and still Eden has not been regained. History is still littered with evidence of man's continuing unfaithfulness. And, the record of the Christian Church has not always been that good!

Q. Can God's purpose ever really be fulfilled?

A. At the end of the first century, John was granted a vision in which he saw down the course of history, through times of trial, to God's final hour, to the blessings of Eden's Garden fully restored and man in Christ reigning at the last as he was intended to do at the beginning. In the time that has passed since then the gospel has spread to many peoples and the end John saw is now nearer than many care to imagine. The power of Word and Spirit that worked in creation, that has upheld God's purposes through history, that has motivated his prophets, that lived in Jesus Christ, that gives us a foretaste of Paradise today, still works for the final recreation of all things. That is our faith!

In Eden there were two special trees: the tree of the knowledge of good and evil and the tree of life. They represent the twin poles or foci of all God's dealings with men, corresponding to his Word and his Spirit. For tampering with the one man needed forgiveness, driven from the garden he lost access to the other. Our drama tells the story of God restoring man to a right relationship with both, first through his promises to the patriarchs, then through the preaching of the prophets, and so forth, but more fully in Jesus, through whose sacrificial death comes the forgiveness man needs and through whose gift of the Spirit comes the life from which man has been excluded.

Now Jesus, while he was himself a prophet, was also more than a prophet. He was The Prophet. In him Word and Spirit come to rest in a unique way, for he alone is 'the Word' incarnate and alone has 'the Spirit without limit' (John 1.14; 3.34). This double aspect of his personality contains within itself the restoration of all that was lost when access to the twin trees of Eden was denied to men. Or, to put it another way, as John the Baptist says, he is 'the Lamb of God, who takes away the sin of the world' and also 'he who will baptise with the Holy Spirit' (John 1.29,33). Jesus' prophetic calling to usher in the New Covenant with its removal of sin and gift of the Spirit is the breakthrough in history that the old covenants looked forward to for setting in motion God's final movement towards restoring Paradise.

But then, in the end time, the matter will be dealt with finally in God's new heaven and earth where men will once more have full and free access to the tree of life (Rev. 22.1f).

2. PROPHETS AND CHARISMATICS

Another title for this book could have been 'A Charismatic's View of History'. This century has witnessed an unprecedented revival of charismatic enthusiasm that has led first to the emergence and growth of the Pentecostal churches and then more recently, over the past thirty years, has strongly influenced the traditional denominations. As we follow the story of the Old Testament prophets, we shall discover how this modern charismatic Christianity has a great deal in common with their ancient faith and experience, so much so that it is hard not to conclude that the one is the direct heir and necessary sequel to the other.

In the New Testament section of this book we shall naturally focus attention on Jesus as Prophet, but it is important in doing so to remember that that only covers one facet of his ministry. In our first volume we looked at Jesus as Priest, in the second as King and in the fourth we shall see Jesus as Lord. A balanced picture will hold these various aspects together. None the less, it is also true to say that in Jesus the Spirit and the Word came among men with greater power than in any other person in history, and so it is not at all misleading to study his ministry as though it were that of the greatest charismatic or prophet that has ever lived.

After that we shall discover that Jesus' followers in New Testament times happily appropriated his prophetic outlook, shared in his charismatic experiences and demonstrated the same kind of spiritual power as he did.

There are basically four different explanations of these facts that are popular among Christians today:

– *Liberals*, who generally prefer to play down the supernatural anyhow, tend to regard the prophetic view-point as simply a particular theological way of looking at things that appeals to some people but need not be adopted by all.

– *Catholics* mostly accept the fundamental truth of the Biblical stories, but believe that the prophetic/charismatic gifts were given to the early apostles and their companions to help them get the Church started, and that once it was established the Spirit and his gifts became the preserve of the institution and its officers, the bishops.

– *Evangelicals* generally hold a view that is not unlike that of the Catholics, for they too believe that primitive Christianity was indeed charismatic, but only until the books of the New Testament were written, for they argue that once the word of God had been encapsulated in the sacred Scriptures, prophecy and the other gifts of the Spirit were no longer needed and so were withdrawn.

– *Charismatics*, on the other hand, believe in a complete continuity of faith, vision and experience that stretches back from today through New Testament times to the Old Testament prophets, and even before them to the patriarchs in Genesis.

The viewpoint in this book is, of course, the last of these four, but you, the reader, should judge for yourself. In the end of the day what others believe is surely for you less important than what you believe yourself and how far you are prepared to share in the call and vision of Jesus Christ and his saints of both ancient times and today.

It may seem surprising to find the words 'prophet(-ic)' and 'charismatic' used interchangeably as if they meant the same. There is a difference, of course. 'Charismatic' literally means 'gifted', or 'endowed with gifts (of the Spirit)'. It comes from the Greek *charisma* (plural *charismata*) which means 'gift' and is used in relation to the spiritual gifts in the New Testament. A charismatic is therefore someone who possesses some or all of these spiritual gifts, such as prophecy, healing, tongues, discernment of spirits, and the like. The word 'prophet' on the other hand is made up from two Greek words, *pro-* and *phetes*, that mean something like 'forth-teller' and is generally used of someone who 'speaks forth' words he has received from God by revelation. In practice, however, we shall find that the Biblical prophets actually used most of the gifts of the Spirit known to us from the New Testament writings and we shall also see that the words 'prophet' and 'prophecy' in both Testaments are often used with a wider meaning that is virtually identical with 'charismatic'. One of the clearest examples of that is in Acts 2.16–18 where Peter readily identifies the tongues-speaking of the first Christian Pentecost with the prophesying foretold by Joel.

Therefore, whilst there are certainly times when the two words 'charismatic' and 'prophet(-ic)' need to be used with their distinctive meanings, it is also perfectly legitimate to use the two words interchangeably when referring in a general and comprehensive way to many of the personalities and experiences of both Old and New Testament times. In other words, the prophets of ancient Israel were charismatics and the charismatics of the early Church were the direct heirs of the faith and experience of the Old Testament prophets.

The story about Moses and the seventy elders in Num. 11 gives us the basic clue to understanding this peculiar continuity of prophetic/charismatic faith. There we see Moses pleading with God that he finds it impossible to carry the burden of the complaining Israelites all by himself. God asks him to summon seventy of his best elders to the Tent of Meeting, and there he endues them with the Spirit that is already on Moses himself and they begin to prophesy. The nature of their prophesying is not explained to us, but when Joshua is offended by it and wants to have it stopped, Moses turns to him and says, 'I wish that all the LORD's people were prophets and that the LORD would put his Spirit on them!' (v. 29).

Clearly Moses recognises that something very precious has happened, so much so he longs for it to be shared by all his people. Much later in Israel's history other men on whom God's Spirit rested were to experience the same longing, but more than that were to realise it was going to be fulfilled one day. For example, Isa. 44.3 speaks of God pouring out his Spirit on Israel's offspring, Ezek. 36.26f tells that the Spirit will be put within them, and Joel 2.28 declares that then they will prophesy. The fulfilment of these prophecies began on the day of Pentecost described in Acts 2, when the disciples of Jesus were filled with the Holy Spirit and spoke in other tongues. It was then that Peter was able to explain that this was the prophesying foretold by Joel, but clearly Moses, more than twelve centuries earlier had glimpsed the potential of it.

This unique outpouring of God's Spirit in Num.11 looks very much like an early foretaste of Pentecost. There we see a first hint of a stream that was to surface from time to time in Israel's history and finally burst forth in full flood in and through the ministry of Jesus and his disciples. It is in fact this stream of the Spirit that gives the Bible-story coherence as it develops, linking the men of faith of the Old Testament with the Christians of the New. Moses glimpsed and longed for it, others (the prophets) later saw it coming, it arrived with Jesus, and the disciples lived and ministered in the fulness of it. It was to bring blessing to all who received it, in line with God's original promise to Abraham (Gen.12.2f), and was to impart new life to them, thus restoring a measure of what man had lost when deprived of access to the tree of life in Eden.

That in brief is the story we are about to trace in greater detail. It is from beginning to end a story about charismatics told by charismatics, and so very much 'a charismatic's view of history.' The challenge involved in studying it is that it still invites us today to enter ourselves into the enjoyment of the vision and experience of these ancient men of God. Pray as you read that the Holy Spirit will, according to the promise of Jesus (John 16.13), 'guide you into all the truth' about these matters so that you can catch the vision for yourself and then learn to live in the good of it.

3. STUDYING PROPHECY

The Prophetic Writings and the Bible
Since the Jews do not recognise our New Testament as sacred Scripture, they do not refer to the Hebrew Bible as 'The Old Testament'. Their name for it is 'The Law, the Prophets and the Writings' (*Torah, Nebi'im uKethubim*).
'The Law' refers to the Pentateuch.
'The Prophets' refers to
  (i) the history books Joshua, Judges, Samuel and Kings ('the former prophets')
  (ii) the prophetic books Isaiah, Jeremiah, Ezekiel and the 12 Minor Prophets from Hosea to Malachi ('the latter prophets')
'The Writings' refers to everything else.
The books in the Hebrew Bible are arranged in that order, which is different from the English order.
The arrangement of the prophetic books themselves has little to do with dates – Amos and Hosea lived over a century before Jeremiah and Ezekiel.
Though Daniel and Jonah are prophetic books, we shall study them in Volume Four. Both of them add more to the theme we shall be following there than to the development of the vision we are tracing here.
There is a lot of discussion about prophecy in the New Testament, but only Revelation is called a prophetic book.

Variety in the Prophetic Writings
Most of the prophetic books of the Old Testament are anthologies rather than continuous narratives and so contain

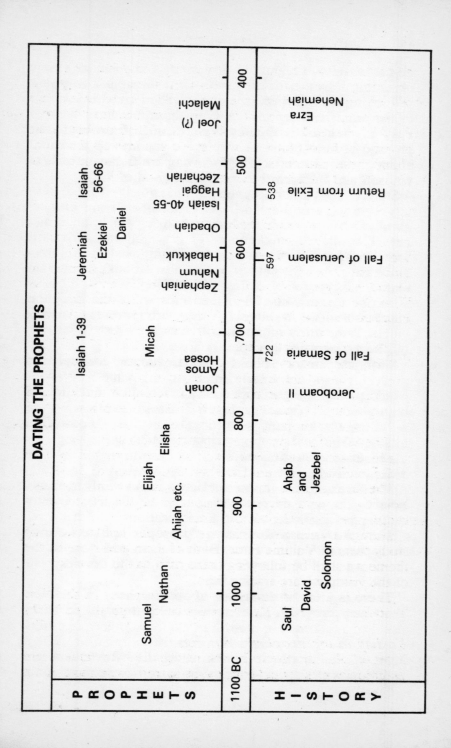

DATING THE PROPHETS

	1100 BC	1000	900	800	700	600	500	400

PROPHETS

Samuel
Nathan
Ahijah etc.

Elijah

Elisha

Isaiah 1-39

Micah

Jonah
Amos
Hosea

Jeremiah
Ezekiel
Daniel

Isaiah
56-66

Zephaniah
Nahum
Habakkuk
Obadiah
Isaiah 40-55
Haggai
Zechariah

Joel (?)
Malachi

HISTORY

Saul
David
Solomon

Ahab
and
Jezebel

Jeroboam II

Fall of Samaria   722

Fall of Jerusalem   597

Return from Exile   538

Ezra
Nehemiah

a great variety of materials. There are, of course, stories in them, but they are for the most part made up of collections of the prophets' sayings (sometimes called 'oracles'). Hence it can often be more profitable to dip into one of them at random than to try reading them through from beginning to end, in much the same way as we would read selections from a book of poetry. The following are the main sorts of material we find ourselves reading.

– Stories: The earlier prophets, from Samuel to Elisha, have left us very few of their sayings. About all we know of these men is told in stories in the history books – which sometimes read like ancient counterparts of our modern charismatic (auto-)biographies. There are also biographical and autobiographical stories in some of the prophetic books themselves (e.g. Amos 7; Hos. 1–3; Jeremiah throughout).

– Prophecies in verse: For the most part the prophets expressed their messages in verse utterances of varying length, some fairly short, and often starting with 'Thus says the LORD' (see, for example, Amos 1–2).

– Sermons: The message is also frequently conveyed by preaching in a prose style, much in the same way as we would preach today. Prose sermons are often much longer than poetic prophecies (e.g. Jer. 7; Ezek. 22,23).

– Psalms: Occasionally the prophets put their visions down in song. The best example is Hab. 3, which even includes instructions about musical accompaniment.

Generally be prepared for variety. Ezekiel in particular uses many different literary devices to convey his message: poetry, sermons, allegories, visions, symbolic actions, autobiography, legal debates, law-codifications. Nevertheless, despite the variety, the individual prophetic books are by no means random in their arrangement. Indeed they usually show a clear progression from one chapter to the next.

The Spirit, the Prophet and his Word

Also be prepared for variety in style. Although 'prophecy never had its origin in the will of man, but men spoke from God as they were carried along by the Holy Spirit' (2 Pet. 1.21), it is still quite easy to distinguish the styles of different prophets. That is because prophets are not impersonal loudspeakers through which God utters his voice. They are more like messengers telling what God has told them to say. So the voice we hear is not in the first instance God's, but the prophet's, though the origin of the message is not the prophet, but God. Like any messenger, he conveys his message in his own voice, with his own dialect, style and intonation. Or, as Paul was later to put it, 'The spirits of prophets are subject to the control of prophets.' (1 Cor. 14.32) The voice of the prophet only becomes the voice of God to the hearer by faith and the witness of the Spirit.

This raises the perennial problem of discerning between true and false prophecy. The Old Testament tussles with this many times. In the New Testament, Paul speaks of 'discernment of spirits' as one of the gifts given to Christians to help deal with this problem, but as we shall see, it still remains an enigma today for very many people.

The Authority of the Prophet

Prophets came from all different walks of life. Amos was a shepherd, Isaiah had free access to the royal court, Nathan was himself a courtier, Hosea was married to a prostitute, Ezekiel and Jeremiah belonged to priestly families, Elisha was a farmer. Some could clearly have claimed a hearing because of their public status, but their authority rested elsewhere, in the revelation of the word of God by the action of his Spirit. Their declaration was never 'Listen to what I have to say', but always 'Thus says the LORD', and they used 'I' as if it were God himself that spoke. Sometimes that led to scorn, persecution and even death, whatever their social status, but their conviction of divine authority remained absolute.

The Message of the Prophets

Prophecy is not clairvoyant prediction. It is the utterance of messages from God, and these may relate to the prophet's present as much as to his future. Furthermore, they are not simply disjointed messages, for they form part of the total, all-embracing message about God's redemptive purpose and man's response to it in repentance, obedience and faith. However, each prophet does present that message in his own style with his own insights and, as we shall see, his presentation can usually be summed up in one or two key words. That is part of the purpose of this book, to help you discern these things as you read, to highlight each prophet's 'word' so that his message can be more clearly understood, taken to heart, and thus received as God's word that gives life.

We shall be covering a span of about 700 years, in which time the Old Testament prophets' message developed considerably as they addressed different social and political crises. But we shall see that there is a general coherence in that message down the centuries and we shall be tracing the growth of revelation in it. As you read, let each prophet's word challenge you, but try also to catch their overall vision for yourself, because in all they spoke they were preparing for the coming of our Lord Jesus Christ, and beyond that, for his coming again. Today we still need their preparation as much as ever.

2

The Birth of Prophecy in Israel

The books of the prophets from Isaiah to Malachi make up about a quarter of the Old Testament and when we add to them the stories about the prophets in the history books the fraction rises to almost a third. That should give us some idea of the importance of the material we are about to study. The teaching of the prophets clearly met a significant need in Israel before it came to hold such a prominent place in sacred Scripture. But what was that need, and where did these people come from who were able to meet it so powerfully?

1. THE PROPHETS OF THE NATIONS (NUM. 22–24)

Other nations in the ancient world also had people we call prophets, but they were very different from the Israelite prophets. They were rather diviners, astrologers, sooth-sayers and the like, people who tried to read the future by observing the stars, animal-behaviour, the weather and other natural phenomena, or who consulted magical charts, almanacs and various divining aids. Sometimes they would seek to induce a trance-condition in themselves in the hope of contacting some spiritual or demonic being that might instruct them what to say. The closest modern counterparts to most of their practices are found in the activities of superstitious and clairvoyant circles. The whole ethos of such prophesying is so much in contrast with the prophesying of the Old Testament that it seems pointless to begin drawing comparisons, even though many books on Biblical

---

MAIN REFERENCES TO PAGAN PROPHETS, DIVINERS, SORCERERS, ETC.

A. Examples of pagan prophets, diviners, etc.:

Egyptian	Gen. 41.8; Exod. 7.11,22 (Pharaoh's counsellors)
Aramean	Num. 23.23; 24.1 (Balaam)
Canaanite	1 Kings 18.26-29 (prophets of Baal)
Philistine	1 Sam. 6.2 (priestly advisers)
Early Israelite	1 Sam 28 (the witch of Endor)
Later Israelite	Mic. 3.7; Jer. 14.14; Ezek. 13.6 (= false prophets ?)
Babylonian	Ezek. 21.21 (royal military advisers)
Babylonian	Isa. 47.9,13 (Babylonian prophets in general)
Persian	Dan. 2.2; 4.7; 5.7 (court counsellors)
Samaritan	Acts 8.9-11 (Simon the magician)
Cypriot	Acts 13.6-11 (adviser of Roman governor)
Macedonian	Acts 16.16-19 (local fortune-teller)
Asian	Acts 19.19 (general local superstition at Ephesus)

B. Pagan prophecy, divination, etc. condemned by:

The Law	Lev. 19.26,31; 20.6,27; Deut. 18.9-14
Historians	2 Kings 17.17; 21.6
Prophets	1 Sam. 15.23; Isa. 8.19; 44.25; Jer. 10.2; 27.9; Zech. 10.2
New Testament	Gal. 5.20; Rev. 21.8; 22.15

---

prophecy do just that, some of them even claiming that Israel learnt its prophecy from the pagan soothsayers. It seems clear, however, that the very opposite is the truth, for the prophets of Israel did nothing but condemn their abhorrent ways. Their practices were strictly forbidden by Israelite law. A mere glance at 1 Kings 18 shows just how much their conduct was held in contempt. Israel's prophets were of a different order altogether. They were the charismatics of their time and, as we shall see presently, were much more akin to what we might call revivalist preachers today.

There is, however, one ancient pagan prophet we need to give some thought to before we turn to the Israelite prophets, and that is Balaam son of Beor, who came from Pethor, near the River (Euphrates). He is remembered in the New Testament as one whose services could be bought with money (2 Pet. 2.15f; Jude 11) and as one whose influence led the Israelites into idolatry and immorality (Rev. 2.14), which is just what we should expect of a pagan soothsayer. What is surprising about his story is that the LORD was able to use him powerfully for his own purposes.

We read in Num. 22 that Balak, the King of Moab, perturbed to see the vast hordes of Israel encamped at Shittim on his borders, sent messengers to summon Balaam, whose utterances he knew to be exceedingly effective, to come and put a curse on the Israelites. But then we hear the LORD speak to this pagan in much the same way as he is to speak to the Israelite prophets in later times. At first he warns Balaam not to go, though when the messengers are persistent, offering even greater rewards, God allows

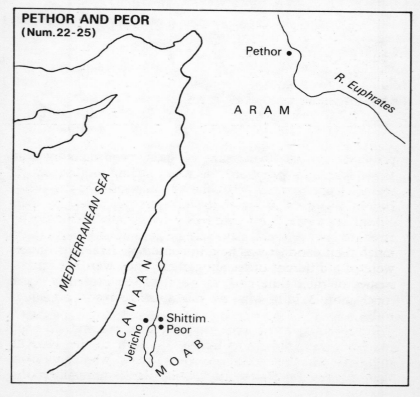

PETHOR AND PEOR
(Num. 22-25)

Pethor

R. Euphrates

ARAM

MEDITERRANEAN SEA

CANAAN

Jericho Shittim
Peor

MOAB

him, on condition that he speak only the words he gives
him to speak. On the way Balaam is shown the utter seriousness of this commission from God when by an astounding
miracle his donkey is enabled to speak and his own eyes are
opened to see an angel with drawn sword standing in his
path reminding him of what God had told him. After such
awesome happenings, we are not at all surprised when
Balaam refuses to curse the Israelites but blesses them
instead (Num. 23–24), even in the face of Balak's anger and
at the cost of losing his promised remuneration (24.10–13).

It is difficult to piece the rest of the story together,
because the Bible does not give us many details. Balaam,
we are told, returned home, as Balak had ordered him to
do (24.11,14,25). In the days that followed some of the
Israelites became sexually involved with local Moabite and
Midianite women and as a consequence found themselves
participating in their pagan sacrificial rites, worshipping the
local Baal of Peor. This episode roused the LORD to anger
and plague swept through the camp (ch. 25). Some time
later the Israelite armies went out to take vengeance on the
Midianites for what had happened and in the battle 'they
also killed Balaam son of Beor with the sword' (31.8). After
the battle we hear Moses laying the blame for all that happened squarely at Balaam's feet: the Midianite women, he
says, 'were the ones who followed Balaam's advice and were
the means of turning the Israelites away from the LORD in
what happened at Peor' (31.16). It seems that Balaam must
have returned to Shittim almost immediately after he got
home, probably regretting that he had not cursed Israel
after all.

It has been important to spend some time looking at this
story because in the middle of it Balaam actually pronounced some astoundingly accurate prophecies. As well as
blessing the LORD's people in a beautifully appropriate way
that would have befitted one of Israel's own great prophets,
he went on to foretell the rise of David and his conquest of
Moab and Edom (24.17–19), the passing of the Amalekites
from history (24.20), the invasion of the Assyrians in the
eighth century (24.21f), and finally even the coming of the
Greeks (Kittim) in the fourth, about 900 years beyond his

own time (24.24). Truly these were amazing revelations to be granted a pagan soothsayer, but after the episode with the donkey and the angel, Balaam must have been, for a time at least, very open to hearing and obeying God. We can almost hear his own amazement as he begins to recount his revelations the third and fourth time:

> *The oracle of Balaam son of Beor,*
>   *the oracle of one whose eye sees clearly,*
> *the oracle of one who hears the words of God,*
>   *who has knowledge from the Most High,*
> *who sees a vision from the Almighty,*
>   *who falls prostrate, and whose eyes are opened.*

(24.15f; cp. 24.3f)

Even though Balaam did once call the LORD 'my God' (22.18), it seems that in these stories we are reading about a sovereign act of God in a basically pagan life. The true Balaam was the man that surfaced afterwards, one who was shown in the end to be nothing more than a foreign diviner. Furthermore, he had just been done out of a potentially rich reward, which may well be the reason why he returned to stir up trouble for the Israelites. However, for a brief space of time he had the privilege of being used by God in a way that was only to become familiar much later in Israel's history. And the means by which all that happened, we are told in 24.1–2, by-passed the sorcerer's techniques he was accustomed to using, for it was by the operation of the Spirit of God that he prophesied, just as it would be among the later prophets of Israel.

We can indeed learn something of value about the Israelite prophets from the stories of Balaam, because for a time he became one to all intents and purposes. But we also need to remember that his experience in that was unique both in his own life and in the history of Israel. Balaam's story does not prove to us in any way that Israel learnt its prophecy from the pagan nations.

2. THE CHALLENGE OF THE WORD (GENESIS – JOSHUA)

The roots of Israel's prophetic tradition lie in her own history, not in external sources. In pre-conquest times there were one or two outstanding individuals who were known to have had the prophetic gift, such as Abraham (Gen. 20.7), Miriam (Exod. 15.20) and Moses (Hos. 12.13), but it was only well after the tribes had settled, in Samuel's time, that anything like a popular prophetic movement began to appear. When it did, it was found to be a movement of energetic reaction to declining religious, social and moral standards in Israel. And the measure of these standards that the prophets upheld was always the revealed will of God as expressed by his word to the nation's forefathers.

God's word of promise revealed to Abraham (Genesis)
God's word is found in two basic forms: promise and command, and these call for two different, though interrelated responses: faith and obedience. When God called Abraham he gave him several promises concerning land, children and blessing. Their gist was that Abraham would be forefather to a growing family that would one day become an important nation living on the soil of Canaan, a nation that would enjoy considerable blessing and would itself become the source of further blessing for all the other peoples on earth (Gen. 12.1–3). The only response to these promises required of Abraham and his descendants was to have faith in them and to live in expectancy of their fulfilment. Most of the dramatic tension in the stories of Genesis can only be understood in the light of that fact, for repeatedly we watch God pick his people up and restore them by reasserting these promises.

The call to live in faith in God's promises is essentially a call to live in a vision (of their fulfilment). Every time Abraham or one of his descendants lost sight of that vision, or let go of faith, things began to go wrong and God had to intervene to rescue him and restore the vision and faith in him. The challenge to live in this faith did not finish at the end of Genesis, of course, but has continued ever since, and we shall see that one major part of the prophets' task was to call God's people back to this faith and to rekindle the vision in them.

God's word of command revealed to Moses (Exodus – Deuteronomy).

The second major element in God's word is the commandment of his law. When God took the Israelites to himself at Mt. Sinai and through Moses gave them his law, he was instructing them, not about how to attain salvation, for he had already granted them that by saving them from their bondage in Egypt, but about how to live in and continue to enjoy the blessings of the salvation he had already given. The pattern is the same as in Christian experience: salvation is God's free gift of grace received by faith, but discipleship is training in how to live the life expected of a Christian. The problem in ancient times, not unlike the problem today, was that the Israelites, having received this salvation then failed to live out the life-style required of them and so forfeited the benefit that should have been theirs through their salvation.

Attached to the law were a promise and a challenge. The promise was that continued and increasing blessing would attend the way of those who lived in accordance with the law's requirements, while corresponding curse would attend the way of those who did not. The challenge, of course, was to choose the way leading to blessing. We are confronted with this challenge many times in the law (e.g. Exod. 23.20–33; Lev. 26.3–45), but one of the best known presentations of it is found in Deut. 30.15–20 (cp. 11.26–28):

See, I set before you today life and prosperity, death and destruction. For I command you today to love the LORD your God, to walk in his ways, and to keep his commands, decrees and laws; then you will live and increase, and the LORD your God will bless you . . . But if your heart turns away and you are not obedient . . . you will certainly be destroyed . . . I have set before you life and death, blessings and curses. Now choose life . . .

Moses uttered these words about forty years after the law was given at Sinai, on the eve of his death and of Israel's entry into Canaan. He did so to remind them of their calling and to re-establish in their minds the basic principles by which they would find success in taking the land and prosperity once settled in it, whilst at the same time warning them of the cost of disobedience. The same message was to be reiterated many times down the centuries thereafter, not least by the prophets whose second main function was to be to call Israel back to the God-given life-style portrayed in the law, and that mainly at times of political, social, spiritual and moral decline, when revival was urgently needed in the nation.

Faith in God's word is vindicated (Joshua).
The first recorded occasion after Moses's death when this message was again preached to the assembly of Israel was actually one when all was going very well. Joshua had led the Israelites successfully into the land and had established the tribes in their territories. There were still plenty of Canaanite settlements to be taken, but the land as a whole was now Israel's. Then at the end of his life, like Moses before him, he sought to remind the people of their responsibility in faith and obedience.

First he summoned the leaders together and challenged them: You see for yourselves how every promise of God has been fulfilled as we have walked his way. Now I am handing over to you and you must be strong, both in maintaining faith in the vision God has given us of the land fully in our possession, and also in holding fast to the way he has taught us in the law. If you persevere in this way you will have the same success, but if not you will lose all we have already gained. (Josh. 23)

Then Joshua assembled the whole people and laid the same challenge before them. They were very eager to pledge themselves to the vision and to obedience, in fact too eager for Joshua's liking, but then they were riding on the crest of a wave of success and so their enthusiasm was understandably high. (Josh. 24)

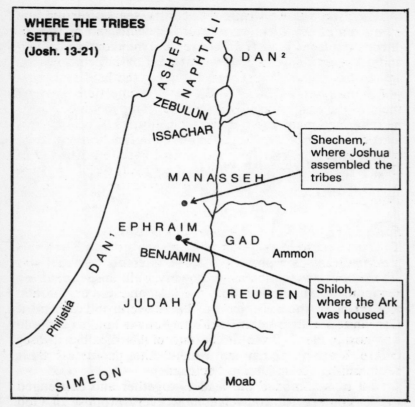

WHERE THE TRIBES SETTLED (Josh. 13-21)

ASHER
NAPHTALI
DAN²
ZEBULUN
ISSACHAR
MANASSEH
EPHRAIM
DAN¹
BENJAMIN
GAD
Ammon
Philistia
JUDAH
REUBEN
SIMEON
Moab

Shechem, where Joshua assembled the tribes

Shiloh, where the Ark was housed

Disobedience and the possibility of repentance

It was not to be long before Israel's fortunes changed drastically as the Israelites lost their grasp of God's promises and slipped progressively into unfaithfulness and disobedience. However, in the economy of God that day had been foreseen and well prepared for in advance. At several points where Moses warns of the consequences of disobedience, he also tells of the way out:

> *But if they will confess their sins . . . I will remember my covenant with Jacob and my covenant with Isaac and my covenant with Abraham, and . . . I will not reject them or abhor them so as to destroy them completely . . .*
>
> (Lev. 26.40–45)

> *When you and your children return to the Lord your God*
> *and obey him with all your heart and with all your soul . . .*
> *then the Lord your God will restore your fortunes . . .*
>   (Deut. 30.2f; cp. 4.29–31)

That was also to become the burden of the prophets' preaching as they challenged Israel in times of decadence to return to God and find restoration. The prophets' vocation was therefore to be essentially two-fold: first, to call God's people back to his ways, to obedience to his commands, while reminding them of the terrible consequences of disobedience, and second, to renew them in vision and rebuild them in faith in accordance with his promises.

The prophets' vocation was to be like Moses' vocation. The prophets' vocation as we have just outlined it bears no comparison whatsoever with the role of the pagan soothsayers and diviners. In times of stress and uncertainty there was always a temptation to turn to them and seek occult knowledge about the future, but these men knew nothing of God's promises that stood right at the heart of Israel's faith, and nothing about the challenge of the two ways God had set before his people. However accurate their predictions, or those of any Israelite who followed their gods, they were to be driven from the land (Deut. 13.1–5). Their ways were absolutely forbidden to the Israelites who would find in their real time of need that God would raise up for them a prophet like Moses from among their own brethren, one who would speak the words God commanded him to speak (Deut. 18.14–22).

Whenever Moses spoke to the Israelites it was with words given him by God and they were always words that inspired faith in his promises or challenged to obedience. The prophetic successors of Moses were to do the same. Theirs was not the way of pagan divinations and predictions, for, as we shall see, they were at heart Israel's revival preachers, calling God's people back to God himself and to the good old-time religion of their forefathers in the faith.

(Different people have identified the prophet in Deut. 18.15,18 who is to be like Moses with various individual prophets in the Old Testament or with Jesus in the New. However, we should probably not be thinking of one prophet in history to the exclusion of all others, but rather of a prophet like Moses in every generation. It seems that what Deut. 18.14–22 is saying is: Whenever your situation becomes so urgent that you feel you could consult some diviner, then cast your eye around and you will find there is already an authentic prophet of the LORD there. Listen to him, for, like Moses before him, he will be speaking words given him by God, not just presumptuous messages. In Samuel's day that prophet was Samuel himself, in Elijah's day it was Elijah, and in Jesus' day it was Jesus. Of course Jesus fits the description better than anyone else in history, but the ministries of the prophets before him were at least foreshadowings of his own and may therefore be legitimately regarded as partially fitting the description as well.)

3. THE SPIRIT AND REVIVAL (JUDGES)

Revival occurs when something or someone that has died or is dying is restored to life, usually through someone else putting something life-giving into it or him. Thus a doctor may revive a dead or dying body by energising its heart and lungs with electrical shock treatment, a politician may revive a dead or dying institution through an infusion of financial or other aid, an orator may revive a crowd's flagging enthusiasm by his dynamic use of language. Similarly the LORD revives his people in times of spiritual decline by fresh outpourings of his Spirit. Revival and the operation of the Spirit are inseparable.

Patterns of revival
Whilst every revival is different from any other, there are fairly consistent patterns that can be recognised. For example, we usually find that there is a widespread movement of repentance and returning to God through overwhelming

conviction of sin. Times of revival are therefore usually accompanied with a mixture of weeping and rejoicing as people find their peace with God. Revivals generally raise up men and women of God who become outstanding instruments of his work in furthering its progress by preaching and teaching. As God touches individual lives there are frequently evidences of his miraculous power in healing and other supernatural signs. Churches grow, books proliferate, enthusiasm abounds, and often persecution follows. But in and through all these external manifestations there is one constant, indispensable factor, namely the powerful activity of God's life-giving Spirit.

One common pattern that we find both in biblical and modern times is that on the eve of revival God's Spirit begins to stir in one man and through his ministry into the lives of others who then become something of a spear-head movement for revival in their nation. And almost always these enthusiasts for revival are charismatics of some description. Prophets and charismatics are, in fact, the shock-troops that God sends ahead into the front line in his battle for revival.

The first time we see this pattern clearly is in Samuel's day, but what happened then was not something entirely new and strange. The story of prophecy, as of everything else that God does with men is indeed full of new things, but new moves of God are never without roots in some earlier preparatory work. Even as the Hebrews descended to Egypt in Jacob's time, God began to prepare them for the exodus that would take place four centuries later (Gen. 46.3f; 50.24). Almost every eighth- and seventh-century prophet whose words are recorded in the Old Testament forewarned of the exile. Some of these, and certainly all of the exilic prophets, foretold the return from captivity. When Jesus came, more than a thousand years of revelation and history had prepared the way for his coming. So also it was with Samuel. He did not suddenly appear with his prophets as from nowhere, for already God had taught Israel much about the ways of his Spirit with men.

And yet something very new did enter history with Samuel, for before his time we never hear of anything that could be called a prophetic or charismatic movement. To be sure, the Israelites were not unfamiliar with prophecy and other supernatural activities of the Spirit, for since Abraham's day they had known that it was possible for a man to receive God's word directly and personally. Abraham had himself been known as a prophet and the stories that were told about Moses, the exodus and the events at Sinai would certainly have familiarised the Israelites with all sorts of miraculous and charismatic phenomena. But perhaps the most significant work of preparation for the birth of Samuel's prophetic movement happened in later times, in the immediately preceding period of the judges.

There again we can pick out the odd prophetic personality, such as Deborah, the prophetess who inspired Barak to fight for Israel (Judg. 4.4–10), or the unnamed prophet who was active in Gideon's time (Judg. 6.8–10), but important as such individuals were, much more important is the whole mood of the age and the overall movement in it of God's Spirit, for it was an age both of decline and dying, but also of first stirrings of revival, and it was out of that melting-pot that Israel's first charismatic movement was to be born.

The spiral of decline and deliverance (Judges 1–12)

Joshua's challenge to the leaders and the people was soon forgotten after his death and the tribal settlement began to run into difficulties. Some of the Canaanites proved hard to dislodge (Judg. 1.19–36), faith in God's promises dwindled and the Israelites began to make treaties with their new neighbours. The results were disastrous, because their pagan presence gradually eroded Israel's faith and proved to be a constant thorn in her flesh thereafter (Judg. 2.1–5). Within a generation many of the Israelites had begun to worship their gods.

The consequence, of course, was that the curse of the law began to operate and the Israelites suffered repeated reversal, invasion and oppression until they cried to God for forgiveness and mercy and he raised up a 'judge' to deliver them. The story was to be a repeating one of disobedience, oppression, repentance and restoration. That

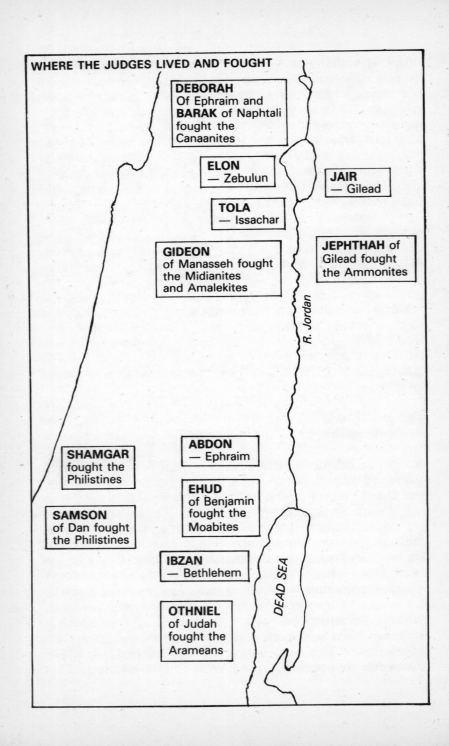

WHERE THE JUDGES LIVED AND FOUGHT

DEBORAH
Of Ephraim and
BARAK of Naphtali
fought the
Canaanites

ELON
— Zebulun

JAIR
— Gilead

TOLA
— Issachar

JEPHTHAH of
Gilead fought
the Ammonites

GIDEON
of Manasseh fought
the Midianites
and Amalekites

R. Jordan

SHAMGAR
fought the
Philistines

ABDON
— Ephraim

EHUD
of Benjamin
fought the
Moabites

SAMSON
of Dan fought
the Philistines

IBZAN
— Bethlehem

DEAD SEA

OTHNIEL
of Judah
fought the
Arameans

pattern embraces most of the stories in Judg. 3–12, where we find folk like Othniel, Ehud, Deborah, Barak, Gideon and Jephthah raised up and empowered by God's Spirit to rescue the Israelites in different parts of the country from various oppressors and invaders and then to establish some kind of respect for the law in the land. But always we read that after the death of the judge the Israelites reverted to apostate ways and so the cycle would start all over again.

The plunge into anarchy (Judges 13–21)

By the time we reach Samson's story in chs. 13–16 matters have deteriorated considerably. The Philistines are now pressing into the territory of the tribe of Dan, and Samson, despite his astounding feats, is unable to deliver his kinsfolk, with the result that the Danites are compelled to leave the region and seek new territory for themselves in the far north where the land is more sparsely populated (Judg. 17–18)

There are many elements in the stories of Samson and the Danites that reflect the declining moral conditions in Israel. Samson's own loose love-life, the priest of Dan's idolatry and the fact that he was made Dan's priest by forcible abduction in the first place all witness, amongst other details in the story, that Israel had largely forgotten the law of God. Then finally we come to the unpleasant and quite unedifying events of Judg. 19–21 where we read of rape, murder, civil war and the like. The portrait of decline is well nigh complete. The verdict the author of the book of Judges passes on this age is unequivocal: 'In those days Israel had no king; everyone did as he saw fit' (21.25).

Israel had plunged into anarchy. Little remained to stop the Philistines, who had been growing stronger by the day, from taking over the country – that is, unless something dramatic happened to stop them and bring Israel to her senses. Never in her short history had Israel so badly needed a thorough-going revival.

Stirrings of revival

Revivals did take place under the leadership of the judges, but they were all fairly localised. Ehud delivered Benjamin from Moabite oppression, Deborah and Barak rescued some of the Galilean tribes from Canaanite domination, Gideon drove Midianite invaders out of Central Palestine, Jephthah dealt with Ammonite oppression in Transjordan. The religious revivals associated with their individual leadership were correspondingly localised, though they must inevitably have had some impact on the rest of the nation. Nowhere, however, do we find record of a national movement of repentance, much as that was needed.

None the less, what we do see is the beginning of a work of preparation for something greater to follow. Already prophetic voices are heard in the land (4.4; 6.8) and most of the judges are said to be charismatic personalities in the sense that they were men in whom God's Spirit worked in life-transforming and supernatural ways. It was because 'the Spirit of the LORD came upon' them that the cowardly Gideon, found hiding in his wine-press, was transformed into a fearless man of war (6.34), and that the half-cast outlaw, Jephthah, was transformed into a respected national leader (11.29). It was the Spirit that empowered Othniel to repel the king of Aram (3.10), and it was only by the power of the Spirit that Samson was able to perform his heroic feats (13.25; 14.6,19; 15.14). None of these men were prophets, but they all displayed charismatic gifting.

The pattern of God's working is regularly the same. When he brings help to his people, it is by the action of his Spirit through men who allow themselves to be used by his Spirit. The local military and religious revivals of the judges already begin to reveal a pattern we are to see emerging more clearly in later times. Without the action of God's Spirit there can be no revival, for it is the Spirit that gives life! And pre-eminently the action of the Spirit turns men into charismatics, and the reason for that is to enable them to become the instruments and leaders of revival.

The charismatic leaders we must now study are those called prophets, men who spoke God's words in the power of his Spirit to restore faith and vision and to call back through repentance to obedience and a new walk with God. Their methods were mainly different from those of the judges, but their basic aim, to restore Israel, was the same, as also was the source of their inspiration in the Spirit of God.

PART TWO

THE EARLY PROPHETS

ELEVENTH – NINTH CENTURIES BC

We meet the early Israelite prophets, from Samuel to Elisha, through stories about them in the books of Samuel and Kings and we know little about their teaching. By contrast, the later prophets, from Amos onwards, are presented to us mainly through the records of their teaching and often we know little about their life-stories. That has caused many biblical scholars to draw a line of distinction between the two groups, think of the earlier ones as 'Spirit-prophets' and later ones as 'Word-prophets', and propound a theory that prophecy evolved out of something fairly ragged, primitive and enthusiastic into something more refined, controlled and theologically articulate.

Whilst it is true that the prophets and their message matured over the centuries, it seems wrong to draw any sharp demarcation between separate movements of Spirit and Word, for in any authentic prophecy, as we have already seen, both must be operative. Anyhow, we shall see that Samuel and his followers, even though we only have brief snatches of their teaching, did have every bit as vital a message to their generation as did the later writing prophets to theirs, and equally that the later prophets were very much men of the Spirit too.

The key to appreciating the continuity between the various movements of prophecy we shall be studying lies, as already noted, in recognising that prophets in every age were essentially charismatic revival preachers, men of God on fire with his Spirit calling his people back to himself, sometimes with miraculous demonstrations of supernatural power, sometimes with dynamic words and messages inspired by God, sometimes with both.

As we read the stories of the early prophets, it is important to recognise what kind of literature we are handling. The nearest modern equivalent to the prophet-stories in Samuel and Kings is found, not in history books or secular biographies, or legends of ancient heroes, but in some of the charismatic biographies found in religious bookshops today. These delight in the workings of God more than of men and tell their stories mainly for his glory. They focus on moments in a man's life when God has worked dramatically, usually starting with some account of how, in a setting of personal, spiritual emptiness and corresponding dryness in his church environment, the Spirit first began to work in and through him, then progressing to tell how his preaching subsequently became more effective, with the result that his hearers' lives were radically changed, some of them receiving the same spiritual anointing as he has experienced. Interwoven with that will be tales of miraculous signs and wonders adding confirmation to the witness of God's power in his life and encouraging others to respond to his preaching with the same kind of enthusiasm he has himself.

The purpose in writing these biographies is normally to encourage those who know the power of such anointing to stand firm in their faith, and to draw those that do not closer to desiring and even experiencing it themselves. To be sure, the Old Testament prophet-stories are preserved as historical records of the words and deeds of the prophets, but as we read them we sense that same delight in the workings of the Spirit as we do in reading their modern counterparts. They are stories written by prophetic men about prophets to encourage other prophetic men and to testify to the workings of God's Spirit through the prophets for the benefit of the rest of God's people. The later prophets sought to draw men back to God by writing down the prophets' teachings, the earlier prophets sought to do the same by writing down the records of his revival power working through them.

3

Samuel and his Successors

Throughout history revivals have come in successive waves, as the Lord has granted them in times of need to maintain a witness for his name. They have established a renewed and reinvigorated 'church' which, after the initial enthusiasm has passed, has sustained its witness for a generation or more, though usually with dwindling effectiveness, so that revival has eventually become needful once more. Such has been the common pattern down the centuries, right from the time of Israel's first prophetic revival.

1. ISRAEL'S FIRST PROPHETIC MOVEMENT AND REVIVAL (1 SAMUEL)

At the close of the period of the judges Israel's history was approaching the end of what we have described as Act 2 of the Drama of Salvation (see p. 5). As we have seen, it was a time of loss of vision, of religious decadence and political instability – a portrait of the state of the nation that is further confirmed when we read 1 Samuel. However, we must also read with the eye of faith that looks to God's word in his promises, sees beyond the immediate circumstances and searches for evidences of his hand at work in history. We may have to look hard for that, but God never leaves himself without a witness and there will always, even in the darkest hour, be somewhere that he is on the move preparing someone to head up the action in the days ahead. Sometimes that search can lead us to the most unlikely people in the most unlikely places.

1 Sam. 1–3: Samuel's infancy and call to be a prophet

Our search takes us to a woman called Hannah who is broken-hearted because she is unable to have children, but who, in answer to prayer, gives birth to a son, whom she appropriately names Samuel (meaning 'God has heard') and dedicates to the LORD's service to be brought up at the temple in Shiloh, where the ark of God was housed and where Eli was the priest. At that time she was inspired to sing a song of gratitude that is like a first prophetic echo of the song Mary was to sing soon before Jesus' birth. (1.1 – 2.11; cp. Luke 1.46–55)

We are made very conscious of the decadent state of religion at the time when we see how the priest Eli, observing Hannah at prayer in the temple, immediately concluded she was drunk. He must have been more accustomed to the sight of drunkenness in the sanctuary than to prayer before he jumped so readily to that conclusion. (1.12–16)

When we are introduced to his sons, Hophni and Phinehas, who were also priests, we begin to understand why. They were men who 'had no regard for the LORD', who thought nothing of overriding the sacrificial customs of the temple to satisfy their own gluttony, who brazenly slept with the women who served at the temple, and who refused to heed their father when he tried to correct them. Such was the school in which Samuel was trained, but strangely the LORD protected him and he 'continued to grow in stature and in favour with the LORD and with men.' (2.12–26)

One day a strange visitor arrived in Shiloh, 'a man of God' who reminded Eli of God's gracious promises to his family and declared that their failure to honour God in return would presently result in their death and the discontinuation of his line as priests at the sanctuary. (2.27–36)

He must have surprised Samuel completely by the way he spoke, with his authoritative 'This is what the LORD says,' which would have been quite unlike anything he could then have heard at the temple, since 'in those days the word of the LORD was rare; there were not many visions.' (3.1)

Samuel must have pondered deeply over that visit, but then he found the same message being confirmed to him directly from God as he lay awake one night in the temple.

SAMUEL'S ISRAEL

Endor
Shunem
Jezreel
Mt. Gilboa ▲

Jabesh Gilead

Aphek
Ebenezer
Shiloh
Ramah
(Ramathaim)
E P H R A I M
Bethel
B E N J A M I N
Mizpah
Michmash
Gilgal
Kiriath Jearim
Ekron
Gibeah
Ashdod
Beth Shemesh
Bethlehem
Ashkelon
Gath
P H I L I S T I A
J U D A H
Gaza

DEAD
SEA

Beersheba

The story shows how little understanding he had of prophetic things at the time, but from that day on the LORD
was with him in a new way and 'all Israel from Dan to
Beersheba recognised that Samuel was attested as a prophet
of the LORD.' He continued receiving revelations from the
LORD 'through his word' and before long his prophetic teaching was being heeded all over Israel. (3.2 – 4.1)

Chs. 4–6: The Fall of Shiloh.
In fulfilment of the word of the LORD, Israel was defeated
by the Philistines, Shiloh was destroyed (see Jer. 7.12–14;
26.6), the ark was captured and the priests were killed. The
ark was eventually returned, but Israel had now hit rock
bottom. The need for revival was more manifest than ever,
but the LORD had already prepared his man.

Ch. 7: Revival breaks out.
The date is about 1050 BC. Samuel has embarked on a
public preaching ministry, calling on Israel to repent and
turn back to God. The people respond by abandoning their
idols and presently Samuel is able to summon a national
revival convention. The scenes of fasting, repentance and
intercession for the nation show how deeply the people were
responding to his message.

The Philistines tried to disrupt this assembly, but were
confounded by a miraculous act of deliverance, and for the
first time Israel witnessed a reversal of her fortunes. The
effect on the nation's morale must have been immense.
Revival had truly started.

Samuel's ministry now takes a new turn. As he goes
around preaching, he finds the mantle of national leadership
falling on his shoulders and has to accept the role the earlier
judges had, but, as the following chapters clearly show, he
lost nothing of his prophetic anointing as he did so.

Chs. 8–11: Israel is given a prophet-king.
The story in these chapters has exactly the same miraculous
flavour as many of the stories we read in some modern
charismatic biographies. It tells how, after much objection,
Samuel agreed to help find a suitable candidate to become

Israel's first king (ch. 8), then leads us into a tale full of wondrous coincidences and happenings. It just so happens that Saul, a farmer's boy out looking for some lost donkeys, is close by Samuel's home when he decides to give up his search; it just so happens that his servant has a suitable gift to give the prophet in his pocket; it just happens that they arrive in the nick of time to catch Samuel before he goes to the evening sacrifice. But more than that, Samuel has been forewarned of their arrival and has a meal already prepared for them. By the time Saul got to the end of that meal and his conversation with Samuel in his home afterwards, he must have been full of amazement and pondering many questions. (ch. 9)

The events of the next day were no less wondrous, for early in the morning Samuel prophetically anointed Saul for the role of leadership he was later to assume, then sent him on his way to meet a band of prophets among whom he also was to receive the Spirit and thus become a prophet/charismatic himself. (10.1–16)

Saul was not to become king immediately, and so he returned to his farming. But now he knew the working power of the Spirit, and some time later the Spirit was to move on him again, rousing him to lead Israel to victory in battle against the Ammonites, after which his kingship was finally confirmed. (10.17 – 11.15)

Samuel's fellowship of prophets.

Saul's story belongs in another volume; for the moment our interest is in prophets. But we have had to glance through his story because it is inextricably intertwined with Samuel's and in it we encounter a group of prophets for the first time in the Old Testament. It seems that Samuel's ministry, whilst it generated revival and hope in the nation at large, also touched some individuals at a much more profound level, men who gathered round him to learn his prophetic experience, to embrace his enthusiasm for God and to help him spearhead the movement for revival in the nation.

Unfortunately we know very little about them. When we first meet them in 10.5–13 we see them worshipping in ways that look familiar to modern-day charismatics, singing to the accompaniment of the ancient equivalent of our guitars, together with other portable wind and percussion instruments, and they were exercising their spiritual gifts during their worship, though we cannot now tell what exactly is meant when it is said that they were 'prophesying'.

We meet them again in 1 Sam. 19.18–24, this time with Samuel superintending their worship. Again present-day charismatics will recognise familiar features in the account of this occasion, as the police who come to arrest David are caught up in the Spirit of the meeting and as Saul when he arrives finds himself laid out on the ground for twenty-four hours, 'slain in the Spirit', as we would say today.

The impression we get is that they were fairly few in numbers at this time, though their impact on the society of their day and their ultimate contribution to history was disproportionately considerable. Saul himself became one of them before he became king, and later they stood firmly behind David who also seems to have shared in some way in their prophetic anointing. Certainly we are told that 'the Spirit of the LORD came upon David in power' from the day that Samuel anointed him at his home (1 Sam. 16.13), and it was with them that he first sought refuge when he had to flee from Saul (19.18).

However, not only did they rescue faith in their own generation and raise up leaders and kings to govern God's people, but they also laid the first foundations on which all subsequent prophetic/charismatic movements were to build – even in our own day, for the challenges to faith, the call to revival-ministry and the opportunities for receiving and exercising the gifts of God remain very much with us today.

Chs. 12–31: Samuel's heartache at the direction the revival takes.

As we have seen, the prophet's call was to preach repentance and a return to the standards of faith and obedience taught by Moses. Samuel had been uncompromising in that call and he clearly expected no less from Saul. His sermon in ch. 12 makes that very clear, and it is precisely over this issue of radical obedience that he separates from Saul:

You acted foolishly. You have not kept the command the
LORD your God gave you; if you had, he would have
established your kingdom over Israel for all time.

(13.13)

Does the LORD delight in burnt offerings and sacrifices
*   as much as in obeying the voice of the LORD?*
To obey is better than sacrifice,
*   and to heed is better than the fat of rams.*
For rebellion is like the sin of divination,
*   and arrogance like the evil of idolatry.*
Because you have rejected the word of the LORD,
*   he has rejected you as king.*

(15.22f)

Through his failure to obey the LORD Saul became proud,
seeking self-aggrandisement, and though the LORD then
directed Samuel to David, 'a man after his own heart'
(13.14), Samuel was broken-hearted at the turn of events
(15.35).

We can understand why. He had, after all, given his whole
heart and life to securing revival for the nation and to re-
establishing it in the ways of God's law, and now he was
watching everything he had worked for being put in jeop-
ardy by the very man he had promoted to power failing to
live by the simple principles of obedience that had formed
the basis of the whole revival. But Samuel knew that, when
it came to the choice, he had to stand by his prophetic
principles rather than the man, even though it rent his heart
asunder.

Samuel did not live to see Saul's final ruin (25.1), though
his words echoed on from the grave haunting Saul with the
reminder of his disobedience (ch. 28). But Saul's loss was
David's gain, for Samuel's men gave him their full support
(ch. 19) and, whereas Saul never again had a prophet to
guide him (28.6), David found one called Gad advising him
in his time of need (22.5). The prophets took their stand
alongside the man they knew would promote the revival
work of God.

2. AFTER REVIVAL – PROPHECY IN THE TENTH CENTURY
(2 SAMUEL 1 – 1 KINGS 16)

There continued to be prophets in Israel, but national recovery and growth rendered their voice less urgent than in Samuel's time. The movement lost its early vitality and the prophet became a recognised functionary in the system of Israel's religious institutions. Whereas Samuel had made and unmade kings, prophets now attended the king in his court. Gad became known as 'David's seer' (2 Sam. 24.11) and Nathan the prophet was readily at hand to be consulted when David was toying with the idea of building a temple (7.1–3). We even find Nathan at the end of David's life actively participating in the political wrangling that attended the succession of Solomon to the throne (1 Kings 1).

However, the first loyalty of these men continued to be to the word of God. When Nathan was consulted about the temple, the word he eventually brought to David was in essence to forget it and get on with building up the nation and governing the people, the job the LORD had raised him up to do (2 Sam. 7.4–16). Later, presumably at the risk of his life, he boldly confronted David with the sinfulness of his affair with Bathsheba (2 Sam. 12). In a similar way, the prophet Gad was to challenge and minister to David when he was conscience-stricken after he had taken census of his fighting men (2 Sam. 24.1–17).

Later prophets were also remembered for the strong stance they took in upholding the ways of the LORD, often very much in opposition to royal authority. Thus:
– Ahijah of Shiloh risked the wrath of Solomon in order to obey the LORD by prophetically encouraging Jeroboam's revolt against the house of David (1 Kings 11.26–40), and then he risked the wrath of Jeroboam by denouncing his sinful ways to his wife (14.1–18).
– When Solomon's son, Rehoboam, wanted to take retaliatory measures against Jeroboam, another prophet called Shemaiah stepped forward with a word from the LORD restraining him from doing so (12.21–24; 2 Chron. 11.1–4). Later in his reign this same prophet was able to call Reho-

boam to repentance and so avert total disaster when Shishak of Egypt invaded Judah (2 Chron. 12.5–8).

– An unnamed man of God from Judah came to Jeroboam while he was publicly offering sacrifice at his new sanctuary at Bethel and at great risk to his own life denounced the king's idolatrous worship (13.1–10).

– In the same vein another prophet called Jehu pronounced judgment on Baasha, Jeroboam's son, for perpetuating his father's sins (16.1–7).

– Then early in the following century we find one called Hanani being put in prison for daring to upbraid King Asa for his unfaithfulness (2 Chron. 16.7–10).

Some of the prophets clearly never lost sight of their calling to stand by the basic revival principles that had called them into being in the first instance, but though there were a few men like that, the movement on the whole seems to have settled into stagnant respectability, even enjoying considerable royal patronage. Such at least is the impression we get from a story like the one found in 1 Kings 22 telling how Jehoshaphat of Judah and Ahab of Israel were able to summon four hundred of them for advice on one occasion. If this impression is correct, then it is little wonder they had made hardly any impact on history for a century or more. Though prophetic forms and life-styles were being maintained, the revival flames had clearly subsided in most of the prophets' hearts. The result was once again a state of social, moral and religious decline in the nation and an encroachment of pagan ways that was to peak in the reign of Ahab in the ninth century. The need for revival was again becoming urgent.

God's Promise to David (2 Sam. 7.5–16).

Amid the various contributions to the flow of history the prophets made in the tenth century, by far the most important of their pronouncements was that made by Nathan to David at the time he was considering building a temple. Apart from telling him to leave aside the building project, his words contained revelations that were to shape the whole future of Israel's faith and history.

The gist of his message was that David had been raised

up for a purpose far beyond erecting a cedar-wood house for the ark (vv. 5–7), but that God's intention was for him to become ruler over a strong independent nation (vv. 8–11) and also to be the father of a house (dynasty) of kings that would rule over his people for ever (vv. 11–16). The promise is quite unconditional: 'Your house and your kingdom shall endure for ever before me; your throne shall be established for ever' (v. 16).

There are, however, some presentations of this promise in the Old Testament that do make continuation of the dynasty conditional on the king maintaining faithfulness in his walk with God (1 Kings 8.25; Ps. 132.12), though there are also others that, like 2 Sam. 7 itself, only make obedience the condition for each king's own personal blessing, and affirm absolutely that his disobedience will not cause the promise, that there should always be a son of David ruling over the LORD's people, to be revoked (cp. 1 Chron. 17.7–14; Ps. 89.30–37). How a promise can be both conditional and unconditional like this defies explanation by our systems of logic, but the fact is that at the time of the exile, precisely because the kings failed to maintain faithfulness, the Davidic succession was discontinued, and yet the promise stood and was not cancelled, for it finds fulfilment today in the eternal reign of Jesus Christ.

We shall return to this promise to David many times, because it was to form the basis for Israel's Messianic hope. For the moment it was simply a promise to David that one of his sons would succeed him, but with hindsight today we can see at a glance how aptly prophetic it was in preparing the way for Jesus' ministry – for example, in its comparison of the king's relationship with God to that of a son with his father (2 Sam. 7.14).

The tenth century may not have been one of the most exciting in the history of Israelite prophecy, but this promise through Nathan was to make it one of the most significant.

4

Elijah, Elisha and the Sons of the Prophets

While revivals all have the same purpose, their character-
istics do differ in each generation. Two distinguishing features of Israel's ninth-century revival are community among
the prophets and miracle-working, which give it a fairly
contemporary feel for many involved in today's renewal
movements. Of course, there are also major differences, but
the similarities are enough to prompt us to learn from their
ancient experience and be encouraged by it.

1. ELIJAH AND THE START OF A SECOND WAVE OF REVIVAL
(1 KINGS 17.1 – 19.18)

When Ahab became king in Northern Israel in 874 BC,
things began to change radically. His wife, Jezebel, a
Sidonian princess, was an ardent devotee of the Canaanite
gods, Baal and Asherah, for whom she built a sanctuary in
Samaria (1 Kings 16.29–33). She introduced her own pagan
prophets (850 of them are mentioned in 18.19), and sought
to eliminate the prophets of the LORD. So thorough was her
purge that at one point Elijah thought he was the only man
of true faith left in the land (19.10,14). For the first time in
its history the prophetic faith, if not the whole faith of Israel,
was in danger of being extinguished. The crisis was different
from that of Samuel's day, but the ultimate danger was
much the same, and again it was the charismatic enthusiasts
who responded to the challenge and ultimately saved the
day.

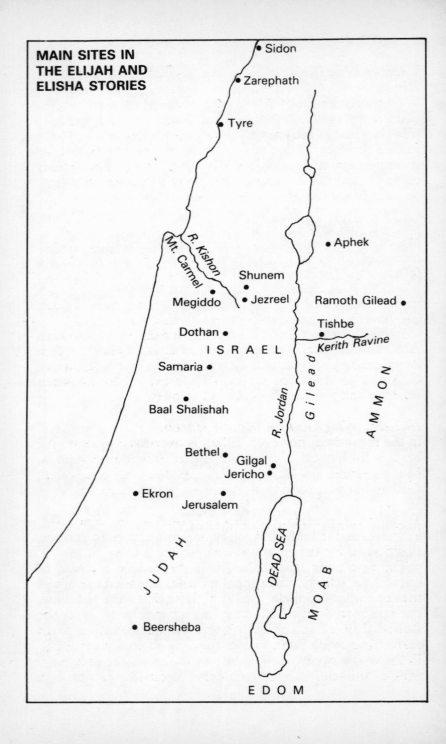

MAIN SITES IN
THE ELIJAH AND
ELISHA STORIES

Sidon

Zarephath

Tyre

R. Kishon

Mt. Carmel

Aphek

Shunem

Megiddo

Jezreel

Ramoth Gilead

Dothan

Tishbe

ISRAEL

Kerith Ravine

Samaria

Gilead

AMMON

Baal Shalishah

R. Jordan

Bethel

Gilgal

Jericho

Ekron

Jerusalem

JUDAH

DEAD SEA

MOAB

Beersheba

EDOM

1 Kings 17: Elijah declares war with the House of Ahab.

We know nothing of Elijah's background, except that he came from Tishbe in Transjordan. Suddenly he appears as from nowhere, confronting Ahab and announcing a prolonged drought. However, these are dangerous times and so he immediately goes into hiding, where he is miraculously cared for, part of the time in the heart of 'enemy territory', up near Sidon, Jezebel's home town.

Ch. 18: His first public victory.

Meantime Jezebel's persecution is creating an underground church. Other men of the Spirit besides Elijah are driven into hiding. Their numbers are apparently quite small (only a hundred are mentioned in v. 4), but like Elijah they are the enthusiasts of the day and Israel's hope rests in their hands. This must have been their darkest hour.

In the third year Elijah comes out of hiding and summons Ahab and the Baal prophets to Mount Carmel where, before a frightened and apathetic crowd, he calls down the fire of God and so starts the revival that is eventually to sweep Baalism and the House of Ahab out of Israel.

19.1–18: With God on Mount Horeb.

In the meantime, however, Elijah is overtaken by fear. All he sees for himself is increasing hatred from Jezebel, so he flees to Horeb (= Mount Sinai). But there he meets with God and is sent back to continue his prophetic work.

These chapters contain some well known stories with excellent lessons for faith, but we must limit comment to their significance for the central theme we are tracing.

The first thing that strikes us is the sudden increase of miraculous activity. Occasional miracles attended the ministries of earlier prophets, as also of those that were to follow, but nowhere do we find them in such profusion as in the stories of Elijah and Elisha, that is, of course, except much earlier and much later, in the days of Moses and of Jesus. In the whole sweep of Bible history theirs are the only main ages of miracle. It is not without reason that it was with

Moses and Elijah, rather than say Joshua, Samuel, David or Isaiah, that Jesus met on the mount of Transfiguration (Luke 9.28–36).

The challenges of the age were similar for all three. They were all great revivalists, but it was never enough for them to call men back to God in repentance. As well as preaching against national apostasy and apathy, they also had to deal with virulent external powers doing their utmost to eradicate faith. In Moses' day the oppression was Egyptian, in Elijah's Baalistic, in Jesus' Satanic. Hence, as well as seeing men's hearts changed through repentance, they had to see these opposing, destructive forces confronted and beaten. For that work God equipped them with miracle-working powers with which to strike at the enemies' strongholds. Today the forces ranged against the Church are no less virulent, and again God is equipping his people in the same way. Our battle has much the same flavour as theirs and the equipping we still need is not much different either.

For Elijah, just as for Moses and Jesus, the battle was a lonely one. There were those who supported Moses, but none who could advise him about God's call; Elijah's prophet friends were all in hiding and so no help to him at all; Jesus' disciples were never able to understand the challenges facing their master, let alone counsel him. But God himself encouraged them. Moses and Elijah both stood on Mount Horeb and spoke with God, both in similar circumstances in which the voice of God was heralded by changing weather phenomena. Just as Moses witnessed thunder and lightning, fire and smoke, and an earthquake preceding the voice of God (Exod. 19.16–19), so Elijah had to watch the wind, earthquake and fire pass by before he heard God speak to him (1 Kings 19.11–13). Likewise, when there was no-one who understood enough to encourage Jesus, on another mountain God allowed him to speak with the only two men in history who had gone anything like the same way before him and again his voice was heard, this time preceded by a brilliant radiance and the appearance of a cloud (Luke 9.29–30,34).

God's commission to Elijah on this mountain was generally to take courage and get back into the warfare. Specifically he was to see that Damascus and Israel got new kings, men who would execute God's judgment on Israel, and to choose Elisha to succeed him in heading up the prophetic battle.

2. THE PROPHETIC VOICE INCREASES AND GROWS IN CONFIDENCE (1 KINGS 19.19 – 2 KINGS 2.18)

19.19–21: *The call of Elisha.*
The story is crisp and dramatic. Elijah acts in obedience to God and then is suddenly appalled at the magnitude of the challenge he has laid on Elisha's young shoulders. Elisha's response is instant and unequivocal. He says goodbye to his parents, burns his farming equipment so that he cannot be tempted back into known securities, and sets out to become Elijah's disciple. We shall not hear of him again until he is ready to take over from his master. Presumably he simply accompanied Elijah in the meantime, in much the same way as Jesus' disciples later followed him, and thus learned the prophetic calling.

Ch. 20–21: *Ahab is confronted again.*
Other prophets must have taken courage from Elijah's public stance, for one of them now joins him in speaking out openly to the king. Ahab is not at all pleased, of course, but the message is now beginning to get through to his heart, and after Elijah confronts him about his sinful seizure of Naboth's vineyard, he shows first signs of repentance.

Ch. 22: *The death of Ahab.*
Ahab's repentance came too late to have any influence on Jezebel's religious policy, for soon afterwards he was killed in battle. But we at least see him prepared to allow Jehoshaphat of Judah's request to consult the prophets of the Lord, though he was quite angry again when one of them, Micaiah ben Imlah, dared to suggest that the Lord still opposed him and then prophesied his coming death.

2 Kings 1.1 – 2.18: The end of Elijah's ministry.

After Ahab's death, Elijah continued his outspoken opposition to the royal patronising of paganism, as when King Ahaziah, Ahab's son, tried to consult Baal-Zebub, the god of Ekron. But his work was now done, and so we read of how he handed on his calling to Elisha together with the power to fulfil it.

In these chapters we see clear traces of resurrection in Israel's faith. The prophets have been creeping out of hiding and gradually making their presence known, and here at the end of his time on earth Elijah is able to pay farewell visits openly to prophetic groups in some not insignificant towns in Israel. But the battle is not yet over, for the official state religion is still Baalism, patronised by Jezebel who is still Queen-Mother and very much an active power behind the throne.

3. ELISHA AND THE 'SONS OF THE PROPHETS' (2 KINGS 2.19 – 13.21)

2.19 – 8.29: Elisha's charismatic ministry.

These chapters are mainly made up of charismatic miracle stories, similar in some ways to the sort of stories we find in modern charismatic biographies. The longer stories tell how:

– Elisha prophesied a flood that confused the Moabite armies (ch. 3),

– raised a Shunamite woman's dead son, a boy whose birth he had originally prophesied himself (4.8–37),

– healed Naaman, an Aramean army commander, of leprosy (ch. 5),

– brought blindness on some hostile Aramean troops (6.8–23),

– and prophesied the lifting of the siege of Samaria (6.24 – 7.20).

The shorter stories are sometimes even more dramatic:

– how he divided the Jordan with Elijah's cloak (2.13–15),

THE AGE OF ELIJAH AND ELISHA

JUDAH	DATE	ISRAEL		

Asa 911-870	880	Omri 885-74
		  Builds Samaria and makes Israel
		  politically strong.
		Ahab 874-53
			H
			O
			U
			S
			E	

Jehoshaphat 870-48
  Judah prospers in his time. He
  lives at peace with Ahab and
  joins him to do battle with the
  Arameans at Jabesh-Gilead
  (1 Kings 22)
	870	Marries Jezebel and allows her to
		  popularise Baalism. Almost all
		  Elijah's ministry was during his
		  reign.
				E
				L
				I
				J

	860		O F	A
		Ahab is killed in battle at Jabesh- Gilead. Ahaziah 853-52 Jehoram 852-41	O M	H
Jehoram 848-41	850	Elisha continues Elijah's revival ministry.	R I	E

Ahaziah 841, killed by Jehu.
Athaliah 841-35
  Pagan daughter of Jezebel,
  deposed in a palace coup.
 	
Joash 835-796
  Boy-king whose reforms restored
  faith in Judah. Elijah's revival
  was now spilling over into the
  southern kingdom.
	840	Jehu 841-14
		  An army officer anointed by
		  Elisha to overthrow the house of
		  of Omri and purge the land of
		  Baalism.
			H
			O
			U
			S
				L
				I
				S

	830	Continuing war with Syria. Period of weakness in Israel.	E	H A
	820		O F	| |
		Jehoahaz 814-798		|
	810		J E H	| | |

Amaziah 796-67	800	Jehoash 798-82
		  Last king to consult Elisha
		  (2 Kings 13)
			U	|
				|

– sterilised the putrid wells of Jericho (2.19–22),
– cursed the jeering youths of Bethel (2.23–25),
– provided a miraculous means of income for a prophet's widow (4.1–7),
– neutralised poison in a pot of soup (4.38–41),
– fed a large gathering with inadequate food supplies (4.42–44),
– caused an axe-head lost in the river to rise to the surface (6.1–7),
– effectively secured the restoration of the Shunamite woman's property (8.1–6),
– and prophesied Hazael's seizure of the throne of Damascus as well as his atrocities against Israel (8.7–15).

Delightful as many of these stories are to read, one of their main values is to show us how the revival had progressed since Elijah first confronted Ahab. The land was still governed by a pagan regime, headed now by Jehoram, Ahab's second son, while his mother, Jezebel, continued to be active in the background. But the voice of the LORD's prophets had also gained strength, and Elisha had gathered around himself a number of supporters who committed themselves to the prophetic cause of working for the revival of Israel's faith. They were known as 'the sons of the prophets'. They came together in some kind of community or fellowship structures to share their lives as they pursued their common vision. At least some of them lived in community (6.1–7) and shared common meals (4.38–44). They were not celibate, for we read of widows and children (4.1–7). They call Elisha 'My lord' (6.5) and are said to 'meet with him' (literally 'sit before him', i.e. be taught by him – 4.38). Although we lack enough detail to make a full comparison, the picture is reminiscent of Samuel and his men, and in many ways bears comparison with revival communities and fellowships today. We are shown nothing of their worship, though the story about Elisha calling for a minstrel to calm his anger and put him in the right mood for hearing God's word (3.14f) compares well with present-day Christian experience of the prophetic word being received most readily in the setting of worship (cp. 1 Cor. 14).

Chs. 9–10: *The overthrow of Baalism.*

In the end it took a military coup to re-establish Israel's religion. Jehu, the commander of the army, appointed to the task through Elisha's ministry in accordance with the word of the LORD to Elijah at Horeb (1 Kings 19.16), overthrew Ahab's dynasty in a blood-bath, in which Jehoram and the King of Judah were both killed, as were Jezebel and seventy other sons of the house of Ahab. Then finally the ministers of Baal were slaughtered. This is not the way we would hope for revival of religion to be consolidated today, but it clearly had the initial support of Elisha and his prophets, and also of another enthusiast, Jonadab son of Rechab (10.15f). He was the founder of the Rechabites, a group that, like the prophets, was totally dedicated to the LORD's work, though they do not seem to have been charismatics. They are remembered more for their asceticism, having pledged themselves to live a nomadic life and to abstain from wine. Jeremiah spoke very highly of their devotion (see Jer. 35).

Jehu's murderous excesses were not allowed to pass without criticism from later prophets (Hos. 1.4f), but it was thanks to his zeal that Baalism was finally expunged from Israel. And so the battle for the faith, that had been spearheaded by the prophets, was finally won by the sword of a man, who like Saul, David and Jeroboam, had been roused to the task by the prophets themselves. This was, however, to be the last occasion in Biblical times, though not the last in history, that a prophetic movement would advocate the use of military force for the defence of faith.

Chs. 11–13: *The restoration is completed.*

The impact of revival in Israel was soon being felt in Judah where Ahab's daughter, Athaliah, had also been introducing Baalism. After she was deposed the temple was restored and refurbished.

Elisha lived on into the reign of Jehu's grandson, Jehoash, but we hear nothing more about him, except that when he was in bed dying the king consulted him about his wars with Aram and he was angry at the king's lack of verve. His own power apparently lived on after him, however, for we hear that a dead man was raised to life through contact with his corpse! (13.20f)

Whilst some in Israel dismissed the prophets as madmen (2 Kings 9.11), many regarded them with awesome respect. They were people who stood very close to God – 'men of God' they were frequently called. Contact with them could bring great blessings, such as healing, the gift of a child, or supernatural provision of food, but it could also prove dangerous, as some discovered to their cost (cp. 2 Kings 1.9–17; 2.23–25). Some sought their guidance and blessing, but others, even of those who stood close to them, feared their holiness and the judgment of God that it could bring into their lives (cp. 1 Kings 17.18). They were men who knew a power of God's Spirit at work in and through them that is not often encountered in religious circles. But then, such power was doubtless needed to rescue faith in a time like theirs. The parallels and lessons for us as we pray for revival today are fairly obvious.

4. THE PROBLEM OF TRUE AND FALSE PROPHECY

There are two prophet-stories that vividly highlight the problem involved in discerning true and false prophecy. The first is in 1 Kings 13 where we read about a man of God who was deceived by a false word from another prophet; his failure to discern the truth cost him his life. The second is in 1 Kings 22 where the prophet Zedekiah is indignant at Micaiah's claim that he and his four hundred prophets are speaking words given them by a lying spirit, and here it is King Ahab who pays with his life for failure to discern the true word.

While we may not be too surprised at Ahab's inability to distinguish the truth, it is a much more serious matter when a man who is himself a prophet has difficulty in doing so. Clearly this is not a problem that can be dismissed with a simple answer.

We can distinguish four groups of prophets in ninth-century Israel:

1. The Elijah-Elisha group.
2. The prophets of Baal and Asherah, alongside whom were doubtless other pagan diviners, mediums, dreamers of dreams, and the like.
3. Solitary prophets who may not have had any group association, like Micaiah – or Nathan, Ahijah and others in the century before.
4. Groups of prophets, like the 400 in 1 Kings 22, who could be called on at any time by the king for advice and guidance, perhaps because they were supported by him in some way. The prophets of Baal and Asherah certainly received royal patronage, for they were said to 'eat at Jezebel's table' (18.19).

The Biblical attitude to the pagan prophets was totally uncompromising and need not delay us here (see above, p. 18). However, it is worth noting some of the differences between them and the Israelite prophets in passing. In 1 Kings 18 we find the Baal prophets dancing around their altar, chanting their endless incantations, slashing their bodies and working themselves into quite a frenzy. They are clearly men with no revelation who can only perform magical rituals in the hope of persuading their god to respond. The contrast with Elijah, the man of faith operating under constraint of the word of God, is striking.

The really thorny problem arose, however, not when a pagan prophet spoke, but when two prophets who both spoke in the name of the God of Israel contradicted each other. Deut. 18.20–22 gives the ultimate test of truth or falsehood when it declares that only the prophetic word that comes to pass is the true one, but sometimes it is necessary to have discernment before the outworking takes place, as 1 Kings 13 & 22 both vividly illustrate.

Both Deut. 18 and 1 Kings 22 contrast the prophet who has received revelation from the LORD and the one who only presumes that he has. The problem remained an urgent one right through Old Testament times. We later hear Jeremiah, for example, criticise prophets who have not 'stood in the council of the LORD', but only speak 'visions from their own minds', filling their hearers with false hopes (Jer. 23.16–18).

Perhaps the 400 in 1 Kings 22 were too much the king's yes-men, giving hopeful prophecies in order to please. Certainly Micah knew of prophets in his day who spoke to please and so line their pockets (Micah 3.5,11), and Ezekiel has harsh words to say about those who give comfortable oracles of 'Peace' when there is no peace (13.10).

Sometimes a prophet without revelation would speak from the confidence of a theological principle, such as that which declared that because the LORD's temple stood in Jerusalem, the city must always be supernaturally protected. Some of the prophets Micah opposed seem to have taken that view (see esp. Micah 3.11), and Jeremiah was familiar with it in his day, though he had no patience with it (Jer. 7). True prophecy must rest on revelation, not doctrine.

The problem of discerning the true and the false was clearly not yet resolved in ancient Israel. It is one we shall have to return to again at a later stage.

PART THREE

THE EMERGING PROPHETIC VISION

EIGHTH CENTURY B.C.

The main concern for most of the prophets of the eleventh to the ninth centuries was revival and the preservation of faith in the face of encroaching paganism. These remained living issues for the eighth century prophets, who were still charismatic enthusiasts fighting for renewal of faith through the power of the Spirit, but now they appear more clearly in the guise of preachers and teachers, as spokesmen of God's word, calling men back to the ancient standards of righteousness and justice (Amos), to knowledge of God and responsiveness to his love (Hosea), or to repentance, holiness and faith (Isaiah).

The main burden of their message is to highlight the terrible dangers of sin and faithlessness. They constantly warn of suffering, destruction and exile that must result, but running through their warnings there is also a thread of hope. We only see a little of it in Amos, but increasingly through Hosea, Micah and Isaiah, we find the growth of a vision that tells of restoration to the homeland, the introduction of a new covenant, the coming of Messiah, and the establishment of a new relationship between God and his people that will affect the other nations of earth and lead ultimately to the re-establishment of Eden. The vision is for the most part quite embryonic and will be developed more fully by later prophets, but all the essential ingredients are there in these eighth-century writings.

This long-term vision will draw our attention increasingly as we approach New Testament times, but for the moment we find the eighth-century prophets generally more preoccupied with the crises and conditions of their own day.

5

Warnings of Approaching Judgment

Though we shall have to give special attention to the long-range visions of the eighth-century prophets because of their importance for understanding the New Testament, it should be borne in mind that most of their utterances actually refer to events that were soon to take place in their own generation, rather than the distant future. Thus the warnings of Amos and Hosea relate mainly to the looming threat of Assyrian invasion, and so to understand their significance properly we need to know just a little about the political background to their ministries.

The Assyrians began to expand their frontiers about 900 BC. In 853, towards the end of Ahab's reign, they engaged a coalition of Palestinian forces at Qarqar on the River Orontes, and in 841 Jehu, almost immediately after becoming king of Israel, was obliged to pay them tribute (both events are known only from Assyrian records and are not mentioned in the Bible), but they were not ready at that time to build their empire in the west and so did not bother the Palestinian states again for a century.

For much of those hundred years Israel was occupied in prolonged wars with Syria (Aram; 2 Kings 13). The revival that set Jehu on the throne was at first followed by political decline rather than resurgence, but it put fibre back into the nation's muscle, and, with the prophets (who included Jonah) still encouraging them, Jehu's successors eventually led Israel forward into an age of considerable wealth and security during the reign of Jeroboam II (782–53 BC; 2 Kings 14.23–29). It was in his time that Amos and Hosea prophesied, but their warnings went largely unheeded by the people of Israel. In 732 the Assyrians took Damascus,

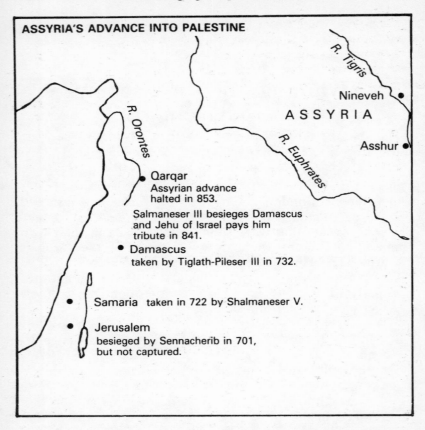

ASSYRIA'S ADVANCE INTO PALESTINE

R. Tigris

Nineveh ●

A S S Y R I A

R. Orontes

R. Euphrates

Asshur ●

● Qarqar
Assyrian advance
halted in 853.

Salmaneser III besieges Damascus
and Jehu of Israel pays him
tribute in 841.

● Damascus
taken by Tiglath-Pileser III in 732.

● Samaria   taken in 722 by Shalmaneser V.

● Jerusalem
besieged by Sennacherib in 701,
but not captured.

and then finally in 722 they took Samaria, deported its
inhabitants and brought the history of Northern Israel to an
end, just as both prophets foretold would happen.

1. A PLEA FOR RIGHTEOUSNESS AND JUSTICE (AMOS)

Amos was a shepherd from Tekoa, a village in the Judean
hills twelve miles south of Jerusalem. He was called to
prophesy in the Northern Kingdom, much to the displeasure
of Amaziah, the priest at Bethel.

The date is about 750 BC. Judging by what Amos says,

much of the affluence of Jeroboam's reign was gained at the
expense of the poor and was accompanied by a horrifying
loss of respect for justice.

Chs. 1–2: Judgment on the nations and on Israel.

The structure of these chapters is quite dramatic. Amos
systematically reviews the surrounding nations, Israel's
immediate neighbours, denouncing various injustices and
atrocities perpetrated by each, and pronouncing God's judgment on them in turn. Then, while his Israelite hearers
would be patriotically approving his judgments, he suddenly
homes in on Judah and Israel and proceeds to declare similar
verdicts against them. The sins of the nations are mostly
war-crimes, but the sins of the Israelites are far more griev-
ous, for they are social crimes committed against their own
people in times of peace and infringements of the law of
God.

Chs. 3–5: Look at your record and repent!

The fact that God has specially chosen you does not automatically ensure your blessing (3.1–2). God has revealed his
plan to his prophet (3.3–8), and it speaks of severe judgment, of invasion and destruction (3.9–15).

You have been warned time and again about the consequences of your oppressive and greedy ways. You have
already suffered judgment through so many natural disasters, 'yet you have not returned to me,' declares the LORD.
(Amos keeps repeating the point: 4.6,8,9,10,11). 'Therefore
. . . prepare to meet your God, O Israel.' (4.12) – And
remember that he is God Almighty, the Creator! (4.13)

There is a way out, however: 'Seek the LORD and live'
(5.4,6). There is so much corruption of justice and
oppression of the poor (5.7–13), but 'Seek good, not evil,
that you may live' (5.14); 'Perhaps the LORD God Almighty
will have mercy on the remnant of Joseph' (5.15). Do not
think the day of the LORD will bring you blessing (5.18–20),
nor that your religious festivals, songs and rituals will
impress God (5.21–27), but let there be justice and
righteousness (5.24). Otherwise it will have to be exile
(5.27)!

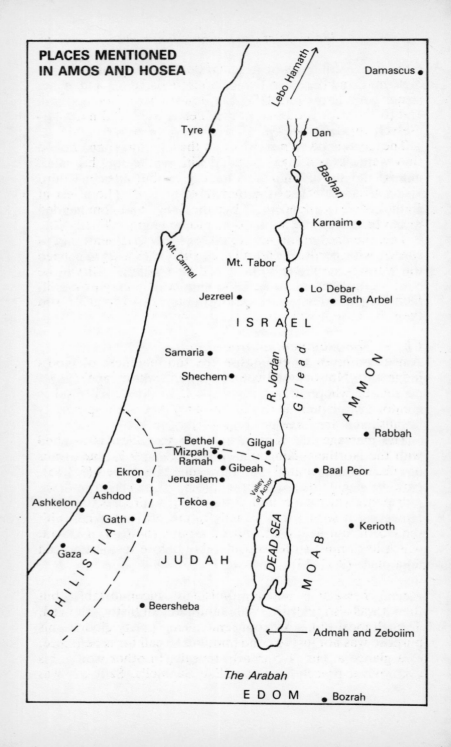

Chs. 6–8: The relentlessness of coming judgment.

You may indifferently lie on your beds, dine and wine, strum your harps and take no thought now, but that will end (6.1–7), for the LORD has spoken, and he will not tolerate your pride (6.8–14).

The LORD showed me visions of the coming judgment and they were devastating. I pleaded with him to stay his hand, and he did show willingness to forgive, but after the third vision I had to accept the inevitable (7.1–9). The priest at Bethel tried to silence me, but the LORD had commanded me to prophesy and so I was not to be stopped (7.10–17).

Then he showed me the totality of the judgment, a land strewn with corpses, and all was silence (8.1–3). So heed the warning now, for soon it will be too late. All will be confusion; it will seem as if the very creation is in turmoil. Don't expect to hear any word from the LORD to guide you then, because it will simply not be there (8.4–14).

Ch. 9: The judgment and beyond.

Amos continues to emphasise the thoroughness of God's judgment: 'Not one will get away, none will escape' (v. 1), no matter where they may try to hide (vv. 2–4). God is creator of all men and will certainly not show partiality because you are Israelites (vv. 5–7).

The message has repeatedly been that God is finished with the Northern Kingdom (7.1–9; 8.1–3; 9.1), but Amos has occasionally hinted that a few might be spared (5.3,15). Now he begins to speak of a future for some beyond the judgment, which he compares to a sieving process (9.8–10). However, it seems that Israel's future no longer lies with the North, but in Judah, centred around the City of David, which itself must suffer considerably before restoration can take place (9.11–15).

Amos' message is uncompromisingly uncomfortable, but then it was also realistic, as the unfolding of history showed. Though most of his pronouncements are pretty gloomy, his purpose was not just to condemn, but to call for repentance, as a glance at chs. 4–5 clearly reveals. In other words, his was revival preaching, not unlike Samuel's. Sadly, it was not received in the same way as Samuel's and so the judgment had to follow. Of course he also saw hope for what lay beyond, but it was not his calling to emphasise that.

In Samuel's and Elijah's day the need for revival was perhaps more evident than in Amos', for his were times of prosperity and seeming security in Israel. Amos' contention was that because that security was based on injustice and oppression of the poor, it could not possibly endure, but must surely call forth God's wrath.

The religion of the day was also generating a false sense of security. The sanctuaries were thriving, the festivals were being observed, tithes were paid and worship was flourishing (4.4f; 5.5,21f), but at base the system was rotten because it had no regard for righteousness and justice, the most basic principles of the law of Moses (5.24). There were even those who looked eagerly for the day of God's visitation, blissfully unaware that he must come in anger (5.18–20). What Amos was up against was quite unlike the near anarchy of Samuel's day or the open persecution of Elijah's, but rather complacency generated by wealth and shallow religion. The reception he got from the priest Amaziah was probably quite typical: 'Go home! Don't bother us here with your religious extremism. Stop causing trouble, because we're happy with things as they are!' (7.10–16) It is surprising how akin such conditions and attitudes are to those we live with today.

It would be wrong to think that Amos' message grew out of his own reasoning about social conditions in his day. He tells us himself that it was based entirely on revelation and the conviction of God's word:

> *Surely the Sovereign LORD does nothing*
> *without revealing his plan*
> *to his servants the prophets.*
> *The lion has roared who will not fear?*
> *The Sovereign LORD has spoken –*
> *who can but prophesy?*

(3.7f)

He prophesied simply because God took him and told him

to do so (7.10–16). His motives were not financial gain, or political ambition, or personal applause, nor had he any desire to justify himself or enter into discussion and debate. He spoke purely from the conviction of the word of God and that word was his only authority. His call was to declare it and he did so with a strength and assurance that speak volumes about the profundity of the experience of his prophetic call.

2. GOD'S ANGER AND HIS COMPASSION (HOSEA)

Hosea prophesied shortly after Amos, during the last years of the Northern Kingdom. These were times of turmoil, very much in contrast with the peace and affluence of Jeroboam's reign, which ended in 753. The Assyrians began to reappear on the northern horizon and when Damascus fell to them in 732 Israel became an Assyrian vassal kingdom. In the three decades between Jeroboam's death and the final fall of Samaria in 722 Israel had six kings, four of them coming to power by assassination.

The turbulence of the times must have shaken Israel out of the complacency Amos had to contend with, but strangely it did not secure a more ready response to Hosea's message than Amos got to his. According to Hosea Israel's religion was in a very sorry state. He speaks of corrupt priests and a people who have no knowledge of God because they are untaught (cp. 4.1–9). But worse still, there has been a wholesale turning, not to the LORD, but to the sexually perverted religion of Baal once more, and that the LORD cannot allow to continue.

Chs. 1–3: *Hosea's prophetic marriage.*
Hosea's prophetic call was very strange: to marry a prostitute as a living symbol of Israel's unfaithfulness, and to show through his marriage-experience the mixture of anger and heartbreak that God felt towards Israel. Thus we find him expressing disgust at his wife's unfaithfulness at one moment, the next calling her back to him, and likewise we

ISRAEL'S LAST YEARS				
JUDAH		DATE	ISRAEL	ASSYRIA
		770	Jeroboam II 782-53 Time of security and wealth in Israel.	No immediate threat to the West from Assyria.
	Uzziah 767-42 Age of peace with Israel.	760		
			Zechariah 753-52 Shallum 752 Menahem 752-42	
		750		
				Tiglath-Pileser III 745-27
I S M A I I C A A H H	Jotham 742-35	740	Pekahiah 742-40 Pekah 740-32	Leads the Assyrian armies west.
	Ahaz 735-15 Asks Tiglath-Pileser to help against Israel and Damascus. Pays tribute to Assyria after 732 (2 Kings 16)	730	Hoshea 732-22 Vassal of Assyria after fall of Damascus.	Takes Damascus in 732 Shalmaneser V 726-22 Takes Samaria in 722.
		720	FALL OF SAMARIA (2 Kings 17) 722	

(Left margin labels: ISAIAH, MICAH, AMOS, HOSEA)

According to 2 Kings 15.27, Pekah reigned for 20 years. Presumably that was as a rival king for about 14 years, until he assassinated Pekahiah and became sole ruler. These were turbulent years.

  2 Kings 17.4 suggests that Shalmaneser managed to arrest Hoshea before he laid siege to Samaria in 724.

hear him one moment declaring that God is finished with his people, even giving his children names to signify that fact, the next that he has compassion on them and wants them back. He knows full well that judgment must come, and yet looks forward to a time when Israel's relationship with God will be healed.

Ch. 4: The main reasons for God's disgust.
The rot is both deep and extensive: 'There is no faithfulness, no love, no acknowledgment of God in the land' (v. 1), and the fundamental laws of the Ten Commandments are neglected (v. 2). The fault lies as much with the leaders as with the people, who 'are destroyed from lack of knowledge', because the priests are ignoring the law and failing to teach it to them (vv. 4–9). The consequence is widespread

drunkenness, prostitution and idolatry, all associated with a wholesale turning to Canaanite paganism (vv. 10–18).

'A whirlwind (Assyrian invasion) will sweep them away' (v. 19).

Chs. 5–7: An extended plea for repentance.

Rebellion has so gripped the hearts of priests, leaders and people that it has caused God to withdraw his protection (5.1–6) and leave them to discover the consequences of their conduct (5.7–12), in the hope that after they have exhausted every other possible source of help, they will admit their guilt and in their misery earnestly seek God's face again (5.13–15).

Heart-felt repentance would, even at this late date, bring restoration, but what love they have evaporates like morning mist and so they must bear the consequences (6.1–6). Strangely, Israel continues in his abominable ways and 'does not return to the LORD his God or search for him.' (6.7 – 7.10). Instead, like a silly dove, he seeks solutions everywhere else, turning now to Egypt, now to Assyria, but all to no avail (7.11–16).

Chs.8–10: The consequences Israel can expect as the result of her sin.

Israel may say, 'O our God, we acknowledge you!', but everything belies such statements – rulers not of God's choice, idolatry in Samaria, running to Assyria for help, disregard for the law, empty sacrifices. 'Israel has forgotten his Maker' and judgment must come. (ch. 8)

Hosea now begins to say more about this judgment and warns it will mean exile to Assyria, but he parallels that with references to an Egyptian captivity. Sometimes he mentions Egypt and Assyria together (9.3; 11.5,11), sometimes Egypt alone (8.13; 9.6), sometimes Assyria alone (10.6). Since there never was an Egyptian exile, nor ever any threat of one, the message must be: Israel will go into exile in Assyria and that will be like going back into the old Egyptian slavery from which they were redeemed at first.

Ch. 11: A Father's love for his son.

Hosea reviews God's past love toward Israel and compares it to that of a father lovingly rearing his infant son. However, the son proved wayward and so he must be cast off. But 'How can I . . .?' the LORD cries. Here we again encounter, as in chs. 1–3, the mixed compassion and wrath of God. Yes, he must punish them, but he will then call them home again.

Chs. 12–14: A final plea for repentance.

Continuing in the same mixed vein, Hosea pleads: You have known the goodness of God in the past, but you are calling down his wrath by your ways now. 'You must return to your God; maintain love and justice, and wait for your God always.' (ch. 12)

You were once prosperous and powerful, but your turning to Baal now means an end to all that. (ch. 13)

Repent and the LORD will turn from his anger. He will heal and love you and then he will restore you to full blessing again. (ch. 14)

The heart-cry of Hosea contrasts vividly with the austerity of Amos, but the message is essentially the same. Hosea, however, speaks of the future beyond judgment with more vision. There will certainly be judgment – Israel cannot escape that, except perhaps by repentance but the coming exile will not be the end of everything for ever. It will be more like a new start.

Yes, the Assyrian captivity will be a return to Egyptian bondage, but just as that was followed by the exodus, so this captivity will be followed by a new exodus, for the LORD 'will roar like a lion (and) his children . . . will come trembling like birds from Egypt, like doves from Assyria' (11.10f). There will then follow a new period of wilderness wandering (2.14; 12.9) ending in a new entry to the promised land (11.11). And the purpose behind this new exodus and wilderness experience will be to create a new relationship between Israel and God, one in which God will no longer be saying, 'Not my loved one,' and 'Not my people,' but 'You are my people,' and Israel will equally wholeheartedly be saying to him, 'My husband,' and 'You are my God.' (2.14–23)

At the heart of this new relationship, just as at the heart of the old one, will be a covenant (2.18). Hosea gives no details about this new covenant except that, like the old one at Sinai, it will be based on the principles of righteousness and justice, love and compassion (2.19). We are also told that it will restore something of the life-quality of the Garden of Eden to the world, so that birds, animals, insects and men will once more live in peace and security (2.18), while God himself provides abundance in the field (2.21f).

While his message is addressed to Israel, like Amos before him, he suggests that Judah will have to have the leading role in the future outworking of God's purposes. Thus he speaks of Judah rescued by the LORD's sovereign power (1.7), the Israelites eventually returning to 'seek the LORD their God and David (the Judean monarch) their king' (3.4f), and the two nations thus fully reunited enjoying the fruit of God's promise to Abraham, becoming 'like the sand on the seashore, which cannot be measured or counted' (1.10f; cp. Gen. 22.17; 32.12). Here, as well as in Amos 9.11, we can see the first glimmerings of what is later to become a full-blown Messianic hope.

It is not that Hosea believes Judah to be that much better than Israel, for he in no way spares her in his invectives against sin (5.8–15; 6.4–11; 8.14; 11.12 – 12.6), though occasionally he does hint that the root of her problem is temptation to follow Israel into its sins, rather than something of her own making (4.15; 5.5). Certainly Baalism flourished more readily in the North, as in Elijah's day, for it was essentially an agricultural religion aimed at securing fertility in the soil and the crops, and Israel with its fertile valleys was good farmers' land, whereas Judah in the south was mainly mountain-terrain more suited to sheep-rearing. But whatever the excuses, Judah also has an appointed judgment through which she must pass before God can use her in his future plans (5.14; 6.11; etc.).

Hosea's vision of the future is an amazingly comprehensive one. Its various ingredients are taken up and developed more fully by later prophets, but already it captures in a few sentences the heart of the total Biblical vision of creation renewed and restored by the sovereign working of God's justice and love. Similarly, his vision of the fatherhood of God and of his disciplining but forgiving love touches the very heart of what is later to become the Christian gospel. Hosea's words still have a living message today.

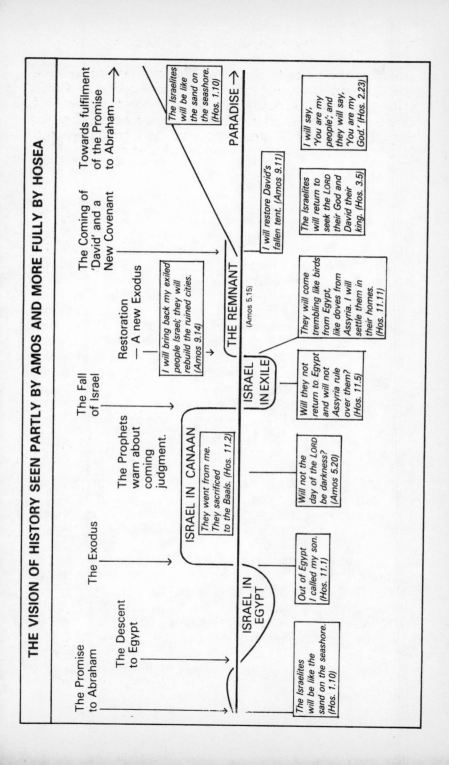

THE VISION OF HISTORY SEEN PARTLY BY AMOS AND MORE FULLY BY HOSEA

The Promise to Abraham

The Descent to Egypt

The Exodus

The Prophets warn about coming judgment.

The Fall of Israel

Restoration — A new Exodus

The Coming of 'David' and a New Covenant

Towards fulfilment of the Promise to Abraham →

The Israelites will be like the sand on the seashore. (Hos. 1.10)

PARADISE →

ISRAEL IN EGYPT

ISRAEL IN CANAAN

ISRAEL IN EXILE

THE REMNANT (Amos 5.15)

The Israelites will be like the sand on the seashore. (Hos. 1.10)

Out of Egypt I called my son. (Hos. 11.1)

They went from me. They sacrificed to the Baals. (Hos. 11.2)

Will not the day of the LORD be darkness? (Amos 5.20)

I will bring back my exiled people Israel; they will rebuild the ruined cities. (Amos 9.14)

Will they not return to Egypt and will not Assyria rule over them? (Hos. 11.5)

They will come trembling like birds from Egypt, like doves from Assyria. I will settle them in their homes. (Hos. 11.11)

I will restore David's fallen tent. (Amos 9.11)

The Israelites will return to seek the LORD their God and David their king. (Hos. 3.5)

I will say, 'You are my people'; and they will say, 'You are my God'. (Hos. 2.23)

6

Vision and Faith for Critical Times

In 735 BC Jerusalem was beset by the joint forces of Samaria and Damascus. King Ahaz of Judah sent to Tiglath-Pileser III of Assyria for help, which brought immediate relief to the city and led directly to the fall of Damascus. However, Ahaz's plea also resulted in Judah itself becoming vassal to Assyria (2 Kings 16). His successor, King Hezekiah, rebelled in 701 and the Assyrians set siege to Jerusalem, but they were prevented from taking it. It was during these four last decades of the eighth century that Isaiah and Micah were prophesying in Judah. Both are remembered for having moved King Hezekiah to seek the LORD, with the result that he was able to work a miracle of deliverance for the city (cp. Jer. 26.17–19; 2 Kings 18–19).

The prophets and prophet-groups between Samuel's day and Elisha's were mostly active in the North. Amos and Hosea spoke of other prophets still active there in their time (Amos 2.11; 3.7; Hos. 6.5; 9.7f). Some of what they said suggests appreciation of these men, some shows them standing apart from them (cp. Amos 7.14f; Hos. 4.4–6). What happened to the members of this old northern movement after 722 is uncertain. Some would have died, others would have been deported. But some may have sought refuge in Judah, and if so, their revivalist longings may have helped inspire the reforms of Hezekiah when he came to the throne in 715 (2 Kings 18.4). Perhaps some of them were among the anonymous prophets who spoke out against the abuses of Manasseh's reign in the first half of the next century, many of them paying for their boldness with their lives (21.10–16).

There is no evidence that the great writing prophets were

74

		THE AGE OF MICAH AND ISAIAH		
DATE	**JUDAH**	**ISRAEL**	**ARAM**	**ASSYRIA**
740	Jotham 742-35			Tiglath-Pileser III 745-27
	Ahaz 735-15 Faithfully paid tribute to		FALL OF DAMASCUS 732 ←	← 734
730	Assyria after 732, but led Judah into	FALL OF SAMARIA		Shalmaneser V 726-22
720	paganism.	722 ←		← 724 Sargon II 721-05
	Hezekiah 715-687 Reforms leading to revival.			
710	Revolt of Judean towns quelled (Hezekiah did not participate).		←	← 711
	Hezekiah leads a revolt against Assyria. Jerusalem is besieged and is miraculously delivered.			Sennacherib
700			←	← 701

products of this older revivalist/prophetic tradition, though they would doubtless have been influenced by it.

1. THE MOUNTAIN OF THE LORD'S TEMPLE (MICAH)

Micah's ministry overlaps Hosea's and runs on into the last years of the eighth century. He foresaw both the fall of Samaria in 722 BC and the siege of Jerusalem in 701 quite early in his ministry (ch. 1). Unlike Amos and Hosea, he lived and prophesied in Judah, not Israel, and so, while his teaching gathers up many of their central themes, particularly concerning justice and mercy, it also incorporates new elements relating to Jerusalem alone.

There was a strong belief in the South that since Jerusalem was God's chosen city, where the temple and the throne of David stood, it enjoyed a divine protection not accorded to

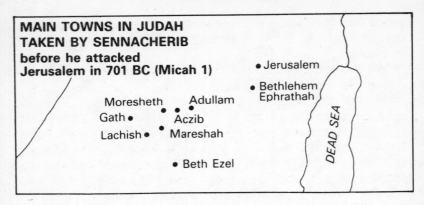

MAIN TOWNS IN JUDAH
TAKEN BY SENNACHERIB
before he attacked
Jerusalem in 701 BC (Micah 1)

• Jerusalem

• Bethlehem
  Ephrathah

Moresheth   Adullam
Gath •   • •
        • Aczib
Lachish •   • Mareshah

• Beth Ezel

DEAD SEA

any other place. This kind of thinking is sometimes referred to as 'Zion-theology' and is reflected in a number of the Psalms (e.g. Pss. 2, 46, 87). Micah warns against taking it too readily for granted, because God also requires justice and mercy, without which the city must forfeit his protection.

Ch. 1: God's judgment on Samaria and Jerusalem.

Micah warns Judah that following the idolatrous sins of Samaria will bring the disaster about to overtake Samaria right to the gates of Jerusalem. After pronouncing Samaria's destruction, he dramatically envisages the Assyrian armies progressing systematically through the towns of Judah up to the walls of Jerusalem. Hosea had also warned Judah about the consequences of following Samaria's sins (see p. 71).

Chs. 2–3: Greedy leaders and false prophets.

The sin of Samaria that Amos denounced was oppression of the poor by the rich. Micah castigates Jerusalem's leaders for the same (2.1–5; 3.1–4). And just as the religious system had waywardly stood by the political in Amos' time, so also in Micah's, though in Jerusalem it expressed itself somewhat differently. The priest at Bethel had tried to silence Amos; the prophets of Jerusalem now seek to silence Micah (2.6f). Together with their leaders and priests, they say 'Is not the LORD among us? No disaster will come upon us.' (3.11; cp. 2.6). Micah's response is that such a naive view of God's protection for Zion is worthless without some accompanying care for people, for justice, and for the ways of the LORD in general.

Micah's invective against the Jerusalem prophets is interesting. As well as criticising them for their unbalanced theology, he also accuses them of prophesying for financial gain, pronouncing words of blessing only if the fee is good (3.5,11). It seems strange that a movement that should have been leading the way in revival as in other ages could have sunk so low. But then the kind of prophecies they gave were apparently just what the people wanted to hear (2.11), and the temptation to preach with an eye on the collection plate is certainly not unknown today – yes, even in charismatic circles!

Micah boldly declares his own motivation, which contrasts sharply with theirs:

> *But as for me, I am filled with power,*
> *   with the Spirit of the LORD,*
> *   and with justice and might,*
> *to declare to Jacob his transgression,*
> *   to Israel his sin.*

(3.8)

And with that anointing he announces God's judgment on corrupt Jerusalem, namely its destruction, the very opposite of the Zion-theology's expectation (3.12). This was apparently the specific word that made the impact on Hezekiah and brought him to seek the LORD for the city's deliverance in 701 BC (see Jer. 26.18f).

Chs. 4–5: 'Now' and 'in the last days'.

But God does not go back on his promises. His purpose for Zion, 'the mountain of the LORD's temple,' will indeed be fulfilled, and wonderfully so, though that will be 'in the last days,' as Isaiah also says (4.1–8; cp. Isa. 2.1–5). Before that there must be judgment: 'now you must leave the city (and) go to Babylon' (4.10).

In these chapters Micah interweaves thoughts of judgment and thoughts of blessing in a way that may seem confusing to the reader, but his general theme is clear. The Assyrians will not take Jerusalem, but will themselves be taken over (5.5f). Judah's exile in Babylon will not be for ever, for 'the LORD will redeem you' (4.10). A new ruler will come from David's home town of Bethlehem and he will gather God's people together like a shepherd 'in the strength of the LORD . . . And he will be their peace' (5.2–5). Then 'the remnant of Jacob' will become what God always intended his people to be, purified and faithful executing their mission among the nations (5.5–15).

Micah's vision is truly amazing. To his contemporaries he seemed to be rejecting God's promise concerning Zion, but actually he was proclaiming the version of it that was to find fulfilment in New Testament times, and that with some surprisingly accurate details.

Chs. 6–7 God's compassion and Israel's ingratitude.
In these chapters we find echoes of Hosea's portrait of God pleading with Israel: I have been nothing but good to you in the past and have shown you very simply that I only wanted you to act justly, love mercy and walk humbly with me, but you have responded with so much corruption and I cannot overlook that (ch. 6).

Micah shares in God's distress, but he sees that judgment will not be the final end of it all, and restoration will come, for God will 'not stay angry for ever, but delight to show mercy,' according to his pledge to Abraham in days long ago (ch. 7).

The attitudes that confronted Micah are mostly still with us today. Many Christians believe that because their church, or their Christian work once had God's blessing, it is therefore bound to continue more or less indefinitely and even eventually blossom. Micah's message is that the LORD's purpose will indeed come to fruition, but not necessarily in the naive way they might want, for there may have to be judgment first. God's will is always to send revival, but sometimes that must start with a pruning.

Micah sees God's future rest with 'a remnant' – those that remain after the judgment of invasion (2.12; 5.7f; 7.18).

Amos had taught the same, but with less certainty (Amos 5.15), and Micah's contemporary, Isaiah, was to say more about it. What it adds up to is a vision of a small group (a 'church') within the wider community of God's people, a group of people who have been refined through God's visitation, purified and renewed to become the nucleus of the future community through which God will fulfil his purposes for men. The same principle still operates in the Christian Church today.

But for the present Micah's challenge is:

He has showed you, O man, what is good.
  And what does the LORD require of you?
To act justly and to love mercy
  and to walk humbly with your God.

(Micah 6.8)

2. THE CHALLENGE OF HOLINESS AND FAITH (ISAIAH 1–12)

Isaiah lived in Jerusalem in Micah's day, but his ministry seems to have started earlier and to have continued longer. Though they never mention each other, they do have one prophecy in common (Mic. 4.1–3 = Isa. 2.1–4), and presumably at least knew of each other's ministries.

Like Micah, and Amos and Hosea before him, Isaiah calls for righteousness and warns of judgment. He elaborates on some of their other themes, such as the remnant and Messiah, and introduces new ones, in particular holiness and faith. Thus his message both added to and further clarified their earlier revelation. In that he was like every other prophet in Israel's history, whose contribution added further clarification to the unfolding prophetic vision until sufficient preparation had been made for the coming of Christ, but it has to be acknowledged that his contribution is far more significant than most.

There is a great deal of debate about how much of this

book actually comes from the eighth-century prophet Isaiah himself. It falls naturally into three main parts:

(1) chs. 1–39, mostly relating to events in the late eighth century.

(2) chs. 40–55, relating to the end of the exile in the mid sixth.

(3) chs. 56–66, relating to the restored community in the late sixth.

Some say we have the works of three different prophets here, some that one prophet was responsible for the whole work, uttering prophecies addressed to people who were to live 200 years and more after his own time, some that the book is the deposit of a school of prophets started by Isaiah and continuing down through two or three centuries. Whatever the truth may be, we shall be studying the book in three separate parts, according to the historical periods to which its message relates. In this chapter we shall only look at the first.

Chs. 1–5: Seek justice.

Isaiah is said to have prophesied in the reigns of Uzziah, Jotham, Ahaz and Hezekiah. The first precise date found in the book is in 6.1: 'the year that King Uzziah died', namely 742 BC. Many take that as the date of his call to become a prophet, but other interpretations are possible. It may be that chs. 1–5, or parts of them, represent Isaiah's earliest teaching, in the reign of Uzziah, probably towards its end, before he had the rich experience described in ch. 6. Anyhow, his early message in these chapters was basically the same as that of the prophets who went before him:

You are a rebellious people and cannot seem to learn from your suffering (1.1–9). Your religion will not save you, for what God wants is repentance and justice (1.10–20). See how you have fallen into wrong ways – a purge must come, and when it does it will be very thorough (1.21–31).

In the end Zion will be established, for it has a great calling and hope (2.1–4; see also p. 77 on Micah 4.1–3). But walk now in the light of the LORD, for the way you are going, God's visitation will be terrible (2.5–22).

Consider the awful consequences of your ways. (3.1 – 4.1; on 4.2–6 see below, p. 89.)

You are like a vineyard that has been lovingly cultivated, but has produced only rotten grapes and will have to be abandoned (5.1–7). Woe, woe, woe to you for your many corruptions (5.8–23). Beware of God's anger against you for rejecting his law and his word – you will see it in the terrifying approach of an enemy from a distant land (5.24–30).

Among the many echoes of the earlier prophets' teaching we hear again, for example, the voice of Amos inveighing against injustice and corruption in chs. 1, 3 and 5, of Hosea pleading the broken-hearted love of God in the song of the vineyard in ch. 5, and of Micah upholding the future of Zion after judgment in ch. 2. We find hints of remnant theology in 1.24–28, and more explicitly in 4.2–6 where it is coupled with a full-blown expression of Messianic hope. Most of the main ingredients of the prophetic message are, in fact, contained in these chapters, but Isaiah's experience of God related in the next was to clothe it in a sense of awe and to give it a vibrancy of expression that is entirely distinctive and has ensured that his voice would continue to ring powerfully down through the ages.

Ch. 6: The Holy One of Israel and the Holy Remnant.
The date is 742. The scene is the temple, transformed in vision into God's throne-room. That was exactly what the Most Holy Place in the temple symbolised to the Israelites and now the symbol springs to life in Isaiah's vision. He himself is in the Holy Place looking down past the altar of incense. The curtain has either melted away or been drawn back and he sees God in his glory enthroned as King over the ark (cp. Exod. 40.34f; 1 Kings 8.10f). The winged cherubim that stood guard on either side of it (1 Kings 8.6f) also come alive and take on the appearance of bright, fiery creatures (*seraph* means 'burning one'). Isaiah hears them sing their eternal, heavenly song (cp. Rev. 4.8) proclaiming everything the Most Holy Place symbolised and the vision portrayed – the holiness of Almighty God in his glory. He

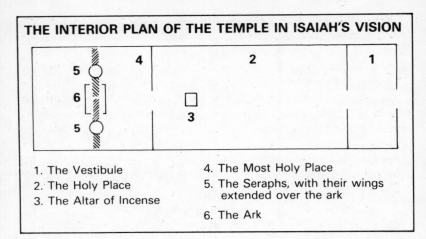

THE INTERIOR PLAN OF THE TEMPLE IN ISAIAH'S VISION

1. The Vestibule
2. The Holy Place
3. The Altar of Incense
4. The Most Holy Place
5. The Seraphs, with their wings extended over the ark
6. The Ark

has been taken right into the court of heaven and into the very presence of God himself.

As the building shakes at the sound of their voices and the smoke of the incense fills the temple, Isaiah's consciousness is entirely of the awfulness of his own and his people's sin in God's sight. His experience of purging with fire from the altar must have been quite terrifying, but its result is total cleansing from all guilt. Then, and only then, does he hear God calling, and he offers himself for what is to prove a heart-rending work, as the summary of the message he is given makes patently clear from the start.

We can make all sorts of interesting analyses of this chapter, for example, pointing out the sequence of conviction of sin, repentance, forgiveness and restoration that is the basic pattern of many of our own liturgical rituals, but whilst such comparisons are interesting, we must not allow them to obscure the absolute majesty of Isaiah's experience. This was no mere ritual sequence for him, but an event so profound and overwhelming that it was to give shape to all he taught. From that day onward his God was 'the Holy One of Israel', to be feared above everything and everyone else (cp. 8.12f), whose purpose was to take Judah through the same experiences of purging by fire in order to prepare them, or the remnant of them that would be left after the purging, for their own future vocation, namely to minister

God's word to the nations that would one day be coming to the mountain of the LORD's temple to be taught his ways (cp. 2.1–4).

According to 1.1 Isaiah was already prophesying before Uzziah's death in 742, and perhaps chs. 1–5 contain some prophecies from those early days, but ahead of him lay critical times, when he would have to stand before the king and speak God's word while the Assyrians were attacking first Damascus, then Samaria and finally Jerusalem itself. And so his message was made alive in his own experience to prepare him in the strength of faith he would need for those critical times.

The LORD also showed him from the start that his words would not be well received, but would even have a contrary effect on his hearers. Yes, the prophet's vocation was to call men back to God in repentance and revival, but Isaiah's revelation was that that was only to come through a very thorough purging, not lightly through any superficial turning and being healed (6.10). God was going to do a complete work this time and Judah would therefore first be felled to the ground like a great tree.

But then 'the holy seed will be the stump in the land' (6.13) and one day 'a shoot will come up from the stump of Jesse' (11.1; Jesse was David's father). It will be the same tree, for God has no intention of rejecting Israel, choosing another nation and starting all over again from scratch as if all past history had been purposeless. However, there will be a difference, for the new shoot will be from a 'holy seed'.

Holiness is of the very essence of God. The word signifies separateness or otherness, what is apart from all that is of man and therefore of sin. Hosea summed it up beautifully in the words: 'I am God, and not man – the Holy One among you' (Hos. 11.9), and Isaiah's own favourite title for God was 'the Holy One of Israel'. In Israel's sacrificial theology priests, places and objects could be called holy if they were specially set apart for God's service. Thus the temple was divided into the Holy Place and the Most Holy Place, the priests were bidden to consecrate themselves, while their garments and the vessels of the temple were all said to be holy (cp. Exod. 29), but in addition to that the

call on the whole nation of Israel was to be holy and to be
God's holy people (Lev. 19.2; 20.7; Deut. 14.2,21; 26.19).
Because of their unfaithfulness and disobedience they failed
to live up to this calling and so God was going to have to
do some drastic purging to make them what he had called
them to be.

Isaiah had already said much of that in 1.24–28, but as
his ministry continues he elaborates on it considerably.
Though the saying about the holy seed being the stump is
not in the Greek version of Isa. 6, it should not therefore
be dismissed as an addition to the Hebrew text, for Isaiah
also said other things that cohere perfectly with it, particularly in those places where he speaks about 'a remnant'. It
was so much an integral part of his message that he even
gave one of his children the name Shear-Jashub, meaning
'A remnant will return' (7.3). Those 'who remain in Jerusalem will be called holy'; they will be washed and cleansed
'by a spirit of judgment and a spirit of fire'; then they will
know the cloud of God's presence among them as in Moses'
day (4.2–6). The remnant will 'truly rely on the LORD', they
'will return to the Mighty God' – but it will only be a
small remnant, the survivors of considerable destruction
(10.20–23). Messiah will be like a banner to which this
remnant will rally from the many lands in which the survivors of judgment have been scattered in exile (11.10f),
and their future with God will be most glorious (28.5f).

Thus Isaiah's teaching about the remnant became the
vehicle by which he expressed his faith that Israel would
never be utterly destroyed nor God's promises withdrawn
from it, for the remnant, cleansed through the fires of judgment, just as he had been cleansed himself by the seraph's
fire, would be heir to those ancient promises. But all that
was for the distant future. First must come the purge, and
prophesying that was Isaiah's immediate charge.

Chs. 7–8: Faith in a crisis.
It is 735. Ahaz, who has only recently become king, is
besieged in Jerusalem by the joint forces of Pekah, king of
Israel, and Rezin, king of Syria (Aram). Their aim is to
overthrow him and replace him with some otherwise

unknown character called Ben-Tabeel. Ahaz and the people are terrified (7.1f).

Isaiah counsels Ahaz to stand firm in faith (7.3–9), offers him the sign of Immanuel (7.10–17), has another prophecy inscribed and sealed before witnesses (8.1f), names his latest son after that prophecy (8.3f) – all as standing signs of his own faith that Pekah and Rezin will be removed in a very short time. He also predicts that the Assyrians will be the instrument by which God will remove them, but warns that they will lay a devastating hand on Judah as well (7.17–25; 8.6–10).

Ahaz refused to trust God and appealed to Tiglath-Pileser for help. The king of Assyria needed no second invitation. Damascus fell to him in 732, Samaria became his vassal, and Ahaz had to pay him tribute. Hence Ahaz's faithless action actually brought about the fulfilment of Isaiah's prophecy! (The story is told more fully in 2 Kings 16.)

Three children are mentioned, each with prophetically symbolic names, like Hosea's children had (Hos.1). Two of them, an older child, Shear-Jashub ('a remnant will return'), and a new-born infant, Maher-Shalal-Hash-Baz (the Assyrian is 'hurrying to the plunder, rushing to the spoil'), are clearly both Isaiah's. The third, Immanuel ('God is with us'), is something of an enigma. He is clearly a baby just about to be born (perhaps not Isaiah's son this time), for he is to stand as a sign to Ahaz that the two kings he is so afraid of will soon be no more, even before the child is old enough to know the difference between good and evil (7.14–16). If Matthew had not identified Jesus with Immanuel (Matt. 1.22f), no further comment would have been needed.

In 7.2,13 Ahaz is very pointedly called 'house of David'. In v. 13 there is even a touch of sarcasm in the title. As the reigning Davidic king, Ahaz was supposed to be the one upholding everything David represented before God, most of which was summarised in Nathan's prophecy to David in 2 Sam. 7 (see above, pp. 45f). The drift of that word was that God had promised a secure future for the Davidic dynasty and kingdom, and all he required of the king was to walk faithfully with him and trust him to fulfil it. It is his

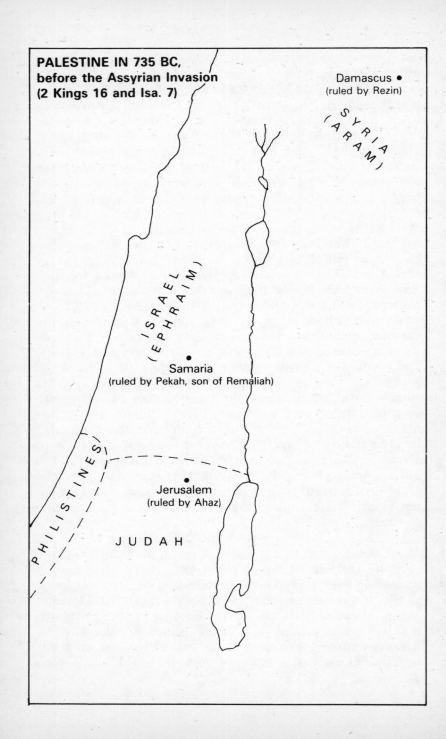

**PALESTINE IN 735 BC,
before the Assyrian Invasion
(2 Kings 16 and Isa. 7)**

Damascus •
(ruled by Rezin)

S Y R I A
(A R A M)

I S R A E L
(E P H R A I M)

• Samaria
(ruled by Pekah, son of Remaliah)

P H I L I S T I N E S

• Jerusalem
(ruled by Ahaz)

J U D A H

own trust in the word of God that enables Isaiah to announce firmly that the things Ahaz fears will not take place (v. 7), but equally he knows that God's promises need to be received in faith:

> *If you do not stand firm in your faith,*
> *you will not stand at all.*

(7.9)

Similar lessons about faith are demonstrated in Jesus' healing ministry, for where there was faith there were many miracles, but where it was scarce there were correspondingly few (Mark 6.5f). God looks for faith before he helps because his purpose is not to overrule our wills like some despot, but to win our co-operation in his work of salvation. Faith is therefore essential if God is to intervene on behalf of his people, even to uphold his promises. Isaiah's whole purpose is to stir Ahaz to the faith he should already be having in God's promise to his forefather, and so he gives him the sign of a child with a name that sums up God's word to David: 'God is with us.' That was the only true ground for faith, namely God's word, and Ahaz needed some constant reminder of it. Perhaps the child was to be born into his own royal household.

In the end of the day, the only child that was ever perfectly to embody all that name stood for was Jesus. Historically his birth was too late for Ahaz's benefit, but theologically his appropriation of the name Immanuel means that the message first given to Ahaz still stands for us today and Jesus is now for us everything that child was meant to be for Ahaz, a constant reminder of the basis of our faith in the promise of God.

Faith is so integral to Isaiah's message at this time that he boldly proclaims that man need fear nothing and no-one but God alone (8.12f). To the man of faith God is a sanctuary, but that same call to faith can be a cause of stumbling for those who find they cannot stand in it (8.14f; cp. 28.16). Isaiah's own stance is clear: 'I will wait for the LORD . . . I will put my trust in him' (8.17). And so he stands with the children God has given him as 'signs and symbols in Israel from the LORD Almighty, who dwells on Mount Zion' (v. 18).

In ch. 8 we also find others besides his children standing with him. In v. 16 he mentions his disciples. In 8.1f he had one of his prophetic words written down and verified by witnesses. Then in vv.16f he has the word sealed and given into the custody of his disciples while he waits for it to come to pass. Here we can see at least one of the reasons why the prophets had their utterances committed to writing – as a testimony to the word of God while it was awaiting fulfilment and as a proof of its authenticity afterwards.

Faith is not merely hope. It is something so certain that Isaiah was prepared to commit everything he had to it – his reputation, his family, his disciples. He knew he could trust God. He knew the king should be leading the people in such trust. They should not be meeting political crises with hearts shaking 'as the trees of the forest are shaken by the wind' (7.2), but firm in faith in the promises God had already given them, in the knowledge that truly 'God is with us.'

9.8 – 10.34: Assyria and Jerusalem.

The historical background is the subjugation of Samaria in 732 and its destruction in 722. Isaiah pictures the relentless onslaught of the Assyrian, coming to execute God's anger that refuses to be quenched (9.12,17,21; 10.4). As fury is vented on Damascus and Samaria, so also it comes to Jerusalem (10.11), but then new factors begin to operate. The Assyrian becomes proud; he oversteps his God-given brief, and so must himself come under judgment (10.12–19). His destruction of God's people will not be total and out of her ashes will arise a remnant that will return to the LORD – but it will be only a remnant (10.20–23).

The LORD's message to Zion is therefore not to fear Assyria, even when he marches through the land reducing city after city and stands shaking his fist at Jerusalem (10.24–34). As we have seen, Isaiah's confidence rests on God's ancient promise to David, but his vision of how that promise is to be fulfilled goes far beyond what was happening in the years 735–22.

Chs. 11–12; 4.2–6; 9.1–7; 32.1–8: The Age of Messiah.
In common with Amos, Hosea and Micah, Isaiah saw that
Jerusalem would have a continuing and a key role to play
in history after God's judgment on the nation had taken
place, but he adds many details to their fairly minimal
vision, particularly with regard to the role of the remnant
and of Messiah in it. He never actually uses the word Messiah ('Anointed One'), but speaks of 'the Branch' (4.2;
11.1), 'the Root of Jesse' (11.10), 'shoot from the stump of
Jesse' (11.1), 'son (who) will reign on David's throne' (9.6f),
'king' (32.1).

When this king comes, he will stand like a banner, sum-
moning the remnant of God's people to himself in a new
exodus from captivity among the nations, calling them back
to reoccupy the promised land. In that day the LORD will
dry up the great River (the Euphrates), just as he dried up
the Egyptian Sea, and he will make a way for his people
from Assyria, just as he once made a way for them when
he brought them from Egypt (11.10–16). Hosea also spoke
of a new exodus (see p. 70), but Isaiah makes much more
of it (see esp. ch. 35).

When all this takes place, the whole feel of life on earth
will change. Life will have a new quality of light and joy
about it (9.2f), for the King will reign in peace, righteousness and justice (9.6f; 11.3–5; 32.1). Even animal and plant
life will experience the change, because his coming will
herald that restoration of Eden that is God's will for his
world (11.6–9).

And in the day that all these things come to pass, men
will rejoice greatly and praise God for his salvation (ch.12).

The source of Messiah's strength will be 'the Spirit of the
LORD' (11.2). The full significance of that for understanding
the New Testament will become clear later, but for now it
is sufficient to note that it means he will have the same
empowering as the prophets themselves, albeit in far greater
measure. He will in fact be 'The Man of the Spirit' *par
excellence.*

With amazing accuracy Isaiah saw that Messiah's light
would shine in Galilee (9.1f). After the Assyrians deported
their Israelite population in 722, Galilee entered six centur-

ies of pagan darkness, but returned into Jewish hands about 104 BC (cp. Matt. 4. 12–16).

3. THE WHOLE WORLD AS GOD'S KINGDOM (ISAIAH 13–27)

As well as challenging men to live in faith and holiness, Isaiah also encouraged them, as we have seen, to live with a vision, one that would stimulate their faith. Ultimately that was of fulfilment for God's ancient promise to bring the whole world back under his own government, but its immediate implications were that his controlling hand was already directing the history of the nations, not just Israel's. Hence, the invading Assyrian, though he did not know it himself, was sent by God to execute his judgment (10.5), but equally would be himself disciplined (10.12). And what was true for Assyria was true for every other nation. In this section Isaiah reviews their immediate destinies (chs. 13–23) and then passes on to consider their and Zion's ultimate future in God's universal kingdom (chs. 24–27).

Chs. 13–23: Prophecies concerning Foreign Nations.
These prophecies come from different times of crisis, but mainly after 715 when Hezekiah succeeded Ahaz. At that time an attempt was made to persuade the new king to join some Judean and Philistine cities in alliance with Egypt against Assyria. Isaiah would have none of it – it was contrary to faith in God. Fortunately Hezekiah, unlike Ahaz some twenty years earlier, heeded him. The rebels were crushed in 711, but Jerusalem escaped unharmed.

Every time Judah was tempted to ally with a foreign power Isaiah's message was the same: Trust God, not men (cp. 31.1–3). His prophecies against the nations explain why: The nations too must fall, for they have no future apart from what God has planned for them. He is your only secure ally.

Babylon will rise to power, but it will end a wasteland, and its king, so proud and strong, will be brought low to the grave (13.1 – 14.23; this prophecy may come from late in Isaiah's life when Hezekiah seemed keen to befriend the Babylonians: ch. 39). Assyria's oppressive rule will also end – after it suffers defeat on the soil of Judah, as happened in 701 when Jerusalem was besieged by the Assyrians, but was relieved by a dramatic miracle (14. 24–27; cp. chs. 36–37).

Nor is there hope in the surrounding nations. In 715 Isaiah warned the Philistines about the futility of their plans to rebel (14. 28–32). About the same time (16.14) he warned that Moab would also be overrun and its distress terrible (chs. 15–16). He asked Jerusalem to shelter its refugees (16. 1–4).

In 735, when Pekah and Rezin attacked Jerusalem, he had predicted the fall of Damascus and the ravaging of Syria and Israel by the Assyrians that followed in 732 (ch. 17).

In Hezekiah's day Egypt was ruled by Cushite (Ethiopian) pharaohs and they were actively encouraging the alliance of Palestinian states against Assyria that revolted in 711. Isaiah said God himself would stop the Assyrians and then the Cushite envoys would come to Jerusalem with gifts of gratitude instead of looking for alliances (ch. 18). He saw clearly that there was no help in Egypt, for it would itself be invaded and thrown into disarray (19. 1–15; Assyria conquered Egypt as far as Thebes in 663 BC). God's plan was not that his people should ally with Egypt, but that both Egyptians and Assyrians should one day come to know the LORD and worship him along with the Israelites (19. 16–25). Isaiah dramatically enacted what would happen to Egypt and its Cushite rulers, by walking around Jerusalem naked, like a prisoner of war, saying, 'See what has happened to those we relied on' (ch. 20).

Isaiah was appalled at what God showed him about the fate of Babylon ('the Desert by the Sea', 21. 1–10); Edom (Dumah, 21. 11f) was granted respite, but that proved temporary (34.5); even remote desert tribes would suffer at the hands of Assyria (21. 13–17).

Ch. 22 concerns Jerusalem, not one of the nations, but placed here it shows the kind of response God looks for. It must date from 701, after Jerusalem's miraculous deliverance. The people did not embrace the message of faith.

Instead of turning to God, they erupted in an orgy of revelry (vv. 1f,13). Their cowardly conduct during the siege suggested little reason for rejoicing (vv. 2f), and though they had put much effort into military preparation, they had not looked to God for help (vv. 8–11). Isaiah therefore warns of God's judgment again (vv. 4–8). He also warns one high official that it is pointless looking for security in earthly splendour (22. 15–25).

Even Tyre, the wealthiest and arrarently most secure commercial city of the day, would fall (as it did to Assyria in 722 and later to Babylonia), to the amazement of her Mediterranean trading partners.

Chs. 24–27: Visions of an end beyond Zion's historical future.

These visions are surprisingly far-reaching, unique in the book of Isaiah. They tell of a day when the world as we know it will be brought to an end (24.1–20) and God will deal with 'the powers in the heavens above' as well as those of earth (24.21–23).

For the LORD's people that will be the day of final blessing when he will invite them to his banqueting table and 'will wipe away the tears from all faces' (25.1–8). Then they will know the full vindication of their faith and will say, 'Surely this is our God; we trusted in him, and he saved us' (25.9–12).

In the day of God's visitation they will be singing psalms of praise to God for the way he has protected and upheld them (26.1–18). Then their dead will rise to a new morning of joy, though first God's wrath must have its way in judgment on sin (26.19–21).

In that day God will also deal with the monstrous beast from the sea (synonymous with the forces of evil, 27.1; cp. Dan. 7.2–8 and Rev. 13.1–10). Then the Song of the Vineyard will no longer be a brokenhearted lament, for Israel will again take root and blossom (27.2–6; cp. 5.1–7). Judgment and exile are not to be for no purpose; they are to correct and to remove sin (27.7–11). But the exile will end and in the final harvest of earth all God's people will be brought home from among the nations (27.12f).

The message of this whole section (chs. 13–27) is clear: there is no long-term security to be had in allying with nations that must themselves be judged, but God has a purpose reaching far beyond the immediate present, one that is for everyone's good. Trust in him!

4. THE TESTING OF FAITH IN A CRISIS (ISAIAH 28–39)

Isaiah's teaching about faith was put very thoroughly to the test in 701 BC. We have a fairly full account of the events of that year in chs. 36–37, which are basically an excerpt from 2 Kings 18.13 – 19.37.

By 701 Hezekiah must have completed his religious reforms (2 Kings 18.1–8) and strengthened Jerusalem's fortifications, which included digging a new tunnel to bring the water-supply from the spring outside the walls into the city (see map below; it is still possible to walk through this tunnel in Jerusalem today). When Sargon of Assyria died in 705, rebellion broke out in the empire. Hezekiah became ringleader of a revolt in Palestine, but Sargon's successor, Sennacherib, systematically crushed the participating cities and set siege to Jerusalem. Hezekiah tried to buy him off (2 Kings 18.13–16), but to no avail, and at that point Isa. 36 takes up the story. It tells of Hezekiah's anguish before the boasting might of Assyria (36.1 37.13), how he turned to God in prayer (37.14–20), was answered first by a prophetic word of encouragement to faith from Isaiah (37.21–35) and then by a miracle of deliverance that still leaves us as astounded as both the Israelites and the Assyrians must have been when it originally happened (37.36–38).

(Ch. 22 also belongs in this setting; see above pp. 91f.)

Chs. 28–32: Trust in the LORD alone.
Isaiah's message has not changed in essentials since Ahaz's day, but he uses fresh images to express it and some of his insights have deepened. Basically his call is still to trust God for Zion's protection, not Egyptian or other alliances (30.1–5; ch. 31). We have already seen that his ground for

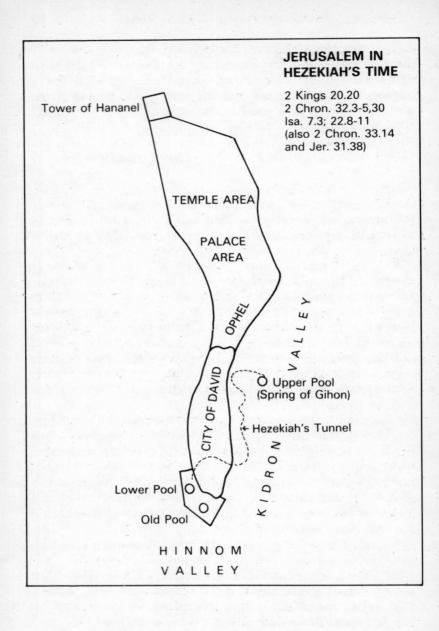

JERUSALEM IN HEZEKIAH'S TIME

2 Kings 20.20
2 Chron. 32.3-5,30
Isa. 7.3; 22.8-11
(also 2 Chron. 33.14
and Jer. 31.38)

Tower of Hananel

TEMPLE AREA

PALACE
AREA

OPHEL

VALLEY

CITY OF DAVID

○ Upper Pool
(Spring of Gihon)

← Hezekiah's Tunnel

KIDRON

Lower Pool ○

○
Old Pool

HINNOM
VALLEY

such a stance is not the naive Zion-theology of Micah's critics, but the realisation that faith enables God to intervene in accordance with his promises.

Anyhow, amid his calls to faith, he has not jettisoned his message of judgment. Jerusalem is still a city of unfaithfulness and injustice, ruled by scoffing drunkards (28.1–13) who rely on totally false securities that are not of God (28.14–29), and so will be brought very low, even until it becomes a ghost-town (29.1–8). The people are spiritually blind and their seemingly religious speech is riddled with hypocrisy (29.9–16).

However, God's purpose still reaches beyond the judgment to a new age when nature and society will be transformed (29.17–24). It is therefore futile to depend on Egypt (30.1–7). The only security is to be found in God (30.8–17) who longs to be gracious to you even now (30.18–26). God's eventual purpose for Assyria is to overthrow it (30.27–33). There is therefore no need to look to Egypt for help (31.1–3), for God will protect Zion and Assyria will fall (31.4–9).

Then God will send his King to usher in the reign of righteousness (32.1–8), and when 'the Spirit is poured upon us from on high', we shall witness the change in our lifestyle promised for the new age (32.9–20).

This is the first time since Moses expressed his longing for all men to become prophets (see above, pp. 3,10f) that we find any positive statement that his longing is some day to be fulfilled. Earlier Isaiah had spoken about Messiah being a man of the Spirit, but now he envisages God's coming age as a time of more general outpouring of the Spirit for everyone's benefit. Later prophets are to elaborate on this primitive perception.

Isaiah's teaching on faith is beautifully summarised in two well-known verses in this section:

> *See, I lay a stone in Zion,*
>   *a tested stone,*
> *a precious cornerstone for a sure foundation;*
>   *the one who trusts will never be dismayed.*

(28.16)

> *In repentance and rest is your salvation,*
>   *in quietness and trust is your strength.*

(30.15)

Chs. 33–35: Entering into God's New Age.

The strength of Isaiah's faith in Jerusalem's future comes out very clearly in these chapters. They probably belong to his later life and are not necessarily associated with any historical event. In them he simply shares a magnificent vision of the future when Zion will enter its era of blessing and peace (ch. 33), the nations that have troubled her will be done away (ch. 34) and the redeemed of the LORD, the remnant in exile, will return to Zion with joy and gladness along the holy highway he has prepared for their final wilderness journey home to the Eden-like life that awaits them (ch. 35).

Chs. 36–39: And the Davidic King – did he learn faith?

After all the encouragement to stand firm in faith he must have received through the relief of Jerusalem (chs. 36–37), and again later through his own miraculous healing and the amazing prophetic sign that accompanied it (ch. 38), Hezekiah finally disappointed Isaiah by befriending some Babylonian envoys who one day came to visit him (ch. 39). Faith in God means alliance with him alone and not with any person who might undermine exclusive trust in him. After all that he had led Hezekiah through in faith, Isaiah's message had still not properly registered. But then, God had warned him right at the start how difficult it would be for men to receive his teaching (6.9f).

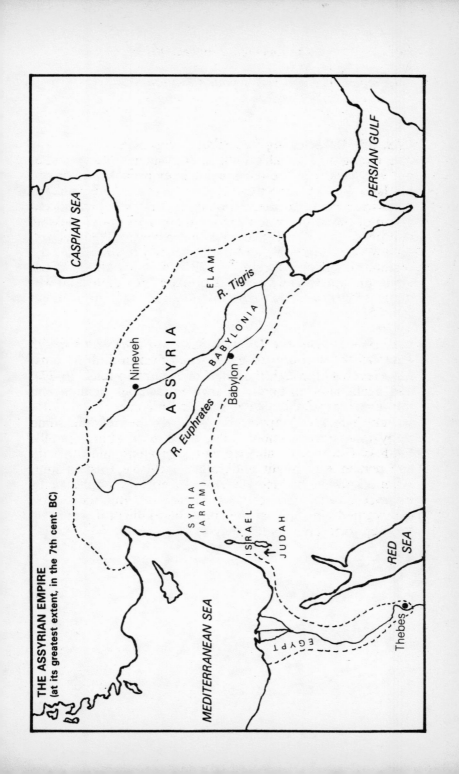

THE ASSYRIAN EMPIRE
(at its greatest extent, in the 7th cent. BC)

CASPIAN SEA

PERSIAN GULF

ELAM

R. Tigris

ASSYRIA

BABYLONIA

Nineveh

Babylon

R. Euphrates

SYRIA
(ARAM)

ISRAEL

JUDAH

RED SEA

MEDITERRANEAN SEA

EGYPT

Thebes

PART FOUR

LIVING THROUGH
GOD'S JUDGMENT

SEVENTH – SIXTH CENTURIES B.C.

We have repeatedly seen how the prophetic voice sounded clearest in times of national crisis: in Samuel's day, in Elijah's, and again in the eighth century. We have seen too that when the LORD's people heeded the prophets they experienced either religious and political revival, or deliverance from oppression, or a mixture of both, but when they refused to heed them they suffered bitterly. The story continues the same way in the seventh century.

In studying the eighth century prophets we concentrated on their message more than their revival impact, but, like their ninth century forerunners, some of them did generate revival. Though Ahaz refused Isaiah's advice, turned to various forms of paganism and superstition, and crumbled in the face of international pressure (2 Kings 16; 2 Chron. 28), his successor, Hezekiah, did heed the prophet. When he came to the throne in 715, his first act was to reform and restore the temple in Jerusalem and that led to a revival that quickly spilled out into the rest of the country (2 Chron. 29–31). National morale rose, Jerusalem was refortified, and when the Assyrians arrived, they found citizens who would not bow in fear and a city that could not easily be taken. At the height of the crisis king and prophet stood side by side in prayer before God (2 Chron. 32.20), and he heard and delivered them.

It was largely thanks to Micah and Isaiah that Hezekiah lived as much in revival as he did (Jer. 26.18f; Isa. 36–39; and see above p. 77), though his stance shifted slightly towards the end of his reign, when he befriended the Babylonians and incurred Isaiah's wrath. Sadly his son, Manasseh, reverted to Ahaz's apostate, paganising ways (2 Chron.

33). There were a few courageous prophets who spoke out against him, men whose names are not preserved, but Manasseh refused to heed them and doubtless many of them were ruthlessly silenced in the course of his bloody purges (2 Kings 21.10–16).

Throughout Manasseh's long and oppressive reign he remained quietly faithful to his Assyrian overlords. His son, Amon, continued his policies for a further two years until he was assassinated in 640. He was followed by the boy-king, Josiah, who, by his eighteenth year as king, restored the faith again with religious reforms as thorough-going as Hezekiah's had been a century earlier. (2 Kings 21–23; 2 Chron. 33–35)

Josiah died in an encounter with the Egyptians in 609 and his successor, Jehoiakim, returned to the faithless ways of Ahaz and Manasseh. Politically he vacillated between Egypt and Babylon, until, twelve years after his accession, in 597, the Babylonians invaded Judah and took Jerusalem. The same vacillation continued through the reign of Zedekiah, and so the Babylonians finally destroyed the city in 587 (2 Kings 24–25; 2 Chron. 36).

Prophets were active all through these years. Hezekiah heeded them and saw revival; Ahaz and Manasseh never knew the LORD's reviving power because they turned a deaf ear; Josiah was probably encouraged in his reforms by Zephaniah and Jeremiah. Prophecy and revival still went hand in hand.

THE LAST YEARS OF THE JUDEAN KINGDOM

DATE	JUDAH	MESOPOTAMIA	
650	Manasseh 687-42 A faithful Assyrian vassal. Age of religious apostasy.	Ashurbanapal 668-27 Height of	A S S
640	Amon 642-40 Josiah 640-09	Assyrian power	Y R
630		Sinsharishkun 629-12	I A N E
620	Josiah's reforms 622	Assyria's decline begins.	M P I
		FALL OF NINEVEH 612	R E

610	Jehoahaz 609
	Jehoiakim 609-597
	    Egypt's vassal until 604/3
	    when he goes over to the
	    Babylonians. Rebels against
	    Babylon 600.
		Nebuchadnezzar 605-562	B
			A
			B
			Y
			L
			O

600	Jehoiachin 597 ←
	JERUSALEM FALLS 597
	Zedekiah 597-87
	    Appointed by Nebuchadnezzar.
	    Rebels against Babylon 589. ←
	JERUSALEM DESTROYED
	                            587*
		— Takes Jerusalem 597.
		First deportation
		
		— Destroys Jerusalem 587.
		Second deportation
			N
			I
			A
			N
			
			E
			M

590			P
580	THE EXILE (Usually dated from the first deportation in 597.)		I R E

(Left vertical column labels: ZEPHANIAH, JEREMIAH, HABAKKUK, NAHUM, EZEKIEL)

* Or 586 according to a different method of calendar reckoning.

7

A Call for Repentance and a Change of Heart

JEREMIAH

The prophetic books are all very different from each other. We know very little about Amos' or Micah's life-story, we can piece together a few impressions about Hosea's and some more about Isaiah's, but Jeremiah's is told in great detail, or at least excerpts from it are. In fact, his message is so intertwined with his story that it is impossible to study the one without the other.

The biographical material in the book is found in its long prose sections, but a lot of Jeremiah's teaching is also in prose, in the style of sermons, much more than in most other prophetic books. There are various theories about why that should be so, but these need not delay us here, for our primary interest is in what the LORD was saying to and through him.

1. JEREMIAH'S CALL AND EARLY MINISTRY (CHS. 1–6)

Ch. 1: Jeremiah is called to be a prophet.
Jeremiah's response to God's call was hardly enthusiastic. In that he was more like Moses than Isaiah (Exod. 3–4; Isa. 6). Right from the start he was unwilling to accept his vocation, but the LORD would have nothing of his excuses. The revelation he received was certainly majestic enough: a word saying God had planned his ministry even before his

JEREMIAH'S LIFE AND TIMES

The Reign of Josiah, 640-09

627: Jeremiah becomes a prophet and begins calling on the people of Judah to "return" to the LORD (Jer. 1-6).

622: Josiah's reforms remove paganism from Judah (2 Kings 22-23).

612: Nineveh, Assyria's capital, falls to the Babylonians.

609: Death of Josiah. His son, Jehoahaz, rules for three months, but Pharaoh Neco, taking control of Palestine after the collapse of Assyria, has him replaced by his brother, Jehoiakim (2 Kings 23.29-37). Pagan cults appear in Judah again (Jer. 7-8).

The Reign of Jehoiakim, 609-597

609/8: Jeremiah's "Temple Sermon" (Jer. 7) results in him being arrested and put on trial (Jer. 26). Some time later he prophesies at the potter's house and is put in the stocks (Jer. 18-20).

605: Nebuchadnezzar becomes King of Babylon. Jeremiah, barred from the temple, dictates his prophecies to Baruch (Jer. 36.1-7).

605-4: Nebuchadnezzar defeats the Egyptians, then marches through Syria into Palestine.

604 (December): Baruch reads Jeremiah's scroll in the temple, but the king confiscates and burns it. Jeremiah and Baruch go into hiding where Jeremiah has another scroll of his prophecies compiled (Jer. 36.8-32).

604/3: Jehoiakim changes his allegiance from Egypt to Babylon — he is to rebel again three years later (2 Kings 24.1).

601: The Egyptians defeat the Babylonians (probably the occasion of Jehoiakim's second defection).

599: Nebuchadnezzar sends advance troops into Palestine.

598: Nebuchadnezzar arrives in Palestine himself. Rechabites (see p. 116) and others seek refuge in Jerusalem (Jer. 35).

597: Jehoiakim dies, leaving his son, Jehoiachin, with a beleaguered city. After three months, he capitulates and is taken into exile in Babylon along with the city's leading men. His uncle, Zedekiah, is made king in his place (2 Kings 24.6-17).

The Reign of Zedekiah, 597-87

595: There is an uprising in Babylon and unrest spreads to the provinces. Foreign ambassadors come to Jerusalem to discuss throwing off the Babylonian yoke. Jeremiah warns them not to do so, but is opposed by Hananiah. He writes to the exiles giving the same warning (Jer. 27-29).

594/3: Zedekiah is summoned to appear before Nebuchadnezzar and Jeremiah sends a prophecy against Babylon with his staff officer (Jer. 51.59-64).

JEREMIAH'S LIFE AND TIMES   *continued*

589: Judah and other Palestinian cities revolt and the Babylonian armies return.

588: Jerusalem is besieged. All the Palestinian cities are taken except Lachish and Azekah. (Jer. 34.7; some fragments of military correspondence known as "the Lachish ostraca", come from this time.) Zedekiah looks to Jeremiah for assurance and a miracle, but the prophet offers no comfort (Jer. 21; 34.1-7).

Lachish and Azekah fall; only Jerusalem remains. Egyptian armies enter Palestine and the Babylonians withdraw from Jerusalem to fight them. Jeremiah predicts a resumption of the seige (Jer. 37.1-10). The slavery affair belongs here (Jer. 34.8-22).

588-7: Jeremiah is arrested on a charge of treason and held in prison for about a year, until the seige ends. It is during this time that he is lowered into a well, and also that he buys his uncle's field at Anathoth (Jer. 32, 37-38).

587: Jerusalem falls in July (2 Kings 25; Jer. 39, 52). Jeremiah is released and offered preferential treatment by the Babylonians, but opts to stay in Judah (Jer. 39-40).

The Governorship of Gedeliah, 587-?

587-?: A courtier, Gedeliah, is appointed Governor of Judah. With Jerusalem in ruins, he establishes his headquarters at Mizpah. Jeremiah joins him, but Gedeliah is murdered and his followers flee to Egypt, taking Jeremiah with them (Jer. 40-43). Jeremiah continues to preach and prophesy there as before (Jer. 43-44).

---

conception, the hand of God reaching out to touch his mouth and giving him the words to say, two visions, one showing him the reliability of the word he was being given and the other revealing the seriousness of God's judgment. But the content of his prophesying was to be fairly gloomy for the most part and the only encouragement God offered was that he would strengthen him and would rescue him when men turned against him. The tension Jeremiah experienced at the very start was to show itself again and again during his ministry, as we shall presently see.

Chs. 2–6: Return to the Lord.

Chs. 2–6 seem to contain Jeremiah's prophecies from the years before 622, when the reforms of Josiah were very much needed. They may even have had some influence on Josiah in planning them.

One word sums up his message at this time: 'Turn' (*shub* = turn or return), i.e., back to God and his ways (3.11 – 4.4). That is essentially the same call as Samuel and every other prophet before him issued, and like them he prophesies that judgment in the form of enemy invasion must follow if there is no repentance.

I gave you everything you have, so why have you turned away from me (2.1–8), to gods that are only worthless idols, broken cisterns that cannot hold water, and to nations that have simply enslaved you (2.9–19)? You gad about restlessly among the Baals and other gods, and yet when you are in trouble you come seeking my help and protesting your innocence – it is all sham (2.20–37). You talk to me as if I were your loving father and friend, but you behave towards me like a faithless wife turned prostitute (3.1–5).

Israel did the same and suffered, yet Judah has not repented (3.6–10). Return to me now, then I will forgive and restore you, for I am your husband and your father (3.11–21). Return, return, return – but with your whole heart (3.22 – 4.4).

Can't you see the trouble coming upon you from the north? (4.5–18) What is about to befall you will be utterly devastating (4.19–31). You have brought it all on yourself (v. 18) – repent now and be saved (v. 14). But you are so accustomed to doing evil that you no longer know how to do that (v. 22)!

This corruption has permeated the whole of Jerusalem, including its leaders, priests and prophets (ch. 5); is there no-one who will heed the warnings and consider the good way before it is too late? (ch. 6)

2. JEREMIAH'S GETHSEMANE (CHS. 7–20)

After the reforms of 622 Jeremiah seems to have stopped prophesying until after Josiah's death in 609, perhaps because the king himself maintained the revival atmosphere throughout his reign. But when Jehoiakim came to the throne conditions rapidly deteriorated again and the worship of pagan gods reappeared throughout the land. Jeremiah immediately started prophesying once more. Most of chs. 7–20 come from the first half of Jehoiakim's reign, before Jeremiah was driven into hiding at the end of 604 BC, that is, after the king burned the scroll of his prophecies (see Jer. 36).

Chs. 7–10: Your religion is corrupt and will not save you.

Near the beginning of Jehoiakim's reign Jeremiah went up to the temple and prophesied its destruction (7.1 – 8.3). His charge was basically the same as Micah's when he had to oppose a presumptuous interpretation of the Zion-theology (see pp. 75ff). People were expecting protection just because 'the temple of the LORD' stood in Jerusalem, but such expectation is utterly false if God's laws are forsaken and if the people worship Baal and the Queen of Heaven and burn their children as a sacrifice to some heathen god. God had made Shiloh the dwelling for his Name at first, but that did not ensure its protection when its ways became corrupt (cp. 1 Sam. 1–4). His judgment remains the same for Jerusalem now.

This 'Temple Sermon' resulted in Jeremiah being arrested and nearly losing his life, but thanks to the intervention of some courtiers who recalled that Micah had prophesied similar things, he was released (see ch. 26).

Undaunted, Jeremiah continues to prophesy, very much in the same vein as before Josiah's reforms. He pleads again for repentance and a turning back to God (8.4–7), castigates prophets and priests for preaching false security (8.8–12) and warns of coming disaster provoked by their sinful ways (8.13 – 9.26). The foreign gods they find so attractive are worthless and cannot protect, mere idols that will be swept aside in the destruction that is on its way (ch. 10). And the reason why disaster must overtake them is 'because they have forsaken my law, . . . have followed the Baals' (9.13f), and 'no-one repents of his wickedness' (8.6).

Chs. 11–20: Jeremiah learns the cost of prophetic ministry.

When Jeremiah was first called, he experienced a tension that made him reluctant to prophesy. In these chapters that tension surfaces again and we begin to see the interplay between the prophet's message and his heart more clearly. At times he is crying out to God with a mixture of anger and anguish, while at others he is prophesying strong words of judgment. We now learn something of what it cost him to be a prophet.

Chs. 11–13: First persecution.

It all stemmed from his prophesying about the need for lives lived in faithfulness to God and in obedience to the righteous demands of his covenant (11.1–17). He discovers that the men of his home town, Anathoth, are plotting to be rid of him, which first evokes an angry prophecy of judgment against them (11.18–23), but after calling to God for vindication of his message and being strengthened by a promise that his word will indeed be fulfilled (12.1–13), he returns to proclaiming his prophecies of warning and judgment (12.14 – 13.27).

Chs. 14–17: The fulness of the cost.

His second experience of persecution is related to some occasion of drought, in which he sees God's hand at work (14.1–10). He finds himself opposed by prophets who preach false messages of peace (14.11– 16), but he knows the bitter truth and it breaks his heart as he weeps for Zion (14.17–22). Even the prayers of Moses and Samuel could not save the city now (15.1–9). As he prophesies this message he suffers yet further persecution, calls out again for vindication (15.10–18), and is encouraged by God to carry on prophesying (15.19–21).

Jeremiah is now learning the personal cost in his prophetic vocation, that it sets him apart from his contemporaries (15.17), and God confirms to him that that is indeed the cost: He is not to marry or have children, he is not to participate in occasions of mourning or festivity (16.1–9), but is only to pronounce his prophetical warnings (16.10 –

17.13), and that again has him crying out for vindication (17.14–18). But his ministry continues, and now he speaks out against Sabbath-breaking (17.19–27).

Ch. 18: At the potter's house.

His third experience of persecution followed a visit to the potter's house where the LORD showed him that Judah must be smashed like a marred pot, but when he prophesies that message his opponents decide to attack him with their tongues and pay no attention to what he is saying, and that makes him call out to God again (ch. 18).

Chs. 19–20: In the stocks.

His fourth experience is even more intense. So far the opposition has been with words and threats, but now it becomes physical. When he went to the Potsherd Gate and smashed a pot prophetically symbolising the threatened smashing of the nation (ch. 19), he was arrested, beaten and put in the stocks by Pashhur, the temple-overseer (20.1–6). This time his cry for vindication is a cry of agony in which he even curses the day he was born (20.7–18).

It is little wonder Jeremiah complained to God and wished he could give up his calling, even that he might die. The passages in these chapters where he calls out to God in this way are sometimes referred to as his 'Confessions' (11.18–23; 12.1–6; 15.10–21; 17.14–18; 18.18– 23; 20.7–18). They mostly take the form of conversations with God, Jeremiah complaining, sometimes very forcibly, and God sometimes telling him to shake himself out of his self-pity (12.5f; 15.19–21). The strongest complaint is the last one, in ch. 20, where he curses the day he was born. He suffers incessant ridicule and when he tries to stop prophesying, he finds he cannot:

> But if I say, 'I will not mention him
>   or speak any more in his name,'
> his word is in my heart like a burning fire,
>   shut up in my bones.

I am weary of holding it in;
indeed, I cannot.

(Jer. 20.9)

With these words Jeremiah found himself in the same place
as Jesus in the Garden of Gethsemane. There is much about
Jeremiah's life that is like Jesus': the message of repentance,
the opposition of the religious, the persecution, trials,
imprisonment – indeed everything short of the cross itself!

3. CONFRONTATION WITH THE RELIGIOUS AUTHORITIES
(CHS. 21–29)

After the death of Jehoiakim and the fall of Jerusalem
in 597, Jeremiah came out of hiding and was soon heard
prophesying again. The section that runs from chs. 21 to 29
contains prophecies and stories from different periods in his
life, but most of them come from the reign of Zedekiah, and
the others are only introduced here because they amplify the
message he was preaching then. At that time the city was
politically divided. Some were saying Jerusalem need not
fear the Babylonians, but Jeremiah prophesied that
rebellion against Babylon would only hasten God's judgment. For that he was to be criticised and eventually
arrested and condemned as a traitor. However, his main
problem at first was dealing with prophets and priests who
were propagating a misleading theology.

21.1 – 23.8: On the future of David's line.
These chapters begin with a review of Jerusalem's recent
kings. Zedekiah asks if the city will be reprieved by some
miracle, but Jeremiah says it will not (21.1–11), adding that
no-one should put any hope in the kings of Judah anyhow,
because they have not kept God's covenant (21.12 – 22.9).
Josiah's son, Shallum (= Jehoahaz) will never return from
his captivity in Egypt (22.10–12), of Jehoiakim it was prophesied that he would have a disgraceful end because of his
oppressive ways (22.13–19), and Jehoiachin has been sud-

denly whisked away into exile in Babylon after only three
months reign, tossed away like a broken pot (22.20–30).
David's line is finished (v.30).

Meanwhile Judah is ruled by 'shepherds' that do them
only harm (23.1–4), but the day will come when God 'will
raise up to David a righteous Branch,' a King (Messiah)
whose name will be 'The LORD Our Righteousness,' and his
people will be gathered to him from all the lands where
they have been banished (23.5–8).

23.9 – 25.38: On false prophetic views about the future.
Sadly the prophets in Jerusalem teach a false hope for the
nation. Like the prophets Micah opposed, they are a corrupt
lot (23.9–15) and their message that says, 'You will have
peace. No harm will come to you,' fills the people with vain
hope and does not benefit them in the least (23.16–40). It
is false, because it is spoken out of their own minds without
revelation, without them having 'stood in the council of the
LORD to see or to hear his word' (vv. 16–18).

The truth is that there are some good folk now in exile
whom God will take back to be the nucleus of his people
once he has brought them to repentance, but the present
inhabitants of Jerusalem are like bad figs, fit only to be
thrown away (ch. 24). What lies ahead is not an immediately
rosy future, but a very long period of suffering – seventy
years – before God brings his people home (25.1–14). The
cup of God's wrath will have to be drunk to the full, not
only by Judah, but by the nations as well (25.15–38).

Chs. 26–27: Jeremiah's prophetic word on trial.
At Jeremiah's trial after his 'Temple Sermon' some elders
recalled that Micah's message, which was basically the same
as Jeremiah's, had influenced King Hezekiah so much that
he sought the LORD and the city was saved. Jehoiakim, by
contrast, had put another prophet, Uriah, who taught the
same things, to death – and Jerusalem fell at the end of his
reign! The priests, prophets and people were being clearly
warned that they were in danger of bringing terrible disaster
on themselves if they did the same to Jeremiah. (ch. 26)

The story is told at this point, rather than after ch. 7, to remind of past reactions from priests, prophets, kings and people to the prophetic word as background to the next chapter where we see Jeremiah still prophesying the same message in Zedekiah's time, and to the same groups of people. The questions raised by the two chapters together are: Will Zedekiah, his priests, prophets and people respond to Jeremiah's word as Hezekiah did, or as Jehoiakim did? Are they too about to bring great disaster on themselves? (ch. 27)

Chs. 27–28: Prophet against prophet.

The setting is a visit from various foreign delegates to Zedekiah to plan a revolt against Babylon. The spirit of rebellion was being encouraged by prophets and various other diviners, mediums and the like who were predicting that Zedekiah would never serve the king of Babylon and that the furnishings and other articles the Babylonians had removed from the temple would soon be returned to Jerusalem. Jeremiah's response to them was unequivocal: They prophesy lies! They will only stir up the wrath of the Babylonians against you. (ch. 27.)

At this time Jeremiah went around carrying a wooden yoke (27.2) prophetically symbolising the yoke of slavery the Babylonians would put on the people of Jerusalem if they rebelled. Hananiah, one of the prophets opposing Jeremiah, came and broke it, claiming that the exiles would be home within two years. Jeremiah's response was to denounce his lies and prophesy that God would replace the wooden yoke (27.2) with an iron one. Hananiah died two months later. (ch. 28)

Ch. 29: Jeremiah writes a letter to the exiles.

The same problem was besetting those who had been taken to Babylon in 597. Among them also there were prophets predicting an early return from exile. Jeremiah wrote a letter advising the exiles to settle down and accept they would have a long stay in Babylon – seventy years, he said (29.10; cp. 25.11). Certainly the LORD's will for his people was not to harm them, but to give them hope and a future, but the prelude to that would have to be repentance, not shallow prophesyings, and that was going to take some time. The prophets in exile were furious and wrote to the priests in Jerusalem demanding that Jeremiah be put in the stocks again, but the only response they got was a further denunciation from Jeremiah himself.

4. RESTORATION AND THE FUTURE BEYOND (CHS. 30–33)

Chs. 30–33 gather together most of Jeremiah's teaching about Israel's future hope. He wrote it all down in one book (30.2), and so some people like to refer to the collection as his 'Book of Comfort'.

Chs. 30–31: Restoration and a new covenant.
Ch. 30 speaks mostly about Judah's future. God will bring the exiles back, break the yoke of their oppressors, raise up a Davidic king for them, and enable them to live in peace and security (vv. 3–11). All the suffering they go through is a healing discipline, but that will end. Jerusalem will be rebuilt, its worship will be restored and its leader will be a man who is close to God (vv. 12–24).

Ch. 31 turns our attention to Israel in the north, which is also to be restored. God's love and tenderness towards Israel that shone through Hosea's prophecies resurfaces here amid portraits of restored joy and plenty (vv. 1–14). There will be no more need for tears. Rachel's children will come home again, repentant after their time of discipline. God's heart still yearns for Ephraim (= Israel), his dear son (vv. 15–22). After a further prophecy about Judah being repopulated, Jeremiah reveals that at least some of these visions came to him in a dream (vv. 23–26).

And now, in 31.27–40, we discover the key to Jeremiah's hope for the future. Here he speaks about Israel and Judah replanted in their land, but this time with no-one blaming his parents for his conduct or its consequences (vv. 27–30), because God will have done a radical work in men to change their very hearts. This is the main point at which Jeremiah adds to the message of the earlier prophets, for, while they also speak about restoration and a future full of hope after a time of judgment, his teaching about the heart and the nature of true repentance is quite revolutionary.

Repentance must be more than a change of ways; it must also involve a change of heart. True repentance has to be with all one's heart (3.10), the heart needs to be circumcised more than the flesh (4.4), and also to be washed clean of all evil (4.14). Unfortunately, as Jeremiah the realist observes, the heart is 'stubborn and rebellious' (5.23), 'deceitful above all things and beyond cure' (17.9), beyond anyone doing anything about it. True repentance is therefore impossible and men are utterly lost in the corruption of their hearts. However, God can change all that, and in fact intends to do so, for the time is coming when he will make a new covenant with his people and write his law 'on their hearts'. Then they will experience full forgiveness, will truly 'know the LORD', and will find a new will within them to live in obedience to his ways (31.31–34).

Once this new covenant is established it will never be revoked as long as God's creation endures (vv. 35–37). In addition to that, a day will also come when Jerusalem will be rebuilt never to be demolished again (vv. 38–40).

Hosea also spoke of a covenant as a prelude to the inauguration of God's new age for Israel (Hos. 2.18), but not with the same depth of revelation. Jeremiah's additional teaching foresees both our forgiveness by the blood of Christ and the love of God formed in our hearts by the Holy Spirit in New Testament (= New Covenant) times.

Ch. 32: Once more fields will be bought.

While in prison during the siege of Jerusalem, Jeremiah is told by God to invest his money in Israel's future by buying a field belonging to his uncle at Anathoth, then in Babylonian occupied territory, as a witness to the worth of his prophecy that 'once more fields will be bought in this land' (vv. 15,43). When Jeremiah prays for further revelation about what he is doing, God's answer again speaks about the change he will work in man's heart and about the lastingness of that work (vv. 38–41).

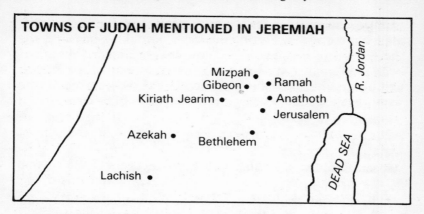

TOWNS OF JUDAH MENTIONED IN JEREMIAH

Mizpah •
Gibeon • • Ramah
Kiriath Jearim • • Anathoth
• Jerusalem

Azekah • • Bethlehem

Lachish •

R. Jordan

DEAD SEA

Ch. 33: *David's throne will be restored.*

Finally Jeremiah speaks about the future of God's covenant with David. After reminding us that the devastation of Jerusalem is because of sin (vv. 1–5), and foretelling forgiveness, cleansing, healing, restoration and joy both in the city and in the countryside (vv. 6–13), he recalls one of his earlier prophecies about Messiah (compare vv. 15f with 23.5f) and assures us that that word too will be fulfilled, that God's promise to David still stands and that it also will endure as long as creation lasts (vv. 14–26).

5. JEREMIAH'S PASSION AND NEAR-MARTYRDOM (CHS. 34–52)

In this last section, Jeremiah has one consistent message: The city is about to fall to the Babylonians again, so prepare yourselves accordingly. The time for a call to national repentance is past; the wheels of judgment are now in motion; Jerusalem's last hour has come.

Ch. 34: *Jerusalem's faithlessness even at the end.*

While the Babylonians were besieging Jerusalem, and Lachish and Azekah were the only two Judean towns that had not yet fallen, Jeremiah warned Zedekiah about what would happen to him personally (34.1–7). Then for a brief moment the pressure was relieved when the Babylonians withdrew from Jerusalem to meet Egyptian reinforcements approaching from the south. During the siege, Zedekiah had ordered the release of all slaves, but now they were forcibly taken back. Jeremiah took the opportunity to warn the officials and others that their faithless action has only stirred God's wrath against them even more (34.8–22).

Chs. 35–36: How will Zedekiah respond to the prophetic word?

We now come to two chapters that remind us about earlier events in Jehoiakim's reign and illustrate the effects of obedience and disobedience to God's revealed will. During the siege of 597 some Rechabites, descendants of the zealous Jonadab son of Rechab who had supported Jehu's religious revolution (see above, p. 55), sought refuge in Jerusalem and Jeremiah, having tested and proved their utter faithfulness to the LORD and to the command of their father, was able to prophesy that they would 'never fail to have a man to serve' the LORD (ch. 35). By contrast, King Jehoiakim, when he laid hands on the scroll containing Jeremiah's call to repentance that Baruch had read in the temple, systematically burned it, thus deliberately rejecting the word of God, and issued an order for Jeremiah's arrest. For him Jeremiah could only prophesy that he would have no descendants 'to sit on the throne of David' (ch. 36). These two stories are introduced here simply to remind us of the options that faced Zedekiah. How will he respond to the prophet's words? Will he be like the Rechabites, or like Jehoiakim?

Chs. 37–39: The prophetic word is rejected and Jerusalem falls.

We do not have to wait long for the answer to the questions raised by the last two chapters: 'Neither he nor his attendants nor the people of the land paid any attention to the words the LORD had spoken through Jeremiah the prophet' (37.2). Jeremiah therefore had only one message for Zedekiah, that the Babylonians would return, take the city and destroy it. For that he was thought to be a pro-Babylonian sympathiser and so was arrested as a traitor, beaten and put in prison. The king enquired of him again, but the prophetic word was still the same (ch. 37).

While in prison, he continued to tell his message to anyone who would listen, advising them to capitulate to the Babylonians before it became too late. An attempt was made, with Zedekiah's permission, to silence him completely by throwing him down a well, but a Cushite courtier called Ebed-Melech persuaded the king to grant him a reprieve. (38.1–13. For that Ebed-Melech was promised God's protection on the day of disaster; 39.15–18.)

When Zedekiah again sought Jeremiah's opinion he did so furtively and Jeremiah, still in prison, could only advise him to surrender to the Babylonians (38.14–28). But he would not, and it became too late to do so. Jerusalem fell, Zedekiah's family was slaughtered before his eyes, he was himself blinded and taken to Babylon, and the city was burned to the ground (ch. 39).

Throughout the story we see that Zedekiah was inclined to listen to Jeremiah, for he consulted him several times, but he was a weak man who feared his own courtiers as well as his political opponents (38.19,24f). At one point we see him reacting to their pressure in much the same way as Pilate was to react to the demands of the Jewish leaders when he agreed to the crucifixion, for when the Jerusalem officials wanted to murder Jeremiah, the king's response was, 'He is in your hands. The king can do nothing to oppose you' (38.5; cp. Matt.27.24). As we have already once noted, the parallels between the lives of Jeremiah and Jesus are often very close.

Chs. 40–44: Jeremiah is released and is taken to Egypt. The Babylonians offered Jeremiah preferential treatment, but he chose to stay in the land and support the newly appointed governor, Gedeliah, who set up his headquarters at Mizpah (ch. 40). However, before very long Gedeliah was assassinated and his followers, against Jeremiah's advice, fled to Egypt, dragging a reluctant prophet with them (chs. 41–43). There the old superstitious worship of the Queen of Heaven and other gods began to creep back in and Jeremiah found himself at the end of his life having to preach the same message and denounce the same aberrations as at the beginning (ch. 44; cp. ch. 7).

Ch. 45: A disciple's lot!
This little chapter neatly catches the flavour of Jeremiah's life. His prophesying had brought him a lot of rejection and persecution. Men had turned against him, mocked him and plotted to take his life. He had been scourged, put in the stocks, banned from the temple, driven into hiding, locked in prison and dropped down a well. One day Baruch, his best friend and faithful scribe, complained to him about the cost of this prophetic ministry and the only comfort Jeremiah was able to offer him was that he would escape with his life.

Chs. 46–51: Prophecies against foreign nations.
These are mostly just warnings to various nations about imminent invasions by the Babylonians: Egypt, invaded by Nebuchadnezzar in 568 (ch. 46); Philistia, overrun before the fall of Jerusalem in 587 (ch. 47); Moab and Edom subdued about the same time (48.1 – 49.22); Damascus, Arabia and Elam, all defeated some ten years earlier (49.23–39). Then in chs. 50–51 we have a prophecy about Babylon itself, predicting its own downfall when the Persians invaded in 539.

These chapters need not occupy our attention further. They contain some beautiful poetry, but add little to the themes we have been tracing, apart from reminding us that God has a purpose not only for his few chosen people, but for the whole world, which must therefore also be subject to his judgment.

Ch. 52: A final ray of hope.
Here we have what is basically an excerpt from the end of 2 Kings giving the historian's version of the fall of Jerusalem. It adds some extra details which tell us there were three deportations, one in 597, the second in 587, and a third in 582. The last one must have followed the assassination of Gedaliah.

The addition of this chapter is no mere afterthought. It

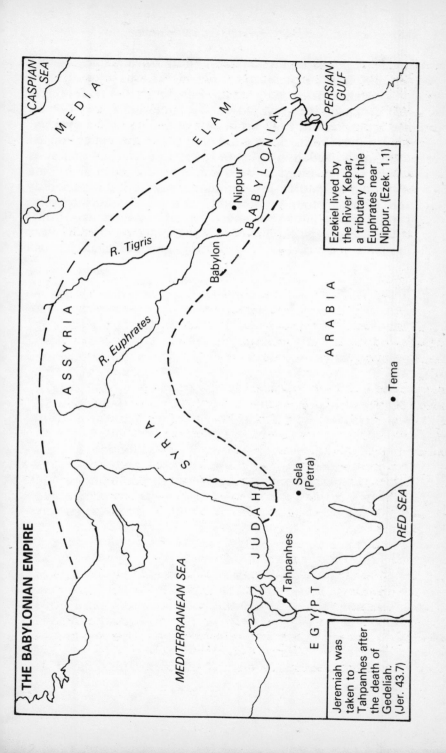

THE BABYLONIAN EMPIRE

CASPIAN SEA

MEDIA

ELAM

PERSIAN GULF

R. Tigris

Nippur

BABYLONIA

Babylon

ASSYRIA

R. Euphrates

ARABIA

SYRIA

Tema

JUDAH

Sela (Petra)

Tahpanhes

MEDITERRANEAN SEA

RED SEA

EGYPT

Ezekiel lived by the River Kebar, a tributary of the Euphrates near Nippur. (Ezek. 1.1)

Jeremiah was taken to Tahpanhes after the death of Gedeliah. (Jer. 43.7)

makes the book end on a hopeful note by reminding us that
Jehoiachin, the king taken captive in 597, was released from
prison and allowed to live at the Babylonian court. Jeremiah
had promised there would yet be hope and that God still
had a purpose for both his people and the Davidic dynasty.
That hope began to see fulfilment when the exiles started
to return to Judah in 537, but it was to be several centuries
before the promised Davidic Son would be born. When he
did come he had to live through many of the experiences
Jeremiah had found so difficult, and even more intensely.
But just as Jeremiah foresaw so clearly, his day would also
witness the breakthrough to true repentance and the change
in man's heart that he longed for so much himself.

8

God's Plan for Israel and the Nations

ZEPHANIAH, NAHUM, OBADIAH, HABAKKUK

In the prophetic books studied so far we have noted a continuing interest in God's plan for the nations. Amos spoke mainly about judgment on them for their sins, but Micah and Isaiah shared a vision of them finally coming to be taught God's ways by his people. There are long collections of prophecies concerning their future in Isaiah and Jeremiah, though we have not looked at these in any detail. Basically they are just particular applications of the same general vision to individual nations, mostly concentrating on the element of coming judgment. However, their incorporation in the prophetic books is important, for it reminds us that God's intention is not just to create a little holy club on earth called 'Israel', 'The Remnant' or 'The Church', but to redeem all men. Israel's and the nations' futures are intimately intertwined. What happens to Israel must affect the rest of mankind.

Hence, when judgment comes to Israel, its effects must spill over into the world around, and equally when blessing is restored, the nations must reap some benefit. Though they have not had the law or prophets to guide them, God is also calling them to submit to him, and is teaching them about that through their involvement in the punishment and blessing of Israel. Sometimes they are his instruments of judgment on Israel, sometimes they are to be punished for belittling Israel, sometimes they are the means of bringing blessing, sometimes they are the recipients of blessing. But always their experience is directly related to their attitude to God and his chosen people.

During Jeremiah's life-time other prophets were also active, that is, besides the false prophets who opposed him. We hear of one called Uriah who was silenced by Jehoiakim (Jer. 26.20–23), and Ezekiel's ministry overlaps Jeremiah's. Four others have their prophecies preserved in the Old Testament, and much of their concern is with the relationship between Israel and the nations.

1. THE DAY OF THE LORD IS NEAR (ZEPHANIAH)

We know nothing about Zephaniah's life-story except that he prophesied during Josiah's reign (1.1) – judging by the strength of his invective against idolatry, before the reforms of 622. His ministry was therefore roughly parallel with the beginning of Jeremiah's.

His message is quite simple and straight-forward. The day of the LORD, that is the day of his judgment, is near (1.7,14). When it comes, it will sweep away everything (1.2f), particularly all your pagan gods and practices, together with their practitioners (1.4–9). The wealthy are in for a shock, especially the complacent among them (1.10–13). Indeed this is no time for complacency, for the day of the LORD is coming quickly. It will bring terrible distress and wealth will provide no security in it (1.14–18). So gather together and seek the LORD now, before that day comes. Perhaps you will be sheltered when it does (2.1–3).

The small nations around Judah's borders had always given them trouble, but the LORD's visitation will deal with them too, 'in return for their pride, for insulting and mocking the people of the LORD Almighty' (2.4–11). The great nations will feel the power of his hand as well, the Cushite rulers of Egypt and the self-confident Assyrians will all perish (2.12–15).

The main focus of God's judgment, however, will be Jerusalem itself, a city whose officials and religious leaders are all corrupt and arrogant (3.1–5). The judgment on Jeru-

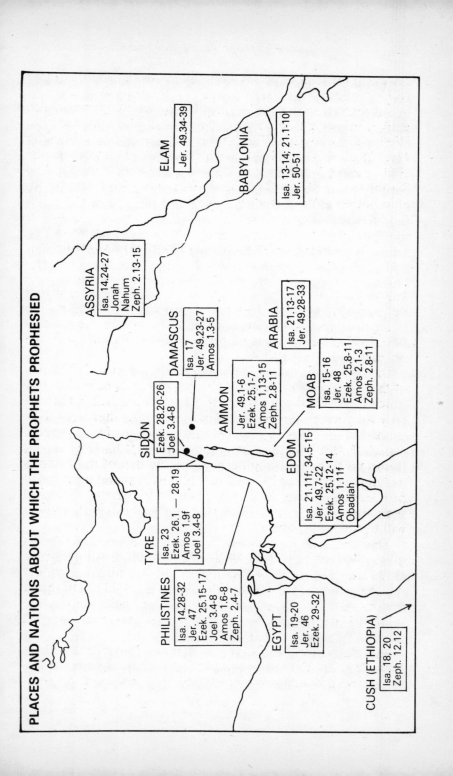

PLACES AND NATIONS ABOUT WHICH THE PROPHETS PROPHESIED

ELAM
Jer. 49.34-39

BABYLONIA
Isa. 13-14; 21.1-10
Jer. 50-51

ASSYRIA
Isa. 14.24-27
Jonah
Nahum
Zeph. 2.13-15

DAMASCUS
Isa. 17
Jer. 49.23-27
Amos 1.3-5

ARABIA
Isa. 21.13-17
Jer. 49.28-33

SIDON
Ezek. 28.20-26
Joel 3.4-8

AMMON
Jer. 49.1-6
Ezek. 25.1-7
Amos 1.13-15
Zeph. 2.8-11

MOAB
Isa. 15-16
Jer. 48
Ezek. 25.8-11
Amos 2.1-3
Zeph. 2.8-11

TYRE
Isa. 23
Ezek. 26.1 — 28.19
Amos 1.9f
Joel 3.4-8

EDOM
Isa. 21.11f; 34.5-15
Jer. 49.7-22
Ezek. 25.12-14
Amos 1.11f
Obadiah

PHILISTINES
Isa. 14.28-32
Jer. 47
Ezek. 25.15-17
Joel 3.4-8
Amos 1.6-8
Zeph. 2.4-7

EGYPT
Isa. 19-20
Jer. 46
Ezek. 29-32

CUSH (ETHIOPIA)
Isa. 18, 20
Zeph. 12.12

salem and the nations will result in a humbling of men and God will call his scattered worshippers, now a remnant, but humbled, trusting the LORD and without deceit, home to Zion, his holy hill (3.6–13). Jerusalem can therefore rejoice in that hope, for God will delight in his people again and make them honoured among the peoples of earth (3.14–20).

Most of Zephaniah's prophecy echoes the teaching of earlier prophets. Particularly striking is the similarity between what he and Amos say about the day of the LORD (cp. Amos 5.18–20). But what he does add is a strong call to humility. The essential purpose of God's visitation, as he sees it, is to remove pride and arrogance from among men and establish the remnant of the humble in the land (3.11f). His call to repentance is accordingly voiced in these words:

> *Seek the LORD, all you humble of the land,*
>   *you who do what he commands.*
> *Seek righteousness, seek humility;*
>   *perhaps you will be sheltered*
>   *on the day of the LORD's anger.*

(2.3)

The vision of humility is presented again, but in greater detail, in the portrait of the suffering servant in Isaiah 40–55 (see pp. 155f) and is eventually lived out in the life of our Lord Jesus Christ (see Phil. 2.5–11).

2. HIS WAY IS IN THE WHIRLWIND AND THE STORM (NAHUM)

A century earlier Assyria had been called by God to be the rod of his anger in executing judgment on Israel (Isa. 10.5), but even then it was foreseen that she would overstep herself, become proud and arrogant, and so have to suffer his wrath herself (Isa. 10.12). Nahum stands close to that moment of wrath, prophesying perhaps just a year or two before Nineveh, her capital city, fell in 612 BC.

The intention of his prophecy, which reads very like some of the oracles against the nations in Isaiah or Jeremiah, is both to offer encouragement to Judah and declare harsh judgment against Assyria. The fall of Nineveh is foretold in vivid detail throughout chs. 2–3, but 1.2 – 2.2 is more wide-ranging, a mixture of descriptions of God's stormy coming, words of judgment against Nineveh and promises of blessing for Judah. The basic theme is that the LORD comes to take vengeance on Nineveh, and with such anger that the very earth trembles at his coming (1.2–6). But 'for those who trust in him' that is no cause for anxiety, for to them 'the LORD is good, a refuge in times of trouble' (1.7). The end of Nineveh's oppressive rule will mean the release of God's people in Judah (1.8–13), and so should indeed be 'good news' to them, a veritable proclamation of 'peace', and the prelude to the restoring of their splendour (1.14 – 2.2).

Though Nahum's depiction of Nineveh's fall is harsh and lurid, the intention of his little book is to offer comfort to the LORD's people. And that, incidentally, is what his name means: 'Comfort'. Perhaps it was really a nickname he got from his message.

3. AS YOU HAVE DONE, IT WILL BE DONE TO YOU (OBADIAH)

This little book is more important than its size suggests, because it reveals why almost every prophet after 587 denounced the Edomites, and why, down into New Testament times, their name continued to be odious to Jews, even though as descendants of Esau they were distantly related to them, their 'brother Jacob' (v. 10). Relationships between the two had never been good, but in 587 the Edomites showed their true colours. Not only did they rejoice over Jerusalem's fall, but also took advantage of the situation to loot the ruined city (vv. 11–14). Obadiah therefore prophesies that the day of the LORD that overtakes all nations will be for them a time when their deeds must return on their own head (v. 15). Then they will be left without survivors in Edom and their territory will be annexed by Israel (vv. 16–21). The lasting message is simple and clear.

The Edomites lived to the south-east of Judah. Their

capital at Sela was a natural mountain fortress that could
only be approached through a narrow gorge. They clearly
believed it impregnable (vv. 2– 4), but it fell to Arabs in
the fifth century and then in the third to the Nabateans
who rebuilt it and called it Petra. Some of the dispossessed
Edomites settled in southern Judah. Their descendants were
the Idumeans of New Testament times. Herod the Great,
the little-loved king of the Jews at the time of Jesus' birth,
was one of them.

4. YET I WILL REJOICE IN THE LORD (HABAKKUK)

Habakkuk's little book is very different from the public
denunciations of other prophets. It is more like the spiritual
diary of a very perplexed man seeking to make sense of all
that was happening in the world around him. The experiences he describes probably happened about the time
Nahum was prophesying, a few years before the fall of
Nineveh in 612.

As he looked at the injustice, violence and oppression of
Assyrian times, he cried to the LORD: How long must this
go on? (1.2–4) and the LORD told him it would soon be
over, for he was raising up the Babylonians who were
powerful and ruthless enough to sweep it all aside (1.5–11).

While Habakkuk accepted that as an immediate answer
to the problem, that through the Babylonians God would
execute judgment (1.12), he was not satisfied that it was
God's ultimate solution to the problem of evil and suffering
in his world (1.13–17), and so he decided to seek the LORD
further, to watch and wait for a more profound answer to
his complaint (2.1).

The LORD first assured him he would get his revelation at
the right time if only he would wait for it, and told him he
must write it down when it came so that others could benefit
from it too (2.2f). Then, in these hours or days of waiting,
in an astounding moment of insight, he realised the truth
of the fact that 'the righteous will live by his faith' (2.4),
that in the midst of all the uncertainties of the world, the

root of stability for God's people, 'the righteous', is their faith in him. That insight was to prove precious and revolutionary, not only for himself, but also for countless others down the centuries, including men like St. Paul who, in Rom. 1.16f, cites Hab. 2.4 as the basic text on which his gospel hangs, Martin Luther who discovered faith when he read Rom. 1.16f, as did John Wesley when he heard Luther's comments on it being read.

In the light of his realisation Habakkuk found he could review the world through different eyes and see only woe for all the unjust extortioners, the oppressive rulers, the wealthy drunkards and the pagan idolaters whose doings had bothered him so much hitherto, for now he knew where his faith lay, namely in the fact that the LORD truly 'is in his holy temple' and that one day, just as Isaiah had said, 'the earth will be filled with the knowledge of the glory of the LORD as the waters cover the sea' (2.4–20; cp. Isa. 11.9).

These insights, however, were only preparatory for the fuller revelation he sought, which he tells us about in song in ch. 3 (to be accompanied by stringed instruments, v. 19). As he waited, now in faith praying for a revival of God's ancient wonders (v. 2), he saw a vision of God coming down from the eastern mountains, his glory covering the heavens like the sunrise, and the earth shook at his coming (vv. 3–7). There was tremendous power and wrath in God as he passed over the earth and through the nations (vv. 8–15). As Habakkuk watched he felt unable to stand for weakness and trembling (v. 16).

Now he had met with God, like Isaiah before him, he knew there was nothing on earth he needed fear any more. Now he could wait in quiet faith for God to work out his purpose with the invading nation (v. 16), knowing that even 'though the fig-tree does not bud' and everything else goes wrong, 'yet I will rejoice in the LORD.' (vv. 17f) The reason for such confidence is nothing other than the knowledge of God's sovereignty (v. 19), that he is truly in charge of history, that his power is indeed mightier than that of any nation, however strong or oppressive.

The source of such confidence can only be a living, personal encounter with God himself discovered through faith in him. This truth, that Habakkuk learned while considering a political enigma, was found also by Job as he wrestled with the problems of his own suffering. He too met with God and in the light of his encounter his questionings gave way to amazement and repentance (Job 42.2–6), whereafter he found his restoration. Similarly in Ps. 73, the answer to the problem of social injustice was found, not in trying to understand, but in God's sanctuary (vv. 16f), and that was followed by one of the most moving expressions of faith, praise and joy in the whole Bible (vv. 23–28).

In New Testament times similar experience lies behind, for example, Paul's statements about rejoicing in his suffering and his injunctions to rejoice in the LORD always (e.g., Col. 1.24; Phil. 4.4). Such rejoicing can only come from a profound faith and a living knowledge of the reality of God's power, but that was something that was to be fairly common among the followers of Jesus Christ – and continues to be today among prophetical men and women in the Church.

9

God's Glory and his Spirit among his People

EZEKIEL

When Jerusalem fell in 597 BC, Ezekiel, the son of a priest and a young man in his mid-twenties, was deported to Babylon, to a settlement by the Kebar River, which was probably a canal or man-made tributary of the Euphrates east of Nippur (see p. 119). His message was therefore delivered first to the exiles among whom he lived, though most of it relates to Jerusalem and so presumably would have been relayed back home by messenger or letter, in much the same way as other exiles were corresponding with Jeremiah and his contemporaries (Jer. 29.1–3,25, 29–31; 51.59–64; cp. Ezek. 33.21). At first he prophesied judgment, warning about the coming destruction, but after 587 his message changed dramatically as he began looking forward to restoration for God's people.

The book is very different from any we have studied so far. It does have the now familiar poetic denunciations, but it also contains many long prose sermons, detailed descriptions of visions, accounts of prophecies symbolically acted in dramatic form, allegories presenting the message in colourful word-pictures, discourses in quasi-legal style, and end-time visions in apocalyptic language.

The word 'apocalyptic' refers to a style of writing that became increasingly popular after 587. Though prophets still uttered warnings about sin and judgment, the future beyond, that the pre-exilic prophets had glimpsed, began to be unfolded in new detail, sometimes in visions described to us in highly picturesque and symbolic language. It is such visions as these we call apocalyptic. We have encountered rudimentary foreshadowings of them in Isa. 24–27, we find them in more developed form in Zechariah and Daniel, but the examples most familiar to Christians are in the New Testament book of Revelation. In fact many of Ezekiel's visions, particularly after ch. 33, are re-echoed there.

Four significant events, one the destruction of Jerusalem and the other three visions, dictated the shape of Ezekiel's ministry, and so also of his book. Each event is carefully dated by Ezekiel, who seems to have written this book himself, since he always uses the pronoun 'I', except in the one verse where he introduces himself (1.3).

1. CALLED TO BE A WATCHMAN (CHS. 1-7)

It all started in 593 BC, Ezekiel's thirtieth year (presuming the date in 1.1 refers to his age). Thirty was the age at which, as a Levitical priest, he would have taken up his duties at the sanctuary if he had not been in exile (Num. 4), but the LORD had a different calling for him to undertake, to be a prophetic watchman. A watchman is someone posted as a look-out, whose job is to watch for the approach of an enemy. Ezekiel's calling was to stand watch on behalf of the house of Israel and warn them about what was coming to them from the LORD, so that they could prepare themselves in advance by turning from their evil ways, that is by repentance. (3.16–21; 33.7–11).

Ch. 1: Ezekiel's vision of the Glory of God.

One day Ezekiel saw what looked like a storm-cloud approaching from the north across the flat Babylonian plain. He became aware of fire in the middle of it, then as it drew nearer, he could distinguish four living creatures in the fire, manlike, but each with four heads and four wings. They stood with their wing-tips touching in the shape of a square, the fire in the centre flashing back and forth among them. The vision was full of vibrancy and the sound of the creatures' wings was 'like the roar of rushing waters, like the voice of the Almighty, like the tumult of an army'. Beneath them were awesome looking wheels, also vibrant with life, with 'the spirit of the living creatures', and over their heads was a platform above which sat enthroned a fiery 'figure like that of a man' with a rainbow encircling his head. Such 'was the appearance of the likeness of the glory of the LORD'.

Ezekiel's experience was essentially the same as Isaiah's when he saw God. The ingredients of the vision are basically the same: winged, heavenly attendants (called cherubim in chs. 10 & 11), fire for dealing with sin (see ch. 10), the throne with God seated on it, and the use of the word 'glory' to describe the vision. These were all represented in the temple where God's glory resided in the Most Holy Place over the ark attended by the cherubim while incense burned on the altar before him (see above, pp. 81f), and John was to see it all in vision again in New Testament times (Rev. 4).

Chs. 2–3: Ezekiel receives his call.

Throughout the book God calls Ezekiel 'son of man'. Jesus used that title for himself in the Gospels, but here it only means 'human being' and shows us how much Ezekiel was aware of his mere humanity in the presence of God's glory. At first he fell on his face overwhelmed and had to be stood on his feet to receive his commission. (1.28 – 2.2) The reaction is so like Isaiah's, and later John's (Isa. 6.5; Rev. 1.17). In the light of it we understand better how Ezekiel could do and say some of the things he did without the fear or embarrassment we might feel if called to do the same. He also needed this overwhelming vision to prepare him, because the people he was to address were so stubborn and obstinate that it was going to be important he should fear God more than them (2.3–8; 3.4–11; cp. Isa. 8.12f; Jer. 1.17–19).

Isaiah's lips were touched by God's fire at his commissioning (Isa. 6.6f), Jeremiah knew God's hand touched his mouth when he received his message (Jer. 1.9). Ezekiel's experiences are often very similar to theirs, but always described in more colourful detail: he was told to eat a scroll

with the words he was to speak written on it. It tasted as
sweet as honey in his mouth, even though the message
was one of lamentation, mourning and woe. But then the
message would be bitter to the disobedient, though as God's
word it was bound to be sweet to the man of God himself
(2.9 – 3.3; cp. Mic. 2.6f).

When the vision left him, he went home and sat overwhelmed for a whole week (3.12–15). Then the LORD
revealed that he was making him a watchman for the house
of Israel, and led him out to the plain to meet with him in
his glory again. Again he had to be raised to his feet to
receive the rest of his commission, which must have been
very hard for him to accept, for he was to become house-
bound and dumb, to speak only when the LORD gave him a
prophetic word to deliver. The dramatic impact of his
strange life-style and utterances on his contemporaries after
that must have been considerable. (3.16–27)

Chs. 4–7: Dramatic prophecies of Jerusalem's fate.

If Ezekiel's call was striking, his first fourteen months as a
prophet were no less so. They started with him playing war
games on a map of Jerusalem (4.1–3), followed by a year
and more lying bound on the ground eating meagre rations
(4.4–17), then shaving his head, burning a third of his hair,
slashing a third of it around the streets with a sword, scatter-
ing a third of it to the wind, and preserving a few strands
in his pocket (5.1–4), all to symbolically drive home his
message that Jerusalem would be besieged, its citizens held
in exile for many years and its remaining inhabitants put to
the sword as punishment for their idolatry and rejection of
God's laws (5.5–17).

Street drama is a common technique used in Christian
evangelism today, but Ezekiel was already a master of the
art. He concluded his year of dramatic prophecy by facing
towards the mountains of Israel prophesying destruction and
further exile (6.1–10), striking his hands, stamping his feet
and crying 'Alas!' over the fate of their people (6.11–14),
then finally and bluntly crying out 'The end! The end has
come. Disaster! An unheard-of disaster is coming. The day
is here! It has come! Doom has burst forth . . . etc.' (ch. 7;

see vv. 2,5,10). Ezekiel certainly communicated the sense of urgency in his message with power.

2. GOD'S GLORY, JERUSALEM'S FAITHLESSNESS, APPROACHING JUDGMENT (CHS. 8–23)

The date is 592. The first phase of Ezekiel's ministry had lasted just over a year when God put his hand on him a second time and showed him a vision that was to make clearer than ever what were his purposes for Jerusalem and his people.

Chs. 8–11: God's Glory leaves Jerusalem.

In his house, with the elders of Judah sitting before him, Ezekiel was transported in vision to the temple in Jerusalem where he was made instantly aware of two things: the glory of God, just as in his call-vision, and a pagan idol. God then showed him various idolatrous rituals taking place in the temple precincts: a room full of elders worshipping animal images, women participating in a mourning rite associated with the Babylonian god Tammuz, and men at the entrance to the temple itself worshipping the sun. Ezekiel was left with no doubts about how God viewed such things. (ch. 8)

He watched God summon six warriors and a scribe, descend from his throne over the cherubim, take his stand majestically at the door of his temple, commission his scribe to mark all the faithful in Jerusalem, send the warriors to slaughter the rest of its inhabitants (ch. 9), and then command the scribe to take fire from between the cherubim and scatter it over the city (10.1–14).

After that he became aware of the cherubim stirring again. As he watched, the glory of the LORD remounted his throne and moved to the east gate of the temple (10.15–22). He found himself being carried there too and told to prophesy against a group of corrupt elders at the gate (11.1–12). As he did so, their leader dropped dead, and that prompted Ezekiel to ask God if the execution of his judgment was going to destroy Israel completely. The LORD's answer is

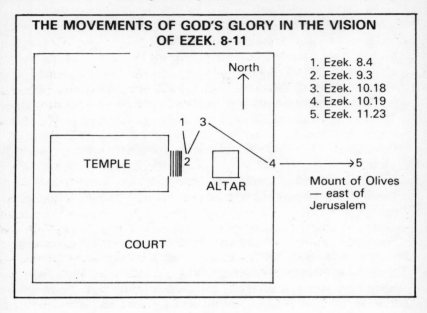

THE MOVEMENTS OF GOD'S GLORY IN THE VISION OF EZEK. 8-11

1. Ezek. 8.4
2. Ezek. 9.3
3. Ezek. 10.18
4. Ezek. 10.19
5. Ezek. 11.23

North

TEMPLE

ALTAR

COURT

Mount of Olives — east of Jerusalem

that he will scatter them among the nations, but will one day regather them, purge them of their idols, change their hearts and bring them into a new wholesome relationship with himself. (11.13–21)

With that, the glory of the LORD left the city and departed over the eastern mountains. Then the vision went up from Ezekiel and he told the exiles all he had seen. (11.22–25)

The message is clear: God is so disgusted with his people that he is about to abandon the city, leaving it for the Babylonians to ravage. And yet God can never go back on his promises. He told Abraham he would redeem this lost world through his descendants and he still intends to do so, though, because of their faithless ways, he must first do something to discipline and reform them for the task.

That was to be the burden of his message for the next six years, until the city fell in 587 BC, and he was to present it over and over with every technique he could employ, in prophecies, sermons, lamentation, arguments, allegories and drama.

Ch. 12: Ezekiel dramatically prophesies the exile.
In front of a watching crowd, he packed a fugitive's bag and
dug through the wall, signifying the mode of King Zedekiah's flight from Jerusalem (vv. 1–16; cp. 2 Kings 25.4–7).
Then he ate food trembling and shuddering as with fear,
just as the people of Jerusalem would soon be doing (vv.
17–20). He followed that by announcing that though nothing
seems to come of his vision now, it will soon be fulfilled
(vv. 21–28).

Ch. 13: He condemns the false prophets.
Like Micah, Isaiah and Jeremiah, he had to deal with prophets who falsely proclaimed peace. They do a cover-up
job, as if white-washing over flimsy repairs in a wall, which
not only fails to secure the wall, but deludes people into
thinking it is safe. They, and women who make magic
charms that also give false security, do more harm than
good.

Ch. 14: God's only word to the elders is 'Repent!'
Some elders come to consult Ezekiel, but the LORD shows
him their secret idolatry and all he can tell them is to repent.
He also warns that it is now too late to save Jerusalem and
the only hope left for righteous men is that their own lives
might be saved.

Ch. 15: Jerusalem is a useless vine.
In Scripture the LORD's people are compared to a vine
several times (Ps. 80.8; Jer. 6.9; Hos. 10.1; cp. Isa. 5.1–7;
John 15.1–8), but unless it produces good fruit a vine's wood
is useless, fit only for burning.

Ch. 16: Jerusalem has been like an unfaithful bride.
The review of Jerusalem's history in this chapter reminds
us of Hosea's comparisons between Israel and a faithless
son, or his own adulterous wife. God loved her, rescued
her, cared for her, made her into a beautiful girl, but then
she used her beauty to attract pagans, the Egyptians, Assyrians and Babylonians. She is worse than Samaria or Sodom,
and will have to be dealt with in the same way, but as Hosea

also saw, God would still love her and in the end bring her back into a new covenant (marriage) relationship that will be everlasting.

Ch. 17: A tree of the Lord's own planting.

The allegory in this chapter tells of an eagle (Babylon) breaking off the topmost shoot of a cedar (Jehoiachin and his nobles) and planting a promising vine (King Zedekiah), which faithlessly stretched out its branches to another eagle (Egypt) and so would be uprooted and stripped by the first eagle. So will the LORD deal with Jerusalem, but in due course he will plant a new cedar shoot of his own (Messiah) which will grow into a splendid tree and give shelter to many birds (God's people). This last image is used again by Jesus in one of his parables of the kingdom (Matt. 13.31f).

Ch. 18: Each individual is responsible for his own salvation.

Each man is responsible before God for his own salvation and should not excuse himself on grounds of heredity, upbringing, or the like. 'The soul who sins is the one who will die', but then God's desire is that everyone should live, not die – and repentance is the door to life. What is needed is that he get himself 'a new heart and a new spirit' (vv. 31f). Of course, as the second of the Ten Commandments states, children do suffer because of the sins of their fathers, even down to the third or fourth generation, but Ezekiel's point is that repentance changes all that.

This is an important chapter in the development of the Bible's message, because it lays a foundation for the challenge to personal faith and salvation that is so important in Christian evangelism. God wants repentance, not excuses – that message is still very valid in our age when we are so often encouraged to seek excuses for unsocial behaviour in upbringing or environment (cp. 33.10–20).

Ch. 19: A lament.

Ezekiel laments the exile of two Davidic kings, of Jehoahaz taken to Egypt by Pharaoh Neco in 609 (vv. 2–4; 2 Kings 23.1–5) and of Jehoiachin taken to Babylon by Nebuchadnezzar in 597 (vv. 5–9; 2 Kings 24.8–17). He then goes on to lament the coming uprooting, stripping and burning of the vine, Jerusalem (vv. 10–14; cp. ch. 15).

Ch. 20: A historical survey.

Ezekiel here takes some elders who come to enquire of the LORD down the centuries in a review of Israel's faithlessness and rebellion to show them how necessary it is that God execute his judgment. But, as in ch. 16, he asserts that God will not abandon his covenant, and will again gather his people to himself, this time to be a holy people.

Ch. 21: Babylon is to be the instrument of God's judgment.

Just as Isaiah had once called Assyria the rod of God's anger (Isa. 10.5), so Ezekiel sees Babylon as the sword of God's justice. He presents his message with dramatic art once more, drawing a map of the junction where one road leads to Jerusalem and the other to Ammon, then envisaging the Babylonian king casting lots to decide which road to take. The lot, of course, falls on Jerusalem. It will be destroyed and its Davidic crown abandoned 'until he comes to whom it rightfully belongs' (vv. 26f).

Ch. 22: The totality of Jerusalem's sin.

Everyone in Jerusalem, its princes, priests, officials, prophets and people are party to the city's sins in some way. God looked for a man to stand in the gap between them and himself, but he found none.

Ch. 23: Oholah and Oholibah.

This chapter takes up the allegory of ch. 16 and elaborates on it, presenting Samaria and Jerusalem as two adulterous sisters called Oholah and Oholibah. Oholah has already been punished, yet Oholibah has refused to learn the lesson. But God will put an end to lewdness in the land.

3. JERUSALEM FALLS AND EZEKIEL'S VISION WIDENS.
(CHS. 24–39)

Ch. 24: The turning point.
In January, 588 BC, the Babylonians set siege to Jerusalem and the whole direction of Ezekiel's ministry began to change. Now for the last time he prophesied the city's doom. It is like a rusty pot full of broth being boiled on a ferocious fire that will burn up the broth and the pot as well. In this allegory the pot is Jerusalem, the rust its sin, the broth its inhabitants and the fire the fury of the Babylonians. Ezekiel leaves no doubt about the finality of this word: 'I the LORD have spoken. The time has come for me to act.' (24.1–14)

At that time the LORD took Ezekiel's wife from him and bade him grieve in his heart without any outward display of mourning. Those who quizzed him about his strange behaviour were told that it symbolised what was soon to overtake them, that Jerusalem would soon be destroyed and because they were in exile for their sins, they would not be able to do more about it than grieve within themselves. (24.15–24)

The LORD also told him that his freedom of speech would be restored when the news of the fall of Jerusalem reached him. He would then have fulfilled the calling he had been given. (24.25–27)

Chs. 25–32: Prophecies concerning foreign nations.
In those days the LORD began to widen Ezekiel's vision. Many of the prophecies against the nations are dated about this time.

The little nations around Judah took vengeful delight at her downfall, but that only earned them God's judgment. (ch. 25; cp. Obadiah) Tyre also rejoiced at first, seeing new trading opportunities for herself now that her southern rival had gone (26.1f), but soon she too would feel Babylon's wrath, as would her neighbour, Sidon. (chs. 26–28) Nor would proud Egypt escape. (chs. 29–32)

Ch. 33: Ezekiel's new appointment and the fall of Jerusalem.

Though Ezekiel's commission to forewarn about the fall of Jerusalem was now fulfilled, the LORD still wanted him to be Israel's watchman. God had not finished with them; they still needed to repent. (33.1–20)

One evening, as promised, the LORD restored his speech, and the next day a messenger arrived with the news that Jerusalem had fallen. Ezekiel immediately began to prophesy again: You will never repossess the land while there are still so many detestable things happening among you. But those who came to hear him seemed to do so simply for entertainment. There was still no sign of repentance, even after all his earlier prophesying and everything that had happened in fulfilment of it. Ezekiel must have found that most depressing, but at least they knew that a prophet had been among them! (33.21–33)

Chs. 34–37: The Lord's plans for Israel's future.

Israel's shepherds (rulers) have been selfish and cruel with little care for the sheep (the people), but the LORD is finished with them. He will shepherd the flock himself, search for the lost (the exiles) and bring them home. The sheep will need discipline, because there has been a lot of bullying among them, but God will set one shepherd over them (Messiah), make 'a covenant of peace' with them and turn their land into a place of security and blessing. (ch. 34)

Edom had thoughts about taking control of the land, but that will not come to pass. (ch. 35; cp. Obadiah)

What will happen is that the land will be repopulated with God's own people and become fruitful again (36.1–15). The exile had to take place because Israel was bringing disgrace on God's holy name – and they still do, even in exile (36.16–21), but God cares deeply for his reputation and intends to show the world that he is true to his word (36.22f). So he will bring his people home, cleanse them from sin, change their heart and spirit, indeed give them his own Spirit, and so enable them to live the life his law requires (36.24–28; cp. 11.17– 21). Then he will begin changing the environment until even passers-by will say it 'has become like the garden of Eden' (36.29–35). This is not something the Israelites can do for themselves, but something God will do for them (36.36–38).

The restoration will seem like the resurrection of a graveyard. The nation is now very dead, but God can take even dried up skeletons, reclothe them with flesh and breathe new life into them (37.1–14). The two old kingdoms, Judah and Israel, will be restored and reunited, the promised Davidic king will be their shepherd, and then God will institute his everlasting covenant of peace (37.15–28).

Ezekiel's teaching here, about Messiah's coming, the new and everlasting covenant, cleansing from sin, the change in man's heart, the gift of God's Spirit, and entry to the security and peace of Eden, is very much in accord with all that Isaiah and other earlier prophets said and clearly foreshadows the work of Jesus Christ in the New Testament. We shall see that more clearly as we progress with our reading.

Chs. 38–39: The LORD's plan for the future of the nations.

The restoration of Israel, the coming of Messiah, the gift of the Spirit and the inauguration of the new covenant will not bring history to an end, but only set a new phase of it in motion. The nations will still be there and will still make plans against the LORD's people.

Ezekiel sees the nations, mustered under Gog, an evil king from the north-lands, marching from every direction against Israel, which is now living at peace, without defensive walls because it trusts in God. Unbeknown to him, Gog is actually brought to do this by God, and earlier prophets had seen it would happen. But no battle with Israel will take place, because God himself will do battle with Gog and the nations. (ch. 38) The weapons of the slain will provide fuel for Israel's fires for years and the dead will take months to bury. The nations will then acknowledge the glory of God, that Israel is his people, that their exile was his judgment, and that their restoration secures the holiness of his name. God's purposes for Israel are not whimsical. God will indeed pour out his Spirit on them. (ch. 39)

With this vision Ezekiel looks beyond Jesus' day into times that John was to describe more fully in Revelation, the day of God's final showdown with the powers of evil, the last battle before the end of history as we know it. Of course, Gog is always there raising his ugly head against the the LORD's people in recurring persecution, and so we are constantly living in something of the experience of chs. 38–39, but what we experience now is only little foretastes of a final mustering against the saints when God will have to deal with Gog once and for all. (See further Zech. 12–14; Rev. 17–19.)

4. THE NEW JERUSALEM (CHS. 40–48)

In 573 BC, twenty years after his call, Ezekiel was granted his final vision, one that carried him far beyond anything he had yet been shown. Isaiah and Micah saw the temple and Mount Zion renewed and gloriously restored (Isa. 2.2–5; Mic. 4.1–5); Ezekiel's vision is similar, though much more detailed.

Chs. 40–42: The plan of the new temple.
Ezekiel was taken to 'a very high mountain' – the mountain in Isaiah's vision was also raised above all others – and on it stood 'buildings that looked like a city'. There he was met by a heavenly architect with a measuring rod who conducted him around the new temple giving very precise details of its dimensions and structure. The pattern was basically that of Solomon's temple, but the details need not delay us here.

Chs. 43–46: The temple springs to life.
Ezekiel had not seen God's glory again in the nineteen years since he had watched the cherubim leave Jerusalem (chs. 8–11). It must have thrilled him to see what he now saw: the glory of God coming back from the east, entering the temple the way he had left, filling the temple and announcing that he was home to stay (43.1–9). As before, Ezekiel fell on his face (44.4).

EZEKIEL'S TEMPLE

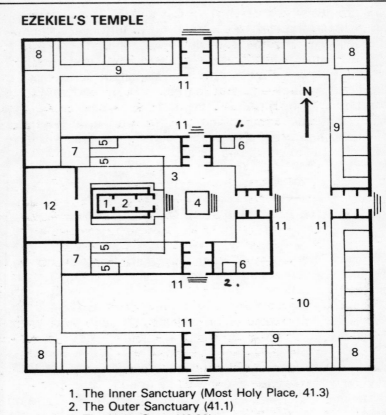

1. The Inner Sanctuary (Most Holy Place, 41.3)
2. The Outer Sanctuary (41.1)
3. The Inner Court (40.28)
4. The Altar (43.13)
5. Priests' Rooms (42.1)
6. Priests' Rooms (40.44)
7. Priests' Kitchens (46.19)
8. People's Kitchens (46.21)
9. Pavement with rooms (40.17)
10. The Outer Court (40.17)
11. Gates with alcoves (40.6,20,24,28,32,35)
12. Building on the west side (41.12)

1. Priests serving in Temple ⎫ descended by
2. "   "   " at the altar ⎬ Zedok - tribe
                                  ⎭ of Levi

He then became aware of the altar and its sacrifices (43.10–27), the prince, the new Zadokite priesthood, the Levites in their role as temple-servants, all of them now pure and holy before God (ch. 44). He saw the land around the temple precinct allotted to the prince and the priests and he learned the new regulations for the festivals and the sacrificial worship (chs. 45–46). Again the details need not detain us. Like the measurements of the temple, they are very precise and basically the same as in the pre-exilic system. The main difference is that there is now a sense of supernatural perfection about them. Ezekiel's temple could be built and its rituals performed today, but not with the purity he envisages. His vision fluctuates back and forth across the borders of practical programme and apocalyptic symbolism. But that is because he is looking through the screen of history to come into the ultimate reality of God's eternity that lies beyond.

Chs. 47–48: The overflow from the temple into the land.

The vision continues in the same mixed vein. Out from the temple flows a supernatural river that no architect could possibly devise. By the time it has flowed just over a mile it has become 'a river that no-one could cross', its banks crowded with trees and swarming with animal life, its waters teeming with fish. The fish provide abundant food, the trees unceasing crops of fruit and their leaves healing virtue.

For centuries Jerusalem had rejoiced in 'a river whose streams make glad the city of God' (Ps. 46.4), hardly a tangible river, but rather the spiritual life-giving outflow of God to its citizens. The exile ended that, but now Ezekiel sees the river flow again. And it is like the primeval river that flowed from Eden watering the garden (Gen. 2.10), for what he sees beyond the temple is a land that, because of this life-giving outflow from God's presence, has again become an Eden-garden with its rich vegetation and abundant animal life (see also Joel 3.18; Zech. 14.8).

Ezekiel's vision was also prophetic of other things, for one day Jesus was to stand in the temple inviting people to come and drink of the streams of living water he would

EZEKIEL'S VISION OF THE REALLOCATION OF THE LAND (47.13 — 48.29)

D A N

A S H E R

N A P H T A L I

M A N A S S E H

E P H R A I M

R E U B E N

J U D A H

The Prince | The Prince

Levites

Temple Priests

City of Jerusalem

B E N J A M I N

S I M E O N

I S S A C H A R

Z E B U L U N

Tamar

G A D

Wadi of Egypt

Kadesh (Meribah)

give, referring, of course, to the Spirit to be given at Pentecost (John 7.37–39). Then at the end, in John's new Jerusalem, the river flows from God's own throne into his eternal
garden of Eden. On each side of it stands the tree of life,
lost to man since he was first driven from the garden. (Rev.
22.1f)

In its imagery Ezekiel's vision gathers up man's total
hope, that one day God will restore the life of Eden. Hence
it is little wonder that, once he sees the land idealistically
reapportioned to the tribes (47.13 – 48.35), he hears the
city given a new, eternal name: THE LORD IS THERE.
As we have seen, this was Jerusalem, and yet more than
that, for what he saw was not a city, but what 'looked like
a city' (40.2). The city the returning exiles would build
would not be this one, but God's intention was that it should
be a prophetic embodiment of it.

PART FIVE

ADDING THE
FINISHING TOUCHES

SIXTH – FIFTH CENTURIES B.C.

King Nebuchadnezzar died in 562 BC and was succeeded by several weak rulers. The longest reigning was Nabonidus (556–39), but he took little interest in the affairs of state and withdrew to Tema in the Arabian desert leaving his son, Belshazzar, in charge. According to the book of Daniel and some intertestamental writings, these later years were times of suffering and persecution for the Jews, but they were not to last long. The power of Babylon was spent and in 539 a little-known Persian king called Cyrus overthrew the Babylonians in a bloodless campaign. Then a year later he published an edict permitting exiles to return home and rebuild their communities (Ezra 1).

The exile had lasted about sixty years, almost but not quite the seventy Jeremiah predicted, that is if we reckon from the fall of Jerusalem in 597, though there was apparently another deportation just under ten years earlier, in 606–5 when the Babylonians first invaded Judah, the year Daniel was taken captive (2 Kings 24.1; Dan. 1.1). Anyhow, the message of the pre-exilic prophets was more than vindicated by the course of events, with the result that prophecy ceased to be so dominated by warnings about coming judgment and began to develop a new role. We saw how Ezekiel's ministry changed after the destruction of Jerusalem in 587, but after 538 the message of Israel's prophets changed even more radically as they found themselves having to address the new crises of the restoration era.

Each new wave of prophecy had to meet the challenge of its age in a different way – Samuel with revival preaching, Elijah and Elisha with miracle-ministry, after Amos with prophetical warnings – but the aim was always the same, to call the LORD's people back to him in repentance. That aim continued to motivate the prophets, though now their message became more one of encouragement, first to get up and go home, then to rebuild, and finally to wait patiently for God to act again and fulfil his earlier promises about the Messiah, the Spirit and so forth.

That long-term vision was already well formulated. Their contribution was to add some finishing touches and so complete the preparation for Christ's coming. Some of their insights are very precious indeed.

THE EXILE AND RETURN

DATE	JUDAH			IMPERIAL	
				← Nebuchadnezzar 605-562	B
590	E		JERUSALEM DESTROYED		A
	Z		587		B
	E		Second deportation		Y
			Murder of Gedeliah		
	K		Third deportation 582		L
580	I	O			
		B			O
	E	A	Ezekiel's final vision 573		N
		D	(Ezek. 40-48)		
570	L	I			I
		A			
		H			A
					N
560				Amel-marduk 562-60	
				Neriglissar 560-56	
				Nabonidus 556-39	E
				Retired to Tema in the	M
				Arabian desert and left his	P
550	ISAIAH			son Belshazzer in charge.	
	40-55				I
					R
					E
540				Cyrus takes Babylon 539	
				Cyrus 559-30	P
			Exiles start to return 537	Issues edict allowing exiles	E
			led by Sheshbazzer.	to return 538	R
			Altar restored autumn 537		S
530		I	Joshua high priest.	Cambyses 530-22	I
		S	Zerubbabel takes over from		A
		A	Sheshbazzer as governor		N
		I	(535?).	Darius I 522-486	
520	HAGGAI	A	Temple rebuilt 520-15		E
	Z	H			M
	E				P
	C	56			I
	H	'			R
	A	66			E
510	R				
	I				
	A				
	H				

10

Preparing the Way for the LORD

ISAIAH 40–55

Opinions differ whether Isa. 40–55 contains the words of the eighth-century Isaiah looking down the years to events that were to happen in the sixth, or whether they were spoken by some anonymous sixth century prophet to his own generation. Whoever he was his words are addressed to Jews living in Babylon about 550 BC or shortly thereafter, though they are also very much in the tradition of Isaiah himself.

When we read Jeremiah and Ezekiel we meet the men behind the books, but in Isa. 40–55 we barely see the prophet at all. There are virtually no biographical notes, just the words of the voice that spoke with him (40.3,6).

The commission and message that voice gave him is summed up in the opening verses of the book: Comfort my people, because their exile is almost ended, God is about to act, the time of discipline is over and the Israelites must get ready to move, for God is preparing a way for their journey home, a new exodus route through the desert (40.1f). It is a powerful message imparting hope and vision to a beleaguered people who must have been quite unable to see how it would all end.

Chs. 40–41: Comfort my people! Say, 'Here is your God!'

Ezekiel's call was to be a watchman, looking out for God's coming, this prophet's to be a herald, announcing his coming, preparing the way for the arrival of his King

(40.3–5). Perplexed by his commission, he calls out, 'What shall I cry?' Immediately one of the most majestic messages in the whole Bible begins to flow.

Men come and go, but God's word remains, and he has made promises to his people that he must keep (40.6–8), so shout it out that he is coming to shepherd them and lead them home (40.9–11). You cannot see how that is possible? Don't you realise your God is the Creator and he cares for all he has made? He is not some puny, man-made idol. He is the one who controls the nations and their history (40.12–26). You think he doesn't care about you! Well, he does. Just wait for him and you will see! (40.27–31)

Let me explain what God is doing: He is raising up one from the east (= Cyrus the Persian; see 45.1) who will drive nations before him (41.1–4). They will turn in fear to their useless idols (41.5–7), but you have nothing to fear, Israel, for you are loved by the LORD and he will help you. Indeed these events will be for your restoration (41.8–16). Your desert will flow with water and folk will see that it was God's doing (41.17–20). No idol can foresee this, but God does and that is why he has sent me to tell you now, before it happens, so that you will appreciate it is his doing (41.21–29).

Chs. 42–43: Israel is called to be a light to the nations. God has a purpose for you beyond what you imagine, that you be his 'light to the nations', to open blind eyes and set captives free (42.5–9). That was his original purpose for Israel, and he has not forgotten it. Praise him now, for he is about to fulfil it (42.10–17). Can't you see it? Israel has only been plundered as punishment for sin. Her present state is not the end of the story (42.18–25).

By no means, for I love you. I have redeemed you. I will protect you and bring you home (43.1–13). Forget the past; I am doing a new thing! I am going to take you home through the desert. It will be like a new exodus. Yes, you have sinned, but I will blot out your transgressions. A new day is about to start for Israel (43.14–28).

On 42.1–4, see below under 52.13 – 53.12.

Chs. 44–47: *I am the* LORD, *and there is no other.*

Many exiles must have found the prophet's message hard
to believe. Some had been in Babylonia for about fifty years,
others had grown up in exile, and in that time many must
have lost hope for Israel's future. There had also been
mockery and persecution (cp. Ps. 137) and some apparently
felt the Babylonian gods had won, that Israel's God was not
so powerful after all. The next four chapters argue to restore
faith that God is all powerful and will indeed be true to his
word.

My promise is still to pour out my Spirit on you and bless
you, to make you mine again, says the LORD (44.1–5). I
who tell you this am LORD Almighty. Apart from me there
is no god (44.6–8). The Babylonian idols are only cast metal
and carved wood; they can do nothing (44.9– 20). But I am
God, the Creator, your Redeemer, and I say Jerusalem
will be rebuilt. I also say Cyrus will make that possible
(44.21–28).

And Cyrus will, for I will enable him to do so, even
though he does not acknowledge me (45.1–6). If I can
create, I can do this. You waste your energy arguing with
me about it! (45.7–13) You may not see how it is possible,
but it is my purpose. I make no secret about it; indeed I
foretold it long ago (45.14–21). So turn to me and be saved.
I have sworn, I will do it and the world will acknowledge it
is I (45.22–25).

The Babylonian gods may seem very powerful to you, but
they are finished. They will not be able to rescue, but will
have to be rescued themselves! (46.1f) I am God – you
cannot compare a cast lump of metal with me! (46.3–7) I
have promised your salvation, and so it will be (46.8–13).

Babylon is also finished, like her gods. So proud and
delicate, but she will be put to shame (47.1–7). So self-
confident, even claiming 'I am, and there is none besides
me,' which is the same as claiming to be God (47.8–11; cp.
44.6; 45.6), so full of sorcery and astrology, but none of
that will save her (47.12–15).

Chs. 48–50: *From now on I tell you new things*.

It was not enough to explain God's programme, nor to argue that he is able to fulfil it. The people needed to be stirred out of despondency and encouraged to look forward to their new future.

I foretold all that would happen to you because of your sins and it has happened (48.1–6), so now when I tell you new things, believe they will happen too. I am true to my word and will not allow my reputation to be defamed! (48.7–12) Pay attention now. If you had attended before you would have had blessing, not punishment (48.13–19). You are leaving Babylon. Start getting excited about it! (48.20–22)

Your exodus and restoration is indeed at hand (49.7–12). Start rejoicing now, because whatever you may say, God has not forgotten you and he has a rich future for you (49.13–21). You will see, the nations will even help to make your restoration possible (49.22–28). You saw my ability to judge your sins; do you think I lack the strength to save you now? (50.1–3)

On 49.1–6 and 50.4–9, see below under 52.13 – 53.12.

Chs. 51–52: *Awake! Depart! Proclaim, 'Your God reigns!'*

The prophet now stirs the exiles to expectancy, so that when the moment comes they will be awake and ready to move. Without such early encouragement few would have been prepared when Cyrus issued his edict. However, thanks to these prophecies, many must have been eagerly waiting for that moment of liberation, full of hope for their future, eager to go home and rebuild for God.

You doubt what I say? Look to your roots: consider the ancient promises to Abraham. The LORD will surely fulfil his word. Even now his salvation is on the way (51.1–8). The fulfilment has already begun: The creator God is on the move and the redeemed of the LORD will come to Zion singing (51.9–16). So wake up and get ready! You have suffered all I intend you to suffer (51.17–23).

Wake up, shake yourself out of the dust (52.1f). Your redemption is not going to cost you anything (52.3–6). Already the herald of good news comes; let Jerusalem's watchmen and all her citizens start rejoicing (52.7–10). Depart from Babylon, but not in frantic haste, for the LORD will go before you (52.11f).

52.13 – 53.12: *The* LORD's *Servant.*

The theme suddenly switches from the joyous home-coming of the exiles to a remarkable preview of the life of Christ as God's suffering servant. We are taken through the whole story of his suffering, death and resurrection, and beyond that to a vision of the many who will be blessed through his ministry.

This passage needs to be read in conjunction with three others we have passed over without comment (42.1–4; 49.1–6; 50.4–9), often referred to as the 'Servant Songs'. In them the servant is introduced as one through whom God's purposes will be powerfully worked out. Much of his ministry is similar to and blends with Israel's, and so in 49.3 he is actually called 'Israel' (Israel is also called God's servant several times in the rest of Isa. 40–55; e.g. 41.8f; 44.1f,21). But there is a difference, because unlike Israel he has 'not been rebellious' (50.5), 'he will not falter or be discouraged' (42.4), he suffers, not for his own sins, like Israel has done, but for the sins of others (53.4–13), and he is sent to restore and revive Israel itself (49.5). However, his mission extends beyond that, for he is also – like Israel – to be 'a light to the Gentiles' (49.6; cp. 42.6).

He is chosen of God to bear his Spirit and bring justice to the world, not violently, but quietly and with compassion (42.1–4). He will spend much of his time on earth simply being prepared for his life's mission, like an arrow polished and kept in a quiver. There will be times when his labour will seem wasted, but through him the LORD intends salvation to reach all mankind. (49.1–6) There will come a time when he will be whipped and beaten, when he will suffer terrible shame, and he will have to live through that with nothing to support him but his faith that God will vindicate him (50.4–9). In the end he will be led, despised and rejected by men, like a lamb to the slaughter. He will face that with quiet humility, but in his death men will see that it is to bear the punishment for their sins that he dies. In fact it is the LORD's will that all this should happen, but after his suffering he will again live and will see how the LORD's will has prospered in his hand (52.13 – 53.12).

The Jews never identified him with Messiah, but his life and mission were lived out and fulfilled by Jesus so exactly that we cannot but be amazed at the miracle of prophecy contained in these passages. Their message, that the way to the world's salvation was to be through the suffering of one man, is quite unique.

Chs. 54–55: Zion's Future Glory.

As in earlier prophetic writings, the vision continues beyond Messiah's coming to glimpse the final, end-time glory of the New Jerusalem as a place of righteousness, peace and plenty, of love, freedom and exceeding joy – of Paradise regained.

Rejoice, and enlarge your vision. You will need a wide vision to cope with the expansion I have in store for you (54.1–3). Don't be afraid. I will not let you down. Yes, I disciplined you for a while, but I am calling you home to make a covenant like the one I made with Noah, one that will last for ever (54.4–10). A glorious future of peace and blessing lies ahead (54.11–17).

So come and join in what I am doing to restore David's throne. You will find that more satisfying than anything else you may labour for, and it will cost you nothing (55.1–5). Seek the LORD, turn to him now (55.6f). His plans are far superior to ours and his word is utterly faithful – you will go home with joy (55.8–13).

The prophet's central vision is of God's people on a joyous exodus journey home along a beautiful highway laid through the desert by God himself. Blessed with God's Spirit, they go rejoicing at the richness of his grace and the brightness of the hope he has set before them. Isa. 35 offers an excellent summary of the same vision. It is a vision that still lives for Christians today, speaking to them of the journey they make through life to God's eternal, heavenly Jerusalem, endued with his Spirit and upheld by his love. This prophet's words, together with his amazing portrait of the suffering servant, have blessed and encouraged the faithful through many generations and will continue to do so through many more.

11

Restoring Vision and Purpose

HAGGAI, ZECHARIAH, ISAIAH 55–66

The exiles began to return soon after Cyrus published his edict in 538. A certain Sheshbazzar was appointed governor of Judah and he led the first returning party. They brought treasures from the old temple with them and some of their leaders gave contributions towards building a new one. In the autumn of 537 they rebuilt the altar and restarted sacrificial worship. The following spring the foundation was laid amid loud rejoicing and a great deal of mixed emotion (Ezra 1–3).

Some of the people in the land were naturally interested and eagerly offered to help, but the returned exiles did not welcome what they regarded as semi-pagan interference. The result was a backlash of opposition that brought work on the temple to a standstill for the next fifteen years (Ezra 4.1–5,24). During that time popular morale also deteriorated as initial enthusiasm gave way to depression after a few bad harvests and other economic disasters (Hag. 1.5–11).

In the meantime Zerubbabel, grandson of the Davidic king Jehoiachin who was exiled in 597 (Matt. 1.12), became governor of Judah. He and Joshua the High Priest had together played a leading part in restoring the altar (Ezra 3.2), and now they were faced with the challenge not only of rebuilding the temple, but of rousing some enthusiasm for the work among the people. There were, however, some men of vision who spoke up to encourage them and once again these were prophets: Haggai and Zechariah. In 520 they restarted the work and soon saw their trust in the

158

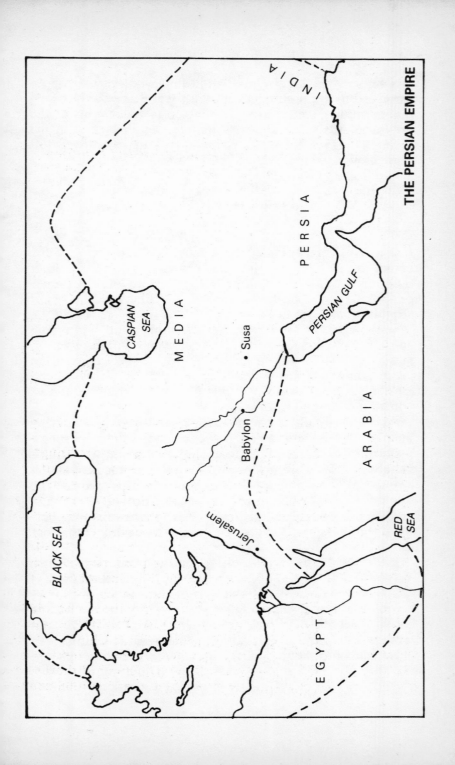

prophetic word wonderfully vindicated when further opposition led to a search uncovering a royal decree authorising the rebuilding and enjoining that costs be met from the provincial treasury. The new temple was dedicated in the spring of 515 amid great rejoicing, particularly over this miraculous means of provision! (Ezra 5–6)

1. WORK, FOR I AM WITH YOU (HAGGAI)

In 520 BC Haggai called on Zerubbabel, Joshua and the people to build, promising that proper harvests and other blessings would soon follow if they would only get their priorities right, stop being so selfishly concerned and start attending to the LORD's house. His message could be summed up in Jesus' words: 'Seek first his (God's) kingdom and his righteousness, and all these things will be given to you as well' (1.1–11; cp. Matt. 6.33). He also assured the people that God was still with them, and his words proved most effective, stirring Zerubbabel and Joshua to almost immediate action (1.12–15).

As well as calling on the people to work and assuring them of God's continuing presence, he sought to renew them in vision, foretelling that the new temple would ultimately be more glorious than Solomon's, the focus of latter-day prosperity and peace (2.1–9). However, his prophesying was not like that of the pre-exilic false prophets who had predicted cheap blessing, for he was fully aware that personal holiness was every bit as necessary as buildings (2.10–19).

Interestingly, he saw in Zerubbabel's governorship a foreshadowing of Messiah's ministry, as did Zechariah also (2.20–23; cp. Zech. 4). That need not surprise us, of course, because, although Zerubbabel was not a king, he was of Davidic descent and was therefore a living reminder and representative of God's promise to his great forefather.

Haggai's prophetic ministry only lasted four months!

2. BE ENCOURAGED, JERUSALEM HAS A GLORIOUS FUTURE (ZECHARIAH)

That same year, 520 BC, Zechariah also spoke to encourage Zerubbabel and Joshua, but his first words, two months after Haggai began prophesying, were addressed to the people in general, reminding them about the lessons their fathers had learned about the consequences of sin and calling on them to return to the LORD in repentance. That, after all, is the point at which all national revival must start. (1.1–6)

1.7 – 6.15: Visions of restoration.
Two months after Haggai's last prophecy, Zechariah saw nine visions containing messages of encouragement for Joshua, Zerubbabel and the people. Read in order they gradually build up a powerful overall vision of restoration and hope for Jerusalem's future:

1.7–17	A new day of blessing is in store for Jerusalem.
1.18–21	Her enemies will be scattered.
Ch. 2	She will become a populous city and God will dwell in her.
Ch. 3	Joshua's priesthood will prefigure Messiah's priestly work.
Ch. 4	Zerubbabel will lay the last stone of the temple – he and Joshua are anointed to serve the LORD together.
5.1–4	All sinners will be banished from the community.
5.5–11	Idolatry will also be banished.
6.1–8	Blessings will be carried to other lands.
6.9–15	And Joshua's ministry will prefigure Messiah's kingship.

1.7–17: Vision 1 – Reporting the state of the nations.
An angel standing in a myrtle grove receives reports from couriers that the nations of earth are at peace, which prompts an expostulation about the need for some blessing to

come Jerusalem's way. God responds that the nations will have their day of judgment, that his purpose is still to prosper Jerusalem, and that his word remains trustworthy.

1.18–21: Vision 2 – Terrifying the horns of the nations.

The nations that harmed Israel will be overthrown. Horns symbolise political power (cp. Dan. 7.7f,24), but however terrifying they may seem on a wild animal, the LORD's power to terrify is even greater.

Ch. 2: Vision 3 – Measuring Jerusalem for expansion.

An architect with a measuring line (cp. Ezek. 40.3) is told not to bother measuring out the boundaries of the city because it will become too populous for walls to contain it. God promises he will protect it himself, calls on the remaining exiles to return from Babylon, and announces he is coming personally to dwell in Jerusalem, to be its glory within (cp. Ezek. 43.1–9).

Ch. 3: Vision 4 – Encouraging the High Priest.

Joshua is depressed, beset by Satan. Amid the temple ruins, all he can see is his own worthlessness. Zechariah's vision must have shaken him out of his doldrums. It shows him reinstated, clothed in new priestly robes, and recommissioned – but more than that, challenged to get on with his priestly duties and act like one whose sacrificial office prefigures Messiah's, which will be to deal finally with sin.

Ch. 4: Vision 5 – Encouraging the governor.

Zerubbabel was also depressed. His small beginnings seemed pathetic and the task of rebuilding seemed mountainous. But what was impossible for him was not so for God. He will indeed complete it, though by God's power, not his own. Furthermore, he shares the same call as Joshua to prefigure Messiah's ministry (cp. Hag. 2.23). Both men are 'anointed (*messiah*-ed) to serve the LORD', to be like two olive trees, a twin source of oil for God's lamp in Jerusalem.

5.1–4: Vision 6 – Purging the community of sin.
Social sin will be banished by an official proclamation of judgment, by an effective decree from God.

5.5–11: Vision 7 – Purging the community of idolatry.
The woman imprisoned in the basket is named 'wickedness'; she is the very personification of sin. And so she is carried from God's land to the place where she properly belongs, a pagan temple in Babylonia.

6.1–8: Vision 8 – Witness to the nations.
But God is 'Lord of the whole world' and what he is doing in Jerusalem will ultimately have its impact for good on other nations as well. The horses and chariots in this vision are his emissaries, 'the spirits of heaven', straining, impatient for the time to go out from standing in his presence and carry his Spirit to other lands. God's final purpose has always been to redeem the peoples, not destroy them.

6.9–15: Vision 9 – Crowning the Messiah.
Joshua is, of course, not the Messiah, but in the vision stands in place of him. As in ch. 3 his ministry prefigures Messiah's, but this time it is Messiah's kingly role that is in mind. His crown is to be lodged in the temple as a reminder of the promise of God prefigured in the High Priest's office.

Chs. 7–8: A call to live in repentance and the vision of blessing.
Zechariah's visions still speak today whenever God's people are confronted with the challenge of taking apparently impossible faith decisions to further his work. They still summon us to rise above negative and depressive thinking, to be people of vision and to act. However, Zechariah never encouraged folly or presumption. His initial call was to walk closely with God. After two years of temple-building he speaks out again to remind the people about these same priorities.

Now that the temple is visibly rising from the ground, the people begin asking whether it is still needful to fast as in the sadder days of exile. Zechariah questions them about the spirit behind their fasting and reminds them of the more basic need for justice and mercy (ch. 7). But he also reminds them about God's promises concerning Jerusalem's blessed future, and affirms that the fast days will indeed become times of joyful festival, though it will still be important to love truth and peace. One day men from all over the world will come seeking out the LORD's people because they will have heard that 'God is with you'. (ch. 8)

Though the building programme was now well under way and the temple would be dedicated in another three years, the community clearly still needed all the encouragement and vision Zechariah could give.

Chs. 9–14: Visions of things yet to come.
These chapters, unlike chs. 1–8, are not dated, and they make no reference to the rebuilding of the temple. Their teaching relates entirely to the distant future, moving towards the end into the realms of apocalyptic. Considering how similar visions generally came late in other prophets' ministries, these chapters should probably be dated well after the temple was completed.

Chs. 9–11: The times of Messiah.
One day Israel's old enemies will trouble her no more (9.1–8), and then Messiah will come riding, not a war-horse, but a peaceful donkey (cp. Matt. 21.5). That will be a joyous occasion and will usher in God's reign of peace (9.9f). It will bring release for prisoners, for the LORD comes in power to establish his people (9.11–17).

Like a shepherd, the LORD will bring home the strays still in exile (ch. 10). Then, in a remarkable passage (ch. 11), we read about a shepherd being appointed by God to rescue his sheep of both nations, Israel and Judah, from oppressive shepherds and care for them, only to experience rejection, be paid off for a mere thirty pieces of silver, which gets thrown away in disgust, but then have to take up his office of shepherd again and heal the sheep. This is partly an explanation of God's dealings with Israel and Judah over the time of their exile and restoration, but it is also clearly prophetic of the life, death and resurrection of Jesus Christ (cp. Matt. 26.15; 27.3–5), and as such reflects common experiences of shepherding and rejection among Christian pastors today. The natural response to such rejection would be to seek revenge, or at least to abandon the flock; the Christian shepherd, however strongly tempted, must follow Christ and resume his pastorate.

Chs. 12–14: The times of the end.

Zechariah sees Jerusalem being strengthened in preparation for a great battle (12.1–9), but before saying more about that, he turns first to scenes of mourning 'for the one they pierced', of 'a fountain opened to the house of David and the inhabitants of Jerusalem to cleanse them from sin', of 'the shepherd' struck and the sheep scattered (12.10 13.9), all pictures that take on fuller meaning in the light of Jesus' crucifixion.

Finally he describes the last battle. Its outcome is that God's enemies are removed and the survivors of all races worship him, though they may need to be disciplined into doing so. The whole earth now becomes God's kingdom and everything in the New Jerusalem becomes 'holy to the LORD'. (ch. 14)

Zechariah's language at this point is dramatic and colourful, more so than Ezekiel's, approximating more closely to the apocalyptic imagery of Revelation, but it does not yet portray that fullness of the vision granted to John in New Testament times. Note that, like both Ezekiel and John, he sees God's river flow from Jerusalem (14.8; cp. also Joel 3.18).

3. ARISE SHINE, FOR YOUR LIGHT HAS COME (ISAIAH 56–66)

These chapters also relate to the early restoration years (see above, pp. 79f). 56.8, for example, speaks of exiles gathered home and the LORD promising to gather still others. The impression is hardly of a community living in enthusiastic, purified holiness, and so the old prophetic proclamation of judgment, repentance and restoration sounds forth again, but the vision of future glory still burns brightly as well encouraging the LORD's people to rise up in faith.

Chs. 56–59: The prophet calls for repentance again.

Salvation is for all who choose to walk wholeheartedly with God, whatever their nationality or social status (56.1–8).

But Israel's leaders are corrupt (56.9–12), good men suffer (57.1f) and idolatry is everywhere (57.3–10). However, idols cannot save, only God can (57.11–13), and he will save and comfort the contrite of heart (57.14–21).

You say God does not heed you, even when you seek him with fasting? Of course he does not while your ways are wrong. Care for the poor and needy, then he will hear and exalt you beyond measure. (ch. 58)

Sin separates us from God and that is why there is no peace (59.1–11). Repentance is what he seeks (59.12–15). Because of sin he rouses himself in anger to intervene, so be sure you are found in repentance when he comes! (59.15–20) God's covenant with penitents is never to take away his word or his Spirit from them (59.21).

Chs. 60–62: He reaffirms the vision of Zion's future glory.

The prophet sees kings and nations pouring into Zion bearing wealth to the city, all because the LORD's glory is there. It is a vision of eternal joy and peace other prophets also saw, and it is experienced in foretaste by many Christians today in churches where men are drawn to seek God when they learn that his glory shines there. (ch. 60)

At its heart stands the portrait of one, a prophetic figure on whom the Spirit of the LORD rests, sent to preach 'good news' and to bring healing and release. His ministry is clearly integral to the establishment of the new age, and for the Christian is also as clearly the ministry fulfilled by Jesus Christ (Isa. 61.1–3; cp. Luke 4.18f). It is shared in our time by all Spirit-filled leaders in the Church.

Inspired by his ministry the people will rebuild and become God's priests, delighting in the LORD and his salvation (61.4–11). Again we see first fulfilments of this vision in the joyous vitality of some churches led by Spirit-filled men today.

It is God's promise that these things should come to pass (ch. 62). He himself will not rest until they be accomplished, nor should his people (vv. 1,7). They should work to prepare for his coming (v. 10).

Chs. 63–64: He prays for God to come and fulfil the vision.

A vision of God coming to judge the nations and save Israel (63.1–6) leads on to a long prayer, recalling God's care in the days of Moses (63.7–14) and crying out for him to return and care for his people now (63.15–19), to come in saving, revival power again, to stop punishing them for their sins and to bring restoration (ch. 64).

Chs. 65–66: God answers that the punishment will give way to glory.

God has already been very patient, but he must deal with sin (65.1–7). That will not mean total destruction, only a purge of sinners (65.8– 16), but then the new day will dawn and all his promises of blessing will be fulfilled. In the new Jerusalem, and new heavens and new earth that stand at the end of God's history, as Isaiah saw in the eighth century, 'The wolf and the lamb will feed together . . .' in the Eden Garden of God (65.17–25).

The temple now being built will have to be undergirded by right spiritual attitudes, not just dressed up with sacrifices (66.1–4), but you can start rejoicing now, for God will not fail to bring this vision he has conceived and carried to birth (66.5–11). He comes to fulfil it (66.12–16).

In a remarkable finale, we see messengers being sent out among the nations, as the New Testament apostles would be, to proclaim God's glory and gather hoards of their people into his kingdom (66.17–24).

We have seen now, over and over again, how it was at times when revival was particularly needed that prophets became most active. So it was in the early years after the exile. Those who returned to Judah faced apparently insurmountable

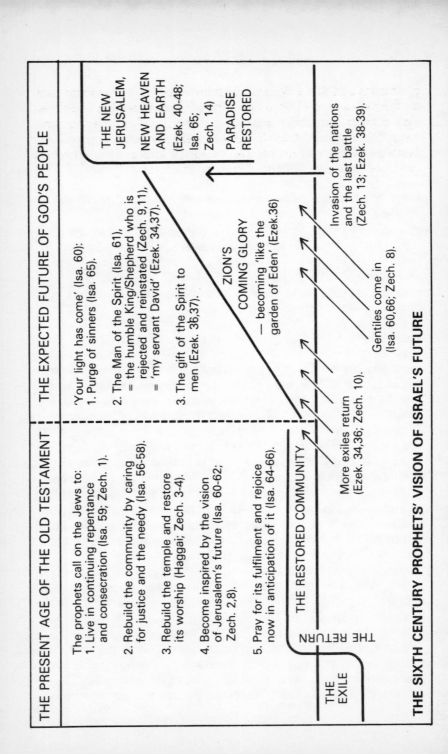

| THE PRESENT AGE OF THE OLD TESTAMENT | THE EXPECTED FUTURE OF GOD'S PEOPLE |

The prophets call on the Jews to:
1. Live in continuing repentance and consecration (Isa. 59; Zech. 1).

2. Rebuild the community by caring for justice and the needy (Isa. 56-58).

3. Rebuild the temple and restore its worship (Haggai; Zech. 3-4).

4. Become inspired by the vision of Jerusalem's future (Isa. 60-62; Zech. 2,8).

5. Pray for its fulfilment and rejoice now in anticipation of it (Isa. 64-66).

'Your light has come' (Isa. 60):
1. Purge of sinners (Isa. 65).

2. The Man of the Spirit (Isa. 61),
= the humble King/Shepherd who is rejected (Zech. 9,11),
= 'my servant David' (Ezek. 34,37).

3. The gift of the Spirit to men (Ezek. 36,37).

THE NEW JERUSALEM,
NEW HEAVEN AND EARTH
(Ezek. 40-48;
Isa. 65;
Zech. 14)

PARADISE RESTORED

ZION'S COMING GLORY
— becoming 'like the garden of Eden' (Ezek.36)

Invasion of the nations and the last battle
(Zech. 13; Ezek. 38-39).

Gentiles come in
(Isa. 60,66; Zech. 8).

More exiles return
(Ezek. 34,36; Zech. 10).

THE RESTORED COMMUNITY

THE RETURN

THE EXILE

THE SIXTH CENTURY PROPHETS' VISION OF ISRAEL'S FUTURE

problems and soon became disheartened, but thanks mainly to the vision and encouragement of their prophets they rose up, rebuilt their city and its temple, and so became re-established as the LORD's people with a renewed and living faith in his purposes for them. Once more prophecy had proved itself an effective instrument of revival.

12

Final Preparation for the LORD's Coming

JOEL AND MALACHI

We now move forward about seventy years from the dedication of the temple. The enthusiasm surrounding its rebuilding had evaporated as time rolled by and the expected new age failed to dawn. By the middle of the fifth century the plight of Jerusalem was again quite desperate. Its walls had not been rebuilt, morale was low in the city, priest and people alike had become careless about the service of God, reform was badly needed.

In 458 Ezra arrived, with the Persian emperor's commission, to reestablish a faith centred on the Law of Moses (Ezra 7–10). Then in 445 Nehemiah was granted permission by the emperor to rebuild Jerusalem's defences (Neh. 1–7). Once more we read of revival (Neh. 8–10), and once again, though now for the last time, it was preceded or accompanied by prophetic activity.

1. I WILL POUR OUT MY SPIRIT (JOEL)

It is impossible to date Joel with certainty. Some would put him as early as the time of Amos, but perhaps the most popular view is that he prophesied somewhere in the middle of the fifth century. However we date him, his message adds a number of valuable insights to everything the other prophets taught about the coming day of the LORD.

170

1.1 – 2.17: The day of the LORD *is coming. Repent!*

Joel sees a locust swarm invade the land and strip everything bare, leaving no food for men or animals to eat, and so he calls on the priests to summon the people and cry out to God (ch. 1). The vision then changes to an army as numerous and devastating as the locusts invading the land (2.1–10). It is led by the LORD, because, like the Assyrians and Babylonians in earlier times, it is to be his instrument of judgment, for his vision, like Amos' or Zephaniah's, relates to 'the day of the LORD' (v. 11). And so once more he calls for repentance, fasting, weeping and crying to God (2.11–17).

2.18–32: God's promise of restoration and of his Spirit.

When they do turn to him, the LORD will have pity on his people, drive back the enemy and restore the land. Trees will begin to bear fruit again and the LORD promises a time of plenty to come (2.18–27). Then will follow the outpouring of God's Spirit foreseen by earlier prophets, but Joel sees how utterly comprehensive that is to be – for men and women, old and young, slave and free, indeed for everyone who calls on the name of the LORD. He also sees that it is to be closely associated with personal salvation and that the event is to take place in Jerusalem (2.28–32). Here we have the amazing crystallisation of a vision that has been growing among the prophets and is to come to fulfilment on the day of Pentecost following Jesus' death and resurrection (Acts 2).

Ch. 3: Proclaim this among the nations.

The restoration of God's people and the giving of the Spirit will, however, only be the prelude to his wider working among the nations, who will be summoned for judgment. They will come as for battle, but the LORD will thunder from Jerusalem (3.1–16) and the world will know that he dwells in Zion. The river Ezekiel and Zechariah saw will then flow from the temple and the land itself will flow with the richness of Eden (3.17–21). The vision has now clearly passed beyond history to the times of the end.

2. I WILL SEND MY MESSENGER (MALACHI)

The name Malachi means 'My Messenger' and so may be a nick-name derived from the prophet's message (see 3.1). There is little reason to doubt that he prophesied in the period immediately preceding Nehemiah's and Ezra's reforms because he speaks of some of the problems they had to deal with, particularly concerning mixed marriages (2.10–16; cp. Ezra 9–10; Neh. 13).

His message is basically that the people cannot expect God to bless them fully unless they, both priests and people, are giving of their own best to him, in worship, holiness, faithfulness, tithing and so forth. He also seems to have a stronger sense than earlier prophets of the nearness of the day of God's coming.

1.1 – 2.16: Why do you break faith?
Part of the problem he had to deal with was disillusionment. A century had passed since Cyrus' edict, but where were the glorious promises of God? The people were asking, 'How has God loved us?' Malachi's answer is to say: Look at your brother Edomites and you will see. God has indeed loved you and so you have been restored, but they are now in ruins and, as earlier prophets predicted, they will never rebuild (1.2–5; cp. Obad., Ezek. 35).

In fact, God has been like a father to you, but how little gratitude you give him in return. Just look at your priests, how they despise my name, sacrificing animals they would be ashamed to offer the governor and viewing their priestly work as a tiresome burden (1.6–14). It is the duty of priests to teach the LORD's ways; instead the Levites have violated their covenant with God, but he will discipline them. (2.1–9)

And the people are no better, for they also break covenant. See the mess their marriages are in, with men leaving their wives for young pagan girls. The LORD hates divorce. He hates your breaking faith as much as the priests' breaking covenant. (2.10–16)

2.17 – 4.6: *Suddenly the* LORD *will come.*

Your ways have wearied God, but he will act. He will send
his herald and then come himself in refining power to purify
first the Levites and then the people, for he must have men
who will bring right offerings and acceptable worship. (2.17
– 3.5)

But God does not change and so is not eager to come in
anger. Return to him now in repentance, bring right offerings, bring your full tithes, and he will forgive and bless you
beyond measure. (3.6–15)

Malachi's teaching apparently made an impact on some.
They consulted together about it and covenanted to honour
God's name. Malachi saw that as a first token of the separ-
ation between the righteous and the wicked that must one
day take place (3.16–18), and was prompted to assure these
good people who revered God's name that for them that
terrible day of his fiery coming would be like the sun rising
with healing in its wings, and would cause them to rejoice
with the fresh vigour of a young calf in springtime (4.1–3).
He therefore reminded them to stand by God's laws while
they waited and encouraged them to watch out for the
coming of his herald who will initiate the work of restoration
in the hearts of men before he comes himself (4.4–6). Interestingly he identifies the herald/messenger (cp. 3.1) with
Elijah. Jews today still watch for his coming, but Jesus
taught his disciples that John the Baptist fulfilled that role
(see below, pp. 184–6).

3. THE FINAL PROPHETIC VISION OF THE NEW COVENANT AGE

In our study of the prophets and their message we have
seen how, as down the centuries they took their stance for
revival, the LORD gradually unfolded to them the vision of
a time when he would act in sovereign power to establish
his kingdom on earth and inaugurate a new age for mankind.

At first the vision was dimly perceived. Amos was mainly
preoccupied with imminent judgment, though he did

glimpse something of what lay beyond. Hosea, whilst he too was largely occupied with approaching judgment, was granted a much fuller appreciation of God's greater purposes, for he saw God bring his people home from exile in an event that would be like a new exodus, complete with a new covenant and a brand new relationship with himself.

Amos and Hosea both recognised that Judah would have a central role to play in God's plan because of his original promise to David, but it was the southern prophets, Micah and Isaiah, who were to discover the fuller significance of these things. Israel's future hope would rest with a remnant left after the inevitable judgment had taken place, and that remnant would find itself led by a descendant of David who would inaugurate a reign of righteousness, justice and peace on earth, leading ultimately to the re-establishment of an Eden-like society.

These prophets, and others that followed them, saw clearly that man needed to change radically if this vision was to work. Amos called for righteousness and justice, Hosea for love and faithfulness, Isaiah for holiness and faith, Jeremiah for repentance, but increasingly they saw that God would have to take the initiative in effecting the necessary change, because man was too lost to do it himself. Thus in the coming new age beyond the judgment of exile Jeremiah saw men being given a new start, with their past forgiven and their heart changed so that obedience to God's law would become possible from within. Ezekiel saw that that change of heart would be associated with God's Spirit being given to men.

Isaiah had also spoken about God's Spirit being given to his people and both he and his exilic successor (? Isa. 40–55) envisaged that gift being like water poured out on a desert land transforming it into a luxuriant garden. Joel saw how comprehensive the gift would be and that it would impart to the LORD's people that same fulness of vision and experience of God that only prophets had hitherto enjoyed.

However, as the book of Isaiah makes clear, these things are not to happen automatically, but must be set in motion by a man sent from God. This man is presented to us as a son of David, as one on whom the Spirit rests, and as God's servant who will take upon himself the punishment for our sins. Then once he has dealt with sin the new age will start. The servant will rise to new life and begin to see the fruit of his work among the Lord's people as the Spirit he bore is poured out on them also.

Other prophets added detail to the picture. For example, Micah saw this man would be born in Bethlehem, Isaiah saw that Galilee would be the place where his light would shine, Malachi saw him heralded by a fore-runner, Zechariah saw him riding into Jerusalem on a donkey. But their main vision was of judgment coming upon the Lord's people to purify them, followed by the re-gathering of a remnant, the coming of this Spirit-filled son of David and through him the establishment of a new age of the Spirit.

All that was only to be preparatory for completing the work God had originally called Abraham's descendants to anyhow, to carry his light to the nations and thus restore blessing to all men. The prophets were also shown that, while the nations would marvel at all God had done for his people, there would be a massive reaction against them culminating in what would become the last battle ever to be fought on earth, when God would intervene himself and finally restore the life of Eden, though that would ultimately involve the creation of a new heaven and new earth.

While the prophets saw that final end beyond history, their central vision relates more to their own day and ours. Much of it was fulfilled in the exile, more was to be fulfilled with the coming of Christ, today we live in expectation of the fulfilment of its end. And at its heart lies a promise of fulfilment for that ancient longing once expressed by Moses, 'that all the Lord's people were prophets and that the Lord would put his Spirit on them.'

By the fourth century enough had been revealed to prepare for history's next phase in the coming of Christ. The prophetic voice then fell silent while men waited and other preparations took place.

The exile left Jews strategically scattered throughout the ancient world. Judah passed from the Persians to the Greeks in the fourth century BC, gained a measure of independence for a while in the second, and finally came under Roman domination in the first. The Greeks had meantime given the world a common language and that, together with the peace and religious toleration enjoyed in the early years of the Roman Empire, made conditions ideal for the spread of the gospel.

Furthermore most Jews had learned the lesson of exile well and now held firmly to faith in the one God and his ways of righteousness. But above all they had become a waiting people, quietly waiting for the coming of their Messiah and the outpouring of the Spirit in the promised New Covenant age. By Jesus' day the work of preparation was truly complete.

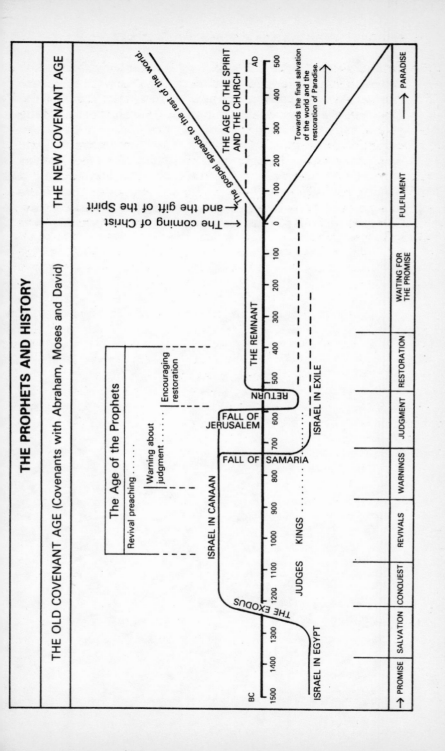

THE PROPHETS AND HISTORY

THE OLD COVENANT AGE (Covenants with Abraham, Moses and David)

THE NEW COVENANT AGE

The coming of Christ → and the gift of the Spirit → The gospel spreads to the rest of the world.

THE AGE OF THE SPIRIT AND THE CHURCH

Towards the final salvation of the world and the restoration of Paradise.

The Age of the Prophets

Revival preaching ....
Warning about judgment ....
Encouraging restoration ....

THE REMNANT

RETURN

FALL OF JERUSALEM

FALL OF SAMARIA

ISRAEL IN EXILE

ISRAEL IN CANAAN

KINGS

JUDGES

THE EXODUS

ISRAEL IN EGYPT

BC 1500 1400 1300 1200 1100 1000 900 800 700 600 500 400 300 200 100 0 AD 100 200 300 400 500

→ PROMISE | SALVATION | CONQUEST | REVIVALS | WARNINGS | JUDGMENT | RESTORATION | WAITING FOR THE PROMISE | FULFILMENT → PARADISE

PART SIX

THE VISION
COMES TO LIFE

FIRST CENTURY A.D.

'Surely the Sovereign LORD does nothing without revealing his plan to his servants the prophets,' said Amos. As we have seen, all the revelation needed to prepare for Christ's coming had been given by the beginning of the fourth century and prophecy had dwindled to extinction. There were some who tried to perpetuate the prophetic gift, but Zech.13.2–6 portrays them as men without true vision who resorted to empty practices, such as wearing hair-cloth garments and indulging in the laceration rituals of paganism. They are dismissed as false prophets, the last representatives of a dying movement clutching at useless straws. Certainly by the second century prophecy was very much a thing of the past, and so, for example, the author of 1 Maccabees, writing about events after the death of Judas Maccabeus in 161 BC, says that Israel's suffering then was 'worse than any since the day when prophets ceased to appear among them' (9.27). However, the final prophetic vision had told of a future rebirth of prophecy associated with the coming of Messiah and heralded by the return of Elijah. The Gospel tells how that came to pass.

The fullest portrayal of the prophetic ministry of Christ and his followers is found in Luke's two volumes, his Gospel and Acts. Together they make up more than a quarter of the New Testament and are longer than the writings of either Paul or John. Hence their witness to the work of Jesus and the Spirit is vitally important for understanding the Christian faith. Whilst Matthew's great theme is the kingdom of God and Jesus as King, Luke's is Jesus as Prophet and his followers as prophetic men of the Spirit. Both volumes were probably written soon before 70 AD.

13

Jesus and the Rebirth of Prophecy

ST. LUKE'S GOSPEL

Our purpose as we read through Luke's Gospel is very specific, to note the prophetic strains in Jesus' life and ministry. However, it should be remembered that Luke's total portrait is much broader. Thus, like the other gospel-writers, he also presents Jesus as Messiah and Son of God, and one of the main emphases in his account of Jesus' death is that he was a good and righteous man, not at all deserving the penalty he suffered. But more than any of the others, he shows us Jesus as a man of the Spirit performing miracles in the power of the Spirit and teaching with the authority of the Spirit, just like the prophets of olden times, though much more fully and perfectly than any of them. Jesus is therefore also seen to be a man of prayer, of praise and rejoicing, with a prophet's care for the poor and the outcasts. Luke's portrait of Jesus is perhaps best summed up in his own words in Acts 10.38:

> *(You know) how God anointed Jesus of Nazareth with the Holy Spirit and power, and how he went around doing good and healing all who were under the power of the devil, because God was with him.*

In both books Luke delights to tell charismatic stories, many of them just like those told in the Old Testament about Elijah and Elisha, but equally to recount Jesus' and the apostles' teachings – hence the many parables in his Gospel and the long sermons in Acts.

181

In the preface to the Gospel he tells us he had access to accounts of Jesus' life 'just as they were handed down to us by those who from the first were eye-witnesses and servants of the word.' That should certainly be true, judging by what we know of him from other sources. Paul tells us how Luke faithfully stood by him while he was in prison, when others had deserted him (2 Tim. 4.11), and also informs us that he was a doctor (Col. 4.14). Eusebius of Caesarea, in his *Ecclesiastical History* (II.4.6, early fourth century), adds that he came from Antioch in Syria, the base from which Paul and Barnabas went on their missions (Acts 13.1–3; 15.36–41). Antioch was a thriving centre of Christianity in the early church where Luke would have met many of the early apostles and evangelists. For example, Mark left Jerusalem to join the community there (Acts 12.25; 13.5,13; 15.37), and Peter once came to visit with a delegation from James, the brother of Jesus (Gal. 2.11). Furthermore, from Acts 16.10 onwards Luke tells the story of Paul's missionary work using 'we' instead of 'they', indicating that from that point he accompanied the apostle most of the time. Thus, as well as travelling with him through Greece and Asia, he stayed at Philip the Evangelist's house in Caesarea, was with Paul in Jerusalem when he was arrested (Acts 21), and finally accompanied him to Rome (Acts 28). Clearly with all these contacts Luke would have had no shortage of early eye-witnesses to tell him the stories about Jesus, as well as about the early Church.

However, when he came to write them down he determined to do so in 'an orderly account'. Of course, that means in chronological order for the most part, but Luke also arranges his material according to theme, and sometimes the thematic order is more important for his purposes. Thus in Acts he arranges the Church's story in three broad surveys relating first to Jerusalem, then to Judea and Samaria, and finally to the rest of the Roman Empire. Similarly the Gospel divides into four broad sections, the first introducing Jesus' own prophetic ministry, the second describing the training of his team of prophet-disciples, the third outlining his prophetic challenge to kingdom living, the fourth

CHRONOLOGY OF JESUS' TIMES
according to Matthew and Luke

B.C.	
39-4	Herod the Great (Matt. 2.1) rules Palestine subject to Rome.
27-14 AD	Caesar Augustus (Luke 2.1) Roman Emperor.
19	Herod starts to rebuild the temple in Jerusalem.
5	Birth of Jesus (?)*
5/4	Visit of Magi, flight to Egypt and slaughter of children (Matt 2.1-18).
4	Death of Herod.
	Palestine is divided between his sons, who are given the title Tertarch:
	Archelaus gets Judea and Samaria (Matt. 2.22).
	Herod Antipas gets Galilee and Perea (Luke 3.1).
	Philip gets Iturea and Traconitis (Luke 3.1).
4/3	Jesus returns to Galilee to live in Nazareth (Matt. 2.21-23).
A.D.	
6	Archelaus is deposed. The Romans make Judea and Samaria a Roman province ruled directly by governors called Procurators.
7	Jesus visits the temple at age 12 (Luke 2.41-50).
14-37	Tiberius Caesar (Luke 3.1) Roman Emperor.
18-36	Caiaphas High Priest in Jerusalem (Luke 3.2).
26-36	Pontius Pilate governor of Judea (Luke 3.1).**
27/28	John the Baptist starts preaching (Luke 3.2-18).
	Jesus, aged "about 30", is baptised (Luke 2.21-23).
	John is arrested by Herod Antipas and put in prison (Luke 2.19f).
30/31	Jesus is arrested, appears before Caiaphas, Pilate and Herod (Matt. 26.47 — 27.31; Luke 22.47 — 23.25).
	The Crucifixion and Resurrection (Matt. 27.32 — 28.10; Luke 23.26 — 24.12).

* Knowing that Jesus' birth coincided with "the first census that took place while Quirinius was governor of Syria" does not help us to fix its date more accurately. Other sources tell us that Quirinius was governor of Syria in 6-9 AD when he held a census that caused a rebellion in Judea, but apart from Luke 2.2 we have no record of an earlier term of office.
** We know from other writings that Lysanias (Luke 3.1) was tetrarch of Abilene about the time of Christ's ministry, but we do not have his dates.

recounting his death, resurrection and final preparation of his prophet-team.

1. THE HERALD AND THE PROPHET OF THE NEW AGE OF THE SPIRIT (CHS. 1–4)

Only Matthew and Luke tell the story of Jesus' birth, and Luke's account is by far the fuller of the two. But it is not the historical details that interest us here so much as the impression created by the way Luke tells the story. And right from the start, we see how enthusiastic he is about its charismatic aspects. He is, after all, telling us about the birth of that prophetic movement of the new age foretold in the Old Testament.

Chs. 1–2: First stirrings of the prophetic Spirit.
Jesus' birth is heralded by a sudden outburst of prophetic activity: We see angels appear with messages, people moved by the Spirit, some even prophesying, and we detect clear echoes of times past in prophetic history.

The story begins with an angel appearing to Zechariah, the priest, and foretelling the birth of his son, John the Baptist (1.5–25). The same angel also visits Mary announcing Jesus' conception (1.26–38). Another angel proclaims his birth to some shepherds who are granted a vision of the host of heaven singing God's praises, rather like Isaiah was (2.8–15).

Men and women are moved by the Spirit and prophesy. When Elizabeth hears Mary's news, she is 'filled with the Holy Spirit' and pronounces an inspired blessing on her and the baby (1.39–45). At John's birth Zechariah 'was filled with the Holy Spirit and prophesied' in a song that pointedly recalls what God had 'said through his holy prophets of long ago' (1.67–80). When Jesus was presented at the temple, Simeon, who had been shown by the Holy Spirit that he would see the Lord's Christ before he died, was waiting, with the Holy Spirit upon him, having been moved by the Spirit to come to the temple at that hour, and he praised God and prophesied concerning the ministry and agony of Christ (2.21–35). Also waiting at the temple was an aged widow called Anna, whom Luke describes as 'a prophetess', and she too gave thanks to God (2.36–38).

John the Baptist, the angel foretold, would be 'filled with the Holy Spirit' and 'go on before the Lord', as the herald of his coming foretold by Malachi, 'in the spirit and power of Elijah' (1.5–25; cp. Mal. 3.1f; 4.5f). Then at his birth Zechariah also prophesied that John would be 'a prophet of the Most High' and 'go before the Lord to prepare the way for him' (1.67–80).

The angel also spoke of the action of the Spirit in connection with the Jesus' conception (1.26–38). But besides that, the stories of his birth and childhood remind us in many ways of Samuel, the founder of Israel's first prophetic movement. Thus, Mary's song (The Magnificat) vividly recalls the psalm Hannah, Samuel's mother, sang at his birth (1.46–55; cp. 1 Sam. 2.1–10); Jesus' infancy associations with the priests in the temple remind us of Samuel's childhood under Eli's tutelage at Shiloh (2.21–50); and we are told that Jesus, just like Samuel in his youth, 'grew and became strong; he was filled with wisdom, and the grace of God was upon him' and that he 'grew in wisdom and stature, and in favour with God and men' (2.40,52; cp. 1 Sam. 2.21,26).

The whole atmosphere is alive with fresh spiritual activity and there can be little doubt about what is happening. The long awaited age of the Spirit has finally begun to dawn. John is the Elijah heralding the new age, the prophetic Spirit is beginning to rest on all sorts of people again, and Jesus, at this early stage of his life, is, like Samuel, the great founder and forefather of Israel's prophetic movements, simply growing up and being prepared for, but not yet ready to undertake his prophetic calling.

Matthew's infancy narratives do also tell of visions, dreams, angelic visitations and the action of the Spirit, but he was presenting a different portrait of Jesus that shows little interest in the rebirth of prophecy. However, the same basic ingredients are there and they do confirm Luke's presentation further.

After the long silence at the end of Old Testament times, the prophetic Spirit is clearly on the move once more!

Ch. 3: 'The Spirit of the LORD is on me.'

The date is about 27/28 AD. John the Baptist, the herald of the new age, comes like some ancient revivalist prophet, preaching repentance, criticising sham religion, urging social justice and care for the needy, and proclaiming the near advent of the One who would bring the promised Holy

Spirit. John is not the founder of the new prophetic movement, only the messenger sent to prepare the way for it. (3.1–20; cp. 7.26f)

The prophets of old had foretold that the new age would be inaugurated by a descendant of David, himself heavily endowed with God's Spirit (Isa. 11.1f; 42.1; 61.1), and so at the Jordan, Jesus, now aged about thirty, is granted his prophetic call-vision and is given the Spirit from heaven. (3.21–3)

Ch. 4: Jesus is attested as a prophet of the LORD.

'Full of the Holy Spirit' he is 'led by the Spirit' in the desert where his call is tested. Then he returns 'in the power of the Spirit' to begin his ministry. (4.1–15)

Back in Nazareth he tells his kinsfolk and friends how Isaiah's prophecy about the giving of the Spirit has found fulfilment in his experience. Their reaction shows him clearly that 'no prophet is accepted in his home town'. (4.16–30)

However, throughout Galilee, and in particular in Capernaum, which he had made his ministry-base (Matt. 4.13), his authority in teaching and healing leaves everyone amazed and talking (4.31–37).

In these selected episodes Luke shows Jesus coming to terms with his calling, his friends rejecting it and the crowds responding to it. Now, in dramatic even-time and dawn-time scenes we watch his vision being kindled for wider ministry throughout the land (4.38–44).

Jesus and the Spirit.

According to Luke, 'the child (Jesus) grew and became strong', at twelve demonstrated amazing understanding, was obedient to his parents, and 'grew in wisdom and stature, and in favour with God and men' (Luke 2.40,46f,51f). The impression is not of a divinely super-charged human being, but of a child who grew up like most others, though with unique qualities. The same impression is given in Hebrews where we read that Jesus was born as a man 'like his brothers in every way . . . suffered when he was tempted . . .

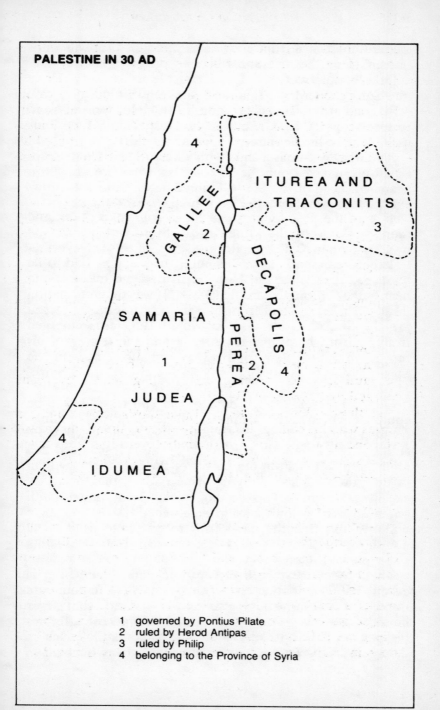

PALESTINE IN 30 AD

GALILEE

ITUREA AND TRACONITIS

3

DECAPOLIS

SAMARIA

PEREA

1

2

4

JUDEA

4

IDUMEA

2

4

1 governed by Pontius Pilate
2 ruled by Herod Antipas
3 ruled by Philip
4 belonging to the Province of Syria

learned obedience from what he suffered . . . yet was without sin' (Heb. 2.17f; 5.8; 4.15).

Luke certainly does not underrate Jesus' divinity. He is 'the Son of the Most High' and 'the Son of God' (1.32,35; 3.38), and at the Transfiguration his disciples were allowed to see 'his glory' (9.32), but in the Gospel story Luke bids us look at Jesus the man.

And what we see is a child with a kind of spiritual perception we ourselves only begin to grasp when we are 'born again' or 'born of the Spirit' (John 3.3–8). Unlike us, however, Jesus was from the very first born of the Spirit as well as of the flesh by virtue of his unique conception, and therefore knew by the witness of the Spirit within that God was his Father (2.49; cp. Rom. 8.15; Gal. 4.6). Nevertheless, before embarking on his public ministry he had to be baptised, experience the Holy Spirit descend on him, and hear Father affirm his sonship (3.21f). It was that affirmation the devil tried to steal from him in the wilderness: 'If you are the Son of God,' . . . prove it! But Jesus emerged from both his baptismal experience and the testing of his revelation with a new, or renewed, relationship with the Spirit, and so began his ministry 'in the power of the Spirit' (4.14).

It is as if Jesus, though born of the Spirit, needed to be equipped with a special anointing of the Spirit for the ministry he had to do. That was how Isaiah had said it would be (Luke 4.18–21), and it is precisely because Jesus lived and ministered as a man in the power of the Spirit, rather than in the power of his inherent divine nature, that we today can live and minister as he did, in that same power, with our awareness of our sonship heightened as his was. Like him, we too find the devil tries to persuade us it is all nonsense, but like him also we can emerge from the testing as prophets of God.

The experience that brings us such an empowering is called 'baptism in the Holy Spirit'. It is what John the Baptist said Jesus would give us (3.16), and what Jesus himself said was given on the day of Pentecost after his resurrection (Acts 1.5). It is not the same as the touch of the Spirit at conversion, but something that turns born-again believers into prophets or charismatics, something similar to the call experiences of the Old Testament prophets. So it was with Jesus, and again, as we shall see later, with the first apostles, as well as with all the early Christians. And so it should be today. These things are not optional for those who would follow in the ministry-footsteps of Jesus. They are what our Drama of Salvation is all about, what the Old Testament prophets foretold would be.

2. PREPARING A PROPHET TEAM (CHS. 5–9)

Besides the crowds who flock to hear his preaching, Jesus' charismatic ministry, just like Samuel's, Elijah's and Elisha's, attracts a number of close, personal followers who gather around him to form a spearhead group in the work for the Christian 'revival' that is about to take place.

Chs. 5–6: *Forming the team and first teaching.*
The call of Peter, who is to become leader of the group, is as sudden and dramatic as Elisha's was. Both had to abandon their livelihood at a moment's notice to follow their prophet-masters (5.1–11; cp. 1 Kings 19.19–21). But as Jesus continues his ministry, others, like Levi, are called in the same sort of way (5.27f). Eventually he has a band of twelve (6.12–16) and begins teaching them the essence of his prophetic message of righteousness, justice and love (6.17–49).

Jesus did not interrupt his work to bring his team together, and so we read about its formation in the context of a busy ministry. Luke's stories of the healing miracles highlight the excitement of the crowds and Jesus' own dramatic power (cp. 5.15,17,26; 6.18f). We can see in them all the flavour of present-day renewal enthusiasm. John's disciples fast often, but Jesus' disciples already manifest that free joy that non-charismatics so often find irksome (5.33–39). Similarly, Jesus' own bold assurance of faith begins to irritate the religious men of the day (5.20f), as also does his fraternising with the non-religious who are open to receive him (5.27–32).

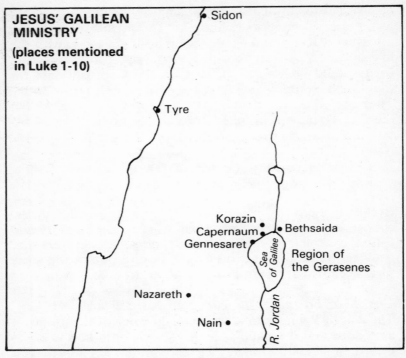

JESUS' GALILEAN MINISTRY

(places mentioned in Luke 1-10)

Sidon

Tyre

Korazin
Capernaum • • Bethsaida
Gennesaret

Sea of Galilee

Region of the Gerasenes

Nazareth •

Nain •

R. Jordan

His teaching too is with authority, just like the proclamation of the prophets of old who did not discuss and debate, but boldly declared God's message with their 'Thus says the LORD.' Jesus demonstrates the same prophetic authority, though his declaration is 'I tell you' (6.27).

Ch. 7: Is he a prophet? 'Are you the one?'

As Jesus continues to heal and teach, his prophetic anointing comes in for a lot of discussion:

– After healing the centurion's daughter and raising the dead boy at Nain, the crowds certainly recognise him as 'a great prophet' (v. 16).

– John the Baptist in prison is naturally beginning to have doubts, though he still hopes Jesus is 'the one who was to come' (vv. 18f).

– the Pharisees cannot believe he is a prophet at all when they see him allow a sinful woman to anoint his feet (v. 39).

– Jesus simply points out that his ministry fulfils certain Messianic promises about the lame walking, the deaf hearing, etc., and that in turn reminds us of the description in Isa. 61.1–3 of one on whom the Spirit rests (vv. 22f; cp. 4.18f).

Chs. 8–9: Ministry training and revelation.

Jesus' training method was basically two-fold: verbal instruction and active demonstration. To receive his teaching the Twelve had to accompany him on his travels, listen to him addressing the crowds and watch him ministering to the sick, but he would also from time to time take them aside and explain the profounder mysteries hidden from others (8.9–15), or involve some of them with him in the ministry itself (8.51). Sometimes his action was highly spectacular, as in the calming of the storm, but his purpose at the heart of it all was to teach faith and, of course, prompt them to question his identity (8.19–25).

After this initial training Jesus sent them on their own mission to do the same things as they had seen him do (9.1–6).

Then came the high-point of their preparation, when their eyes were opened to see who he really was. The whole land by this time was buzzing with questions about him, and everyone, even Herod, was discussing his prophetic identity (9.7–9). Though the crowds had no doubt he was a prophet (9.18f), the truth was much deeper. Peter was the first to realise it, that he was 'The Christ of God' (9.20). Then at the Transfiguration Peter, James and John were granted a full revelation of his sonship, even hearing for themselves the voice and the words Jesus had heard at his baptism (9.35).

When we studied Elijah's story we saw why it was with him and Moses that Jesus spoke on this occasion (see p. 50). They were giants among Israel's men of the Spirit, both with powerful ministries attended by signs and wonders, both deliverers of their people in critical times, both men who had stood on the holy mountain and spoken with God. Jesus was about to set out for Jerusalem to do battle with sin and death (9.21f,44), and the sequel shows how little of that his disciples were able to understand. He had a lonely path to tread, but Father allowed him spiritual encouragement by talking with the only men in history who had walked some of that lonely way before him.

There are times in most Christians' ministries when no man can give the depth of comfort and encouragement they need because the issues are beyond common understanding. At such moments strength can come only from God. Some of the prophets experienced this loneliness and need for spiritual encouragement very deeply – Jeremiah in particular.

We realise when we hear them argue about who is to be the greatest, how little the disciples understood their own prophetic vocation, for which Jesus had been preparing them, (9.37–50). However, both his and their call remained unchanged and Jesus had to press on. Their basic training was now complete, and so Jesus set out on the next phase of his ministry, turning his face to Jerusalem and challenging any who would follow him to do so wholeheartedly (9.51–62).

3. JESUS' PROPHETIC CHALLENGE TO KINGDOM LIVING
(CHS. 10–18)

With prophetic insight Jesus had foretold his suffering, death and resurrection. Also, as a prophet he knows his trial must take place in Jerusalem: 'No prophet can die outside Jerusalem!' he says (13.33). The turning-point was in 9.51, where we read that 'he resolutely set out' for the city.

Luke's account of this last journey incorporates a great deal of teaching, including many parables which we do not have space to study in detail. In our comparison with the Old Testament prophets this section would correspond to their collections of prophetic sayings. Much of it is the same kind of crisis preaching, challenging to decision and spelling out the cost of discipleship, while other elements speak assurance for the poor, the lost and all who come to repentance.

There is now less sense of excited rejoicing over ministry victories and an increasing sense of urgency and challenge as the time grows short.

Ch. 10: The ways of Kingdom mission.

As well as a prophet, Jesus is now also seen as the King coming to his throne city, the City of David, and so, like any king, he sends messengers ahead to prepare the way before him (9.52). Seventy-two of them go with the same commission as he gave the Twelve earlier, to heal the sick and announce the kingdom, and they return exultant about the effects of their mission (10.1–17). At that moment we are granted a fascinating glimpse of Jesus, 'full of joy through the Holy Spirit', praising God for their new understanding of the power of God available to them (10.18–24).

The parable of the Good Samaritan teaches care for the needy and the story of Mary's attentiveness to Jesus reminds us of the crucial importance of heeding God's word, both common themes of prophecy.

Ch. 11: The ways of the Spirit, of sin and of religion.

Here we have three broad contrasting portraits: the Spirit - filled life (vv. 1–13), the demonised and sinful life (vv. 14–36), and the religious life (vv. 37–52). The life-style to which Jesus' followers are called is obvious!

The first portrait focuses on prayer. Jesus' instruction about that is minimal, only a few brief, though profound and comprehensive, words and an injunction to pray for the Holy Spirit. Strangely, Jesus does not give much teaching about the Spirit in Luke's Gospel (he does in John's), but at the end we see he must have taught them a lot more than Luke relates (cp. 24.44–49).

Luke's version of the Lord's prayer is shorter than Matthew's (Matt. 6.9–13) and significantly opens with the one word 'Father', which is precisely the form of address the Spirit inspires (Rom. 8.15; Gal. 4.6).

One of the main points being made in the second portrait is that it is utterly important for the man delivered from an evil spirit to be filled with something else (God's Spirit), lest his final condition be worse than the first. Our body needs to be filled with light (v. 34).

The third portrait shows how religiosity (vv. 37–44) and theological doctrinalism (vv. 45–52) are not only sterile, but burden those who long to draw close to God, even lock them out from his presence. Like the prophets before him, Jesus made quite a number of enemies by saying such things!

Ch. 12: Right attitudes for the last days.
The times are urgent. These are not days for concern about personal reputation (vv. 1–12), for hoarding wealth (vv. 13–21), and for anxiety about tomorrow (vv. 22–34), but for watchfulness (vv. 35–59). It is not some future time that Jesus refers to here, but rather 'this present time' (v. 56). This is already the day the prophets foretold, and so in vv. 49f we see Jesus impatient to release its 'fire' (of the Spirit: cp. 3.16; Acts 2.3), but also knowing full well that he must first undergo a baptism himself (the crucifixion) and that the fiery effect of Pentecost must mean judgment for many.

Ch. 13: Repent or perish.
The call to repentance has always been the prophets' call as the day of the Lord approaches. Here the blessing available to those who repent is contrasted with the hardness that sends Jesus to the cross. Jesus knows he can expect no more than any other prophet before him.

Ch. 14: Care for the poor, whatever the cost.
The prophets also regularly called on their hearers to care for the poor (e.g. Amos 5; Isa. 58). Following Jesus means adopting that same prophetic care for the poor, and that can be a costly calling.

Ch. 15: Love the lost.
God's love for the lost is uncompromising. He searches until he finds them and welcomes them home as a father his son. Such too is Jesus' attitude, and will also be that of his prophet-followers.

Ch. 16: The day foretold by Moses and the Prophets has arrived.

Most people recognise a good thing when they see it and will do their utmost to lay hold of it, sometimes by whatever means. Likewise, many are pressing into God's kingdom, though sadly others will fail to enter, some because they find it too costly, others because they want proofs, such as someone returning from the dead, to convince them of its worth. But the new age the Law and the Prophets spoke of is here.

Ch. 17: Come now with repentance and faith.

Jesus challenges his disciples about inner attitudes of repentance, faith and humility. Faith heals lepers, even Samaritan ones. Christ's kingdom and salvation too are received now by right inner attitudes. Hosea, Jeremiah and other prophets said the same in their generation.

18.1–30: Further teaching on right attitudes.

Persistent prayer, true humility, childlike faith and open-hearted generosity are of the very essence of kingdom living.

Jesus' teaching continues in the same vein as the story progresses, and with an even greater sense of urgency as his arrest draws closer. But now, at the end of ch. 18, we begin to pass from teaching to action as his journey to Jerusalem nears its end.

4. THE CULMINATION OF THE PROPHET'S MINISTRY AND THE COMMISSIONING OF HIS DISCIPLES (18.31 – 24.53)

Before reading these last chapters of the Gospel, it is important to recall that, though we are highlighting the prophetic aspects of Jesus' life and ministry, he was much more than a prophet. We shall continue to trace the prophetic marks, but we shall also find just as much that speaks about Jesus as Messiah and Son of God.

Another aspect Luke emphasises more strongly than the other gospel-writers do is Jesus' innocence. This can be seen most clearly in some of the details he gives that are additional to the information given by the others. Thus, Herod mocks Jesus, but can find no fault; Pilate pronounces him innocent and three times tries to have him acquitted; Jesus himself pleads for forgiveness for his executioners; even a criminal crucified beside him recognises his innocence; and when he dies the centurion in charge of the crucifixion declares, 'Surely this was a righteous man' (23.1–47). This same theme of Christian innocence is emphasised again in the accounts of Paul's trials in Acts. It seems to have been important for Luke to highlight it, probably because he hoped by doing so to avert some of the persecution that was beginning to come on the Church in his day.

18.31–19.48: From Jericho to Jerusalem.

Intermittently we have been reminded throughout chs. 9–18 that Jesus is on his way to die in Jerusalem, and now, his journey almost over, he reminds the disciples again, though they still do not understand what he is talking about (18.31–34).

When he arrives in Jericho the excitement begins. First a blind man hails him as 'Son of David' and follows him healed (18.35–43). Then Zacchaeus the tax-collector receives him (19.1–10). Amid growing excitement about the kingdom, Jesus speaks about God's expectation of those he entrusts with its ministries (19.11–27).

From Jericho he proceeds rapidly to Jerusalem. He comes

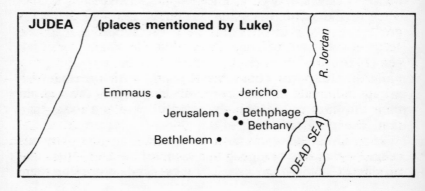

to the city amid songs of Messianic acclaim, riding on an ass, in fulfilment of prophecy (Zech. 9.9). In v. 37 (cp. John 12.17f) Luke points out that the acclaim was in acknowledgment of Jesus' charismatic healing ministry as much as of his Messiahship (19.28–40).

As the city comes in view, Jesus weeps because he sees in prophetic vision how one day it will be besieged and destroyed (19.41–44).

Once in the city he enters the temple, and like Jeremiah of old, denounces the profanation of God's house that he finds there (cp. Jer. 7). The consequences for him were much the same as for Jeremiah, because the priests, teachers and leaders then sought to kill him (19.45–48).

As well as Messiah, Jesus is clearly a prophet walking in the steps of his great prophet forebears.

Chs. 20–21: Jesus' Final Challenge.

Luke tells us less about Jesus' teaching in his last week than Matthew or Mark (e.g. 21.37f corresponds to Matt. 24.36 – 25.46), but what he includes is very pointed.

'Tell us by what authority you are doing these things' (20.1–8). The request is put by the chief priests and other religious leaders. Amos and Jeremiah were confronted by the same people with the same question (Amos 7; Jer. 20; 26). Every prophet speaks with authority when he says 'Thus says the LORD', but Jesus exercised a more striking authority when he spoke, for his words were '*I* tell you' (cp. 19.40).

The parable of the tenants, strategically placed after the question about authority, implies that Jesus comes in succession to the Old Testament prophets, but also that he is greater than any of them, for he is the Son. The response Jesus got was no different from what Amos and Jeremiah got (20.9–18).

Further disputes about his teaching with other Jewish groups culminate in Jesus pointedly challenging them about their attitudes to Messiah as David's Son – and more than that, David's Lord (20.19–44).

Then finally he warns his own disciples against pompous religiosity, again very much like some of the Old Testament prophets (20.45–47; cp. Isa. 22.15–19), and lays before them the challenge of true piety shown by the widow offering her last penny to the Lord (21.1–4).

Like most of his Old Testament prophet forebears, his teaching ministry ends with prophecy that takes us beyond historical times. While telling of the coming distress leading up to the fall of Jerusalem which was to take place in 70 AD (21.12–24), his eye sees beyond the catastrophe to a more ultimate act of God in the more distant future, to his own return 'with power and great glory'. (21.8–11,25–36)

Chs. 22–23: The Prophet's last hours.

Luke's account of Jesus' last hours contains more pronounced prophetic elements than we find in the other Gospels:

– At the Last Supper Jesus emphasises his prophecy about not eating or drinking again of the fruit of the vine until the kingdom of God comes by repeating it twice (22.16,18).

– He shares a vision of the Twelve around his table in his kingdom (22.30).

– He not only foretells Peter's denials, but also his restoration and leadership (22.31–34).

– 'An angel from heaven' appears to him in Gethsemane (22.43).

– Also in Gethsemane Jesus uses his charismatic healing power to restore the High Priest's servant's right ear (23.51).

– Before his trial the soldiers scorn his prophetic claims by blindfolding and beating him, saying, 'Prophesy! Who hit you?' (22.64).

– During his trial the only significant words Jesus speaks, apart from admitting his identity, prophesy his enthronement at God's right hand (22.69).

– Herod's only real interest in him is to see evidence of his miraculous capability (23.8).

– Even as his cross is carried through the city, he prophesies to the women of Jerusalem about greater trials to come (23.28–31).

– And then, on the cross, with his dying breath Jesus, the Prophet, commits his 'spirit' to his Father (23.46; cp. Ps. 31.5).

Luke tells the same story as the other gospel-writers, with

all the same dramatic flavour and without modifying the message they convey that the man who died was Messiah, King of the Jews and Son of God, but as he tells it he highlights its prophetic/charismatic moments, some of which are in the other gospels, some that are not.

Ch. 24: Final preparation of the prophet team.

After recounting the story of the resurrection Luke tells us about three episodes when Jesus was with his disciples:

On the road to Emmaus he walks with two of them who do not recognise him. They speak to him about Jesus of Nazareth, 'a prophet, powerful in word and deed.' He leads them through the Scriptures, 'beginning with Moses and all the Prophets', explaining what has happened (vv. 13–35).

Back in Jerusalem with the gathered group he again runs through the Scriptures, 'the Law of Moses, the Prophets and the Psalms', to help them understand what has happened. Then he reveals that the long awaited moment, for which all history and his own life have been a preparation, is about to arrive, for the Father is soon to send his promised 'power from on high', the Holy Spirit promised of old by the prophets. And they, the disciples, are to be the first to receive the promise (vv. 36–49).

Having thus prepared his disciples fully and finally for the moment when they too will become prophets, empowered to continue his work on earth, he departs from them and they return to Jerusalem, understandably with great excitement, to await the day of fulfilment (vv. 50–53).

We shall never know precisely what Jesus said as he led the disciples through the Scriptures, but it seems he must have summarised the Biblical vision for his life, death and resurrection, and beyond that for the coming of the Spirit in fulfilment of God's promise through the prophets, just as we have tried to do in this volume.

For Luke, Jesus is a prophet, or rather The Prophet, come to usher in the new prophetic age of the Spirit. The sense of excited anticipation seen at the end of the Gospel can be traced throughout, from the moment John the Baptist leaped for joy in his mother's womb (1.44), Mary sang her song of rejoicing (1.47) and the angels proclaimed 'great joy for all people' (2.10). Jesus himself 'rejoiced in the Holy Spirit' (10.21); his disciples rejoiced (10.17); and he even urged them to 'rejoice and leap for joy' (6.23). There was, after all, much to rejoice about – a new day was dawning for mankind!

14

The Growth of the Christian Prophetic Movement

ACTS AND PAUL'S EPISTLES

We systematically trace the history of the early Church through Acts and Paul's epistles in Volume Two. Here, in this chapter, we shall only be looking at a few stories and passages that illustrate how the early Christians were, as Peter pointed out in one of his sermons, 'heirs of the prophets' (Acts 3.25).

It has often been said that The Acts of the Apostles would have been better named The Acts of the Holy Spirit. Whatever we think of that, it is true that in Acts as much as in his Gospel Luke delights in stories that highlight the activity of the Spirit, and it should therefore not cause any surprise to discover that the story he tells is basically about the acts of prophetical men and about the birth and growth of a Christian prophetic movement.

1. HEIRS OF THE PROPHETS

Luke's second volume opens with a reminder that what we are about to read is a history of God's latter-day prophets. The first of them have already been called and prepared by Jesus, who now tells them that they are presently to receive 'the gift my Father promised' and 'be baptised with the Holy Spirit' (1.1–5). As it had been for Jesus himself, so for them the Spirit will mean 'power', and by virtue of that they will become his 'witnesses' (1.8). The Old Testament prophets had proclaimed the coming of Jesus' day, the New Testament prophets are to proclaim or witness that his day has arrived.

'I will pour out my Spirit . . . and they will prophesy.'
(Acts 2.17f)
The Old Testament prophets who told us something about their call all spoke of some living experience of God at or near the beginning of their ministries. From the time Moses and the elders first glimpsed the prophetic potential, that experience was regularly linked with the action of the Spirit, until finally Joel saw that at some future date God would pour out his Spirit freely and that men and women, old and young, slave and free, would prophesy too. Peter tells us (vv. 16–21) that it is the fulfilment of that promise we now witness as we read the story of the day of Pentecost in Acts 2.

Amid wind and fire, recalling the experiences of Moses and Elijah on Sinai (Exod. 19.16–20; 1 Kings 19.11–13), 'all of them were filled with the Holy Spirit and began to speak in other tongues as the Spirit enabled them' (Acts 2.4). There is no record of prophets or anyone else in the Old Testament speaking in tongues, but here the experience can be interpreted as a reversal of the curse of Babel (Gen. 11.9), for the disciples were understood by pilgrims of many different nationalities to be 'declaring the wonders of God' in their own native languages (Acts 2.11). Whether the miracle was that they were actually speaking their hearers' native languages, or simply that the hearers were enabled to understand, the fact is that in their worship the language barrier had been crossed. If man is ever to regain the Garden of Eden, which after all is God's ultimate purpose for his world, he must get back behind the hostility and suspicion created by sin, and to that end something like what happened at Pentecost is essential. Today Christians still find something of that unity as they worship in tongues together.

But Pentecost was more than speaking in tongues. Peter explained it all in terms of the latter-day prophecy foretold by Joel (2.14–21), but then went on to point out how it

THE PROMISE OF THE FATHER TO SEND THE HOLY SPIRIT

"I wish that all the LORD's people were prophets and that the LORD would put his Spirit on them!"

(Moses in Num.11.29)

. . . . till the Spirit is poured upon us from on high . . . .

(Isa.32.15)

> For I will pour water on the thirsty land,
>   and streams on the dry ground;
> I will pour out my Spirit on your offspring,
>   and my blessing on your descendants.

(Isa.44.3)

> "The Redeemer will come to Zion,
>   to those who repent of their sins,"
>   declares the LORD .

"As for me, this is my covenant with them," says the Lord. "My Spirit, who is on you, and my words that I have put in your mouth will not depart from your mouth, or from the mouths of your children, or from the mouths of their descendants from this time on and for ever," says the LORD .

(Isa.59.20f)

I will give them an undivided heart and put a new spirit in them; I will remove from them their heart of stone and give them a heart of flesh . . . .

(Ezek.11.19)

I will give you a new heart and put a new spirit in you; I will remove from you your heart of stone and give you a heart of flesh. And I will put my Spirit in you . . . .

(Ezek.36.26f)

I will put my Spirit in you and you will live.

(Ezek.37.14)

I will no longer hide my face from them, for I will pour out my Spirit on the house of Israel, declares the Sovereign LORD .

(Ezek.39.29)

> And afterwards,
>   I will pour out my Spirit on all people.
> Your sons and daughters will prophesy,
>   your old men will dream dreams,
>   your young men will see visions.
> Even on my servants, both men and women,
>   I will pour out my Spirit in those days.

(Joel 2.28f)

originated with Jesus (vv. 22– 36): He was himself very
much a man of the Spirit (v. 22), and it was no accident,
but all part of God's plan, that he died as he did (v. 23),
for God's purpose was to raise him from the dead, lift him
up to be at his right hand in heaven and give him the
promised Holy Spirit to pour out on his followers (vv.
24–33). It is therefore all to do with Jesus, from first to last,
and God has now made him Lord and Christ (vv. 34f).

The significance of Jesus in all this is more profound than
we have space to discuss now, but what we need to note
here is that Jesus' own ministry started with something like
a Pentecost, and that was how he intended his disciples'
ministry to start. He himself became a prophet to fulfil his
role and the disciples had to become prophets to fulfil theirs.
To continue his ministry on earth they had to receive their
prophetic anointing from his hands. Jesus, God's own Son,
was the one appointed to inaugurate God's new age of the
Spirit, and so it is only through him that anyone can enter
into its blessing and ministry.

And its blessings are for all who will receive them, who
will turn to God in repentance, be baptised and accept the
forgiveness offered in Christ (v. 38). In accordance with
Joel's prophecy, the promise is for all men everywhere who
hear God's call, whether Jews or from far off lands, whether
adult men and women or children (v. 39). That very day
some three thousand pilgrims from all over the world
entered into their inheritance and the prophetic movement
of the last days was thus well and truly launched (vv. 40f).

'Did you receive the Holy Spirit when you believed?' (Acts 19.2)

Several other stories show that the Spirit continued to be
given in the same prophetic fashion throughout the period
covered by Acts. Some of these even suggest that Christian
experience without such Spirit-endowment was deficient.

In ch. 8 we read about converts in Samaria who had
believed in Jesus and had been baptised, but had to have
Peter and John lay hands on them so that they might receive
the Holy Spirit. Whatever happened when they did so must
have been very dramatic, since Simon, a local magician,

offered to pay them to give him the ability to do the same (8.9–24).

After his dramatic encounter with the Lord on the road to Damascus, Paul also had to have hands laid on him so that he would receive the Holy Spirit (9.17).

With Cornelius, the Roman centurion, it all happened back to front, for he and his household received the Spirit while Peter preached to them and had to be baptised after, but either way they too received the same charismatic endowment and spoke in tongues (10.44–46). It was because of that alone that the church back in Jerusalem was able to accept the authenticity of his conversion (11.1–18).

Much later, in Ephesus, we encounter an enthusiastic evangelist called Apollos. 'He had been instructed in the way of the Lord, and he spoke with great fervour', but two of his hearers, Priscilla and Aquila, recognised that he lacked something (18.24–26). The problem was, we are told, that 'he knew only the baptism of John'. However, we are also told that he 'taught about Jesus accurately', which must mean that he knew everything about Jesus' life up to the resurrection or the ascension. Presumably, therefore, the missing ingredient in his faith was that he knew nothing about Pentecost and the gift of the Spirit. That was certainly the lack in his converts' faith, as Paul discovered when he arrived in Ephesus, but when Paul baptised them and laid hands on them they too spoke in tongues and prophesied (19.1–7).

2. CHARISMATIC COMMUNITIES AND PROPHETIC GROUPS

There are a number of passages in Acts where we catch a glimpse of community life in the early Church, and in them we see the early Christians showing many traits similar to the prophets of Old Testament time.

At our very first encounter with them on the day of Pentecost we are reminded of Samuel's followers coming down from their high place prophesying, for there we see

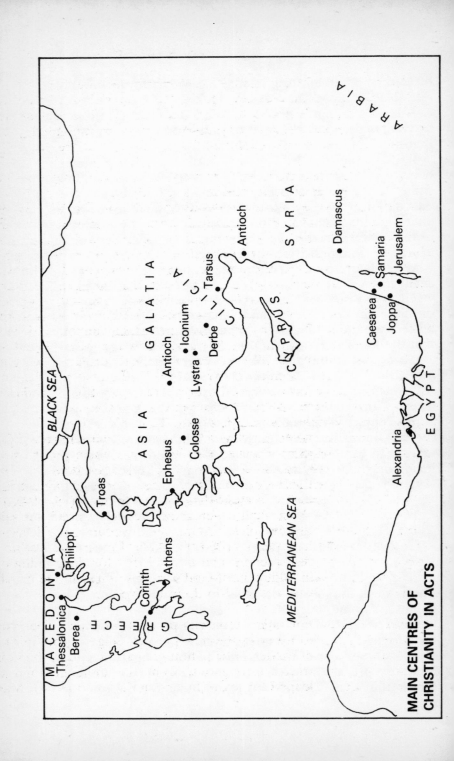

MAIN CENTRES OF
CHRISTIANITY IN ACTS

bystanders scorn their exuberant behaviour, just as they had scorned Samuel's men (2.12–17; 1 Sam. 10.11f).

Just as in Elisha's day, the new Christian prophets sought each other's fellowship and established forms of communal living. Apparently that involved daily meetings for worship, fellowship in homes, sharing possessions, and being taught by the apostles, but we are not given enough information to describe their forms in any detail. However, we could not do that when we read the Elisha stories either (2.42–47; 4.32–35).

Their happy, praise-orientated meetings clearly proved attractive to some (2.46f), but were also sufficiently unusual to keep most observers standing aloof (5.12f). Their leaders' ministries were attended by 'many wonders and miraculous signs', just as Elijah's and Elisha's were (2.43; 5.12,15f). And their preaching quickly stirred up opposition and persecution, just as the preaching of the Old Testament prophets often did too (4.1–3; 5.17–40). But as they prayed together the Lord visited them with renewed Pentecostal blessings, filling them again with his Spirit so that they could speak his word boldly (4.23–31).

It is this general impression rather than specific details that makes our comparison valid. Peter himself suggests the same when he points out that his gospel stands firmly in the tradition of the ancient prophets: 'Indeed, all the prophets from Samuel on, as many as have spoken, have foretold these days. And you are heirs of the prophets . . .' (3.24f).

When the Church spread beyond Jerusalem it took the same prophetic forms with it. The early church in Samaria was established with many miracles and great joy (8.6–8). The church in Antioch was also founded amid plentiful 'evidence of the grace of God' (11.19–26) and it openly welcomed Agabus and other prophets from Jerusalem (11.27f). It was led by men who were themselves 'prophets and teachers', and it was during one of their prayer-meetings that Barnabas and Paul were prophetically prompted by the Spirit to undertake their first missionary journey (13.1–3). The prophetic gift also continued to operate in the homes of Christians, as we see so clearly in the account of a meeting in Philip the Evangelist's house in Caesarea, where, in the company of his four prophet-daughters and Paul's companions, Agabus prophesied Paul's arrest (21.8–14).

The fullest account of worship in a Christian prophetic gathering is in 1 Cor. 14, but we shall look at that in some detail presently.

There can be little doubt that the fellowship of Christians in the early church was and continued to be thoroughly charismatic.

3. CHARISMATIC LEADERS AND CHARISMATIC MINISTRIES

Prophets and charismatics have always delighted in recounting the more dramatic stories about their leaders' lives and ministries. The Elijah-Elisha stories and our modern charismatic biographies both testify to that, but so also do some of the early stories in Acts, among which the following are particularly notable.

Chs. 3–4: Peter and John's miracle and their boldness. The story of the healing of the lame beggar is dramatic in itself. Peter's sermon after it proclaims that it was effected by faith in Jesus, and explains how his ministry was foretold by the prophets, how he was the prophet Moses said would come, and how we in 'these days' are heirs of the prophets. But equally as impressive as the miracle and the sermon is the supernatural boldness and wisdom with which both he and John conducted themselves before the Sanhedrin afterwards. These 'unschooled, ordinary men' (4.13), 'filled with the Holy Spirit' (v. 8), astonished their hearers as they gave witness to what they had 'seen and heard' (v. 20), proclaiming salvation in no other name than Jesus' (v. 12). We are reminded of the authority with which the prophets declared their message and the authority of Jesus that so amazed the crowds in Galilee.

Chs. 6–7: Stephen's dynamic witness and martyrdom. Stephen was an ordinary church member, chosen along with six others to help with the distribution of the community's food. However, he was a man 'full of the Spirit and wisdom' and miracles were soon happening while he was performing his duties. Persecution followed, but his opponents 'could not stand up against the wisdom or the Spirit by which he spoke' (6.10). Like Peter, he too testified boldly before the Jewish court, but unlike Peter, had to pay for it with his life. As he died he was granted a vision that would have been the envy of any prophet, of 'the Son of Man standing at the right hand of God' (7.56), and like his Master died praying for his executioners' forgiveness and for the Lord to receive his spirit (vv. 57–60).

Ch. 8: Philip's powerful evangelistic ministry.
Apart from all the miracles that attended his preaching in Samaria, impressive enough to convert Simon the magician, Philip found himself communing with an angel, being sent on a mystery trip down the Gaza road, being guided by the Spirit to speak to the Ethiopian eunuch and, after leading him to faith, being whisked away by the Spirit. Only men like Elijah could rejoice in such experiences.

9.1–31: Paul's dramatic conversion.
There are many accounts of conversations with God in Scripture, but for majesty Paul's encounter with Christ ranks alongside Isaiah's temple vision or Ezekiel's vision of the glory of God. Paul was left every bit as stunned as was Ezekiel when he sat dumbfounded for a week before the LORD fully revealed his calling to him (Ezek. 3.15f). Similarly Paul had to sit blinded for several days before Ananias was led by a vision to come and pray for him to be filled with the Spirit and give him prophetic revelation about his calling and future ministry.

9.32–43: Peter's miraculous healing ministry.
The miracles recorded here remind us of similar ones performed by Jesus. But we also find echoes of Elijah's and Elisha's ministries, particularly in the story of the raising of Tabitha (cp. 1 Kings 17.17–24; 2 Kings 4.18–37).

Ch. 10: Peter's vision leading to Cornelius' conversion.
This chapter is filled with prophetic material. An angel
appears to Cornelius giving supernatural guidance about
sending for Peter. Meantime Peter is prepared for meeting
him in a thrice-repeated vision and the story culminates in
Cornelius being filled with the Spirit.

11.19–30: Barnabas' pastorate at Antioch.
The story of Barnabas ministry at Antioch contains none of
the spectacular detail we find associated with Peter's ministry, but we are told that 'he was a good man, full of the
Holy Spirit and faith' and under his care the church grew
rapidly, so much so that he had to send for Paul to help
him. The prophetic quality of their work is seen in their
readiness to respond to Agabus, and later to follow the
Spirit's lead by leaving Antioch to go on mission (13.1–3).

The Spirit of the New Age.
There can be little doubt that it was Jesus' Spirit-empowered, prophetic ministry that the early Christians took out
into the ancient world. Like Jesus, they too were prophets.
They healed the sick, they saw visions, they spoke with
angels, they prophesied, they created communities of love
and joy, they showed themselves to be truly men with a
'new heart and new spirit' (Ezek. 11.19; 18.31; 36.26).

The fire of their enthusiasm was contagious and soon the
good news spread through the Palestinian coastlands. After
Paul joined them the gospel spread rapidly through Asia and
into Greece. Tales of miracles, visions, signs and wonders
continue as he preaches the word 'with demonstration of
the Spirit's power' (1 Cor. 2.4). The accounts of his missions
in Acts are replete with such tales, but perhaps more telling
than any of them is a story like that of his imprisonment in
Philippi, where we see him and Silas, their backs sore with
flogging, chained in a foreign dungeon, not knowing what
tomorrow holds, and yet in the middle of the night not at
all distressed, but 'praying and singing hymns to God'. Here
indeed is life in a new dimension (Acts 16.22–25). These
were men filled with a joy inspired by the Spirit that the

world knows nothing about, men who had, as it were, one foot on earth and one in Paradise.

Christians with similar charismatic gifts were soon to be found all over the ancient world. Hence when Paul wrote about the gifts, fruit and ministries of the Spirit to the churches in Rome, Corinth, Galatia, Ephesus and Thessalonica, he could do so without having to explain everything from the start (Rom. 12.1–8; 1 Cor. 12–14; Gal. 3.1–5; 5.16–26; Ephes. 4.1–16; 1 Thes. 5.19–21). The Church everywhere was indeed thoroughly charismatic.

Enduement with the Holy Spirit did not solve every problem for the early Christians any more than it did for the Old Testament prophets, but what it did do was turn them, like their Israelite forebears, into powerful revival preachers who in a very short time turned their world upside down.

The Garden of Eden had only been recovered in foretaste. There were still plenty of tensions, problems, squabbles and the like, and Luke does not camouflage that fact. For example, in Acts 15 he tells something of Paul's quarrel with the Jewish Christians in Jerusalem and of his disagreement with Mark and Barnabas. But the message of good news Luke conveys through his Gospel and his history of the early Church is that the promised age of the Spirit has come, first in Jesus and then in his disciples, who show themselves to be men not unlike the Old Testament prophets, Spirit-empowered, evangelistic, revivalist preachers, men such as the ancient prophets believed God would eventually raise up in order to bring about the fulfilment of his purpose to restore blessing to all the families of the earth.

4. PROPHECY AND PROPHETS IN THE NEW TESTAMENT

The prophetic gift operates at three different levels. Firstly, there is a general prophetic endowment common to all Spirit-filled Christians; secondly, there is a more specific gift of prophetic utterance; and thirdly, there is a highly specialised ministry of prophecy.

The General Prophetic Endowment.

The common prophetic (or charismatic) endowment is what
is given to all Christians the moment they are baptised with
the Holy Spirit. It enables them to appreciate more fully
the deeper realities of God and to enter into a general
exercise of all the charismatic gifts, such as those listed in
1 Cor. 12 and those we have seen operative in the ministries
of the Old Testament prophets, Jesus and the early Christians in Acts. It is mainly this level of prophetic activity we
have been studying throughout this chapter.

The best explanations about how this Christian prophetic
endowment works are given by Paul in his letters to the
Corinthians. In 1 Cor. 2 he draws a distinction between two
kinds of wisdom: 'men's wisdom' and 'God's secret wisdom'
(vv. 5,7). The former is the common learning of man
acquired by teaching and study, the latter is something that
cannot be learned by any human means, 'the deep things
of God' himself, 'a wisdom that has been hidden and that
God destined for our glory before time began' (vv. 7,10).
It is, however, revealed by the Spirit (vv. 10,12) to those
that are capable of understanding it (vv. 6,14). In fact, it is
to enable them to appreciate this divine wisdom that men
are given the Spirit in the first place, for he alone can show
them its truths (vv. 12f). Although the word 'prophet' is not
used in this chapter, we could paraphrase its teaching by
saying that no-one can properly appreciate prophetic
insight, vision and experience except one on whom the prophetic Spirit rests.

This supernatural wisdom is above all else concerned with
the significance of Christ (v. 2) in the total, primordial plan
of God (v. 7) and the interpretation of the gifts given to
believers (v. 12). Thus it enables men to understand how
the purposes and promises of God in the Old Testament
find fulfilment in Christ, and then in Christians themselves
as they experience the spiritual or prophetic blessings of the
age of the Spirit that has dawned with his coming. That is,
it gives them the same kind of understanding of God's purposes as the Old Testament prophets had.

In 2 Cor. 3 Paul makes the distinction a little more explicit
when he contrasts Jewish and Christian appreciation of the

old covenant Scriptures. The Jew, he says, reads his Bible with a veil over his mind, but for those in Christ that veil is removed 'whenever anyone turns to the Lord' (vv. 14–16). And for Paul's argument in this passage 'the Lord is the Spirit' and the new illumination he is writing about 'comes from the Lord, who is the Spirit' (vv. 17–19). This new enlightenment therefore belongs exclusively to those who recognise Jesus as the long-awaited Messiah and who receive his endowment with the Spirit promised by the prophets for these last days.

On such grounds Paul was able to draw a contrast between 'the man without the Spirit (who) does not accept the things that come from the Spirit of God, for they are foolishness to him, and he cannot understand them, because they are spiritually discerned, (and) the spiritual man (who) makes judgments about all things (because he has) the mind of Christ' (1 Cor. 2.14–16). The distinction was not unlike the one the Old Testament prophets drew when they criticised those who 'speak visions from their own minds', who 'follow their own spirit and have seen nothing' (Jer. 23.16; Ezek. 13.3).

If the nature of Christian charismatic endowment was essentially prophetic, so also was its expression. As we have already seen, both Israelite and Christian prophets had their records of miracles, visions, angelic communications, supernatural discernment and the like. In the New Testament there are four passages where the Spirit's gifts are listed, all different from each other.

– Rom. 12.6–8: prophesying, serving, teaching, encouraging, contributing, leadership, showing mercy.
– 1 Cor. 12.8–10: word of wisdom, word of knowledge, faith, gifts of healing, working of miracles, prophecy, discerning of spirits, divers kinds of tongues, interpretation of tongues (AV translation).
– Ephes. 4.11: apostles, prophets, evangelists, pastors and teachers.
– 1 Peter 4.9–11: hospitality, speaking, serving.

Some of these gifts are of a more homely nature, others more administrative, some more supernatural and spectacular, others almost natural endowments. Our concern here is not to examine these gifts in detail, but to note their relationship with prophecy. Most of them were exercised in some measure by the Israelite prophets, the most significant exceptions being tongues and its twin, interpretation.

We already discussed the relationship between prophecy and the initial gift of tongues accompanying baptism in the Spirit when we looked at Acts 2, but there was also a continuing gift for use as a language of prayer to edify the speaker himself (1 Cor. 14.4), which when interpreted could also edify the hearers (14.13–17). At that point tongues joins hands with prophecy, for the function of prophecy was also to edify the hearers (14.1–5). There is, however, one important difference between the two: tongues, unlike prophecy which is God's word to men, is first and foremost prayer addressed to God (14.2), and so interpretation's function is to enable hearers to say 'Amen' to the prayer offered in tongues (14.16).

Prophecy, tongues and interpretation, and every other gift of the Holy Spirit have two basic points in common, first that they are given for building up the body of Christ (the church), and second that they are to be exercised in a context of love. That is stated explicitly in each of Paul's three letters, where the gifts are only discussed in the context of love in the body of Christ. Essentially they are all intended to fulfil the same ultimate function as prophecy has, to strengthen God's people for the work to which he has called them.

The purpose of the gift of God's Spirit is therefore to make men prophets, to help them understand their prophetic calling, to enable them to minister with prophetic power, to become like their Prophet-master, Jesus, the Man of the Spirit. To that end the Spirit's presence in the life of the believer also moulds character, or produces 'fruit', as Paul puts it (Gal. 5.22f). But that also was part of the prophetic vision for the new age when the Spirit would create a new heart and a new spirit in man (Ezek. 36.26f).

The Gift of Prophecy.

The New Testament preserves few examples of Christians prophesying (only Agabus in Acts 11.27f & 21.10f) and almost no record of any prophetic words outside Revelation, but it does contain some discussion about the gift of prophecy, particularly in 1 Cor. 14. The main points to note are:

1. Prophecy is mainly a word for believers, 'for their strengthening, encouragement and comfort', and its purpose is to 'edify the church' (vv. 1–5).
2. Its twin gifts, tongues and interpretation, have the same effect, though tongues itself is not prophecy, but prayer addressed to God (vv. 1–5).
3. It can sometimes have convicting power over an unbeliever, though the implication of the text is that that happens in a co-incidental sort of way, 'if an unbeliever or someone who does not understand comes in while everyone is prophesying' (vv. 24f).
4. It is an orderly gift, not taking control of the prophet, but subject to the control of the prophet himself, who can exercise wisdom and discernment about how he uses it (vv. 26–33).
5. The place where it will commonly be used is in the congregation assembled for worship (vv. 26–33).
6. Interestingly, women were not allowed 'to speak' in church (v. 34), but they were allowed to pray or prophesy provided they had their heads covered (1 Cor. 11.5).
7. It is recognised that our prophecy is imperfect (or 'in part'; 1 Cor. 13.9) and so needs to be tested (1 Thes. 5.20f).
8. It was, however, held to be one of the most valuable gifts given to God's people (1 Cor. 14.1; 1 Thes. 5.20).
9. There could also be false prophecy – see below.

The fact that prophecy is mainly for the believing church is not altogether surprising. The unconverted were reached by preaching and evangelism, rather than by prophecy, and the New Testament clearly distinguishes the two ministries.

Prophecy in the Old Testament was mostly a word to God's people, Israel, calling them back to him in repentance, encouraging them to faith and holiness, and looking forward to the coming of his kingdom and its Messianic King; prophecy in the New Testament is the same word to God's new people, the New Israel, but now proclaiming that their King has already visited them in Jesus. Whether the prophecy encourages men to look forward to Christ's first or second coming, or back to his sacrificial ministry, the Spirit's function is ultimately the same, namely to bear witness to him and bring him glory (John 15.26; 16.14).

Revelation, the only book in the New Testament described as 'prophecy', is also a word for believers (God's 'servants'), written to bless (edify) those of them who take it to heart. It is called 'revelation' or 'testimony of Jesus Christ', mainly because it bears witness to Jesus. (Rev. 1.1–3)

The Ministry of Prophet.

Certain individuals were recognised in New Testament times as having a particular prophetic ministry and so were called 'prophets'. Acts 11.27f mentions 'some prophets' who came from Jerusalem, one of them called Agabus. We meet Agabus again in Acts 21.10f. We find two others in Acts 15.32, Judas and Silas, speaking 'to encourage and strengthen the brothers' at Antioch, where the church leadership itself included some who were known as prophets (Acts 13.1).

In 1 Cor. 12.28 and Ephes. 4.11 Paul lists prophets, alongside apostles, teachers, etc., among the leading ministries

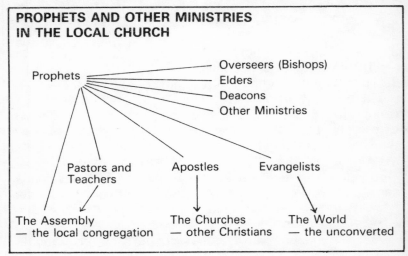

PROPHETS AND OTHER MINISTRIES IN THE LOCAL CHURCH

Prophets — Overseers (Bishops)
— Elders
— Deacons
— Other Ministries

Pastors and Teachers · Apostles · Evangelists

The Assembly — the local congregation
The Churches — other Christians
The World — the unconverted

of the churches. Perhaps the best way to understand their function is to see them as encouragers of the other ministries. Pastors and teachers have to care for and teach their congregations; apostles have a wider ministry to the churches at large; evangelists are called to reach the unconverted; overseers (or bishops), elders and deacons have the general responsibility for the welfare and running of their churches; and all engaged in these ministries, as well as in every other supporting ministry, need the encouragement of the prophetic word that it is granted to some to give them.

Of course, the overseer, pastor, or evangelist, for example, may have exercised this prophetic ministry as well as his own ministry of oversight, pastoral care, or evangelism. We are never told that one man could not exercise both. But regularly in the churches someone was recognised as having a special ministry of prophecy that helped encourage everyone else in his own faith or ministry.

DISTINGUISHING TRUE AND FALSE PROPHETS

We encountered the problem of false prophecy in the Old Testament. The same problem rears its perplexing head again in Christian times, cp. Mark 13.22; Matt. 7.15; 24.24; 1 John 2.18f; 4.1. In these passages Jesus and John both stress how important it is to test or recognise the kind of prophet who speaks, as does Paul when he advises: "Do not put out the Spirit's fire; do not treat prophecies with contempt. Test everything. Hold on to the good." (1 Thes. 5.19-21)

So how do we test the prophet and his word? Putting the insights of both Old and New Testaments together we do have a helpful overall pattern to guide us:

1. Do his words find fulfilment? (Deut. 18.17-22)

2. Is his teaching orthodox; that is, does it accord with the truth of your faith in Christ? (Deut. 13.1-5; 1 John 4.1-3)

3. Is he one who you recognise has had intimate counsel with the Lord? (Jer. 23.16-22; 1 Kings 22.19-25)

4. Does his teaching lead the brethren into wrong ways of thinking or acting? (Mark 13.22)

5. Does he claim that his word is above being questioned or tested? The New Testament actually commands us to test all prophecy. (1 Thes. 5.19-21; 1 John 4.1)

6. What is his way of life like? Is it like Christ's? Or does it seem self-opinionated, proud, greedy, desirous of approval, etc.? (Matt. 7.15f; 1 John 2.6)

7. How does his word strike you? You too have the Spirit, and among his gifts is discernment of spirits. (1 Cor. 12.10)

8. Does his word strengthen, encourage, comfort, edify? Sometimes this can be done through a disquieting call to repentance, of course. (1 Cor. 14.1-5)

9. Is his word pure, peaceloving, considerate, submissive, full of mercy and good fruit, impartial and sincere? Or does it cause a fear and anxiety, that are not of God? (James 3.17)

10. Do his words glorify Christ, or reveal more deeply the hidden mysteries of Christ, or interpret his gifts to you? (John 16.14; 1 Cor. 2.6-16)

11. Does the prophecy seem to be a matter of the prophet's own interpretation, or does he seem to speak from God, inspired by the Holy Spirit? (2 Peter 1.20f) Sometimes you can recognise that a person is giving his own thoughts in "prophetic" language; of course, that depends partly on how well you know him, or on your exercise of the gift of discernment.

12. Does he seem to be "taken over" in his spirit when he speaks? The spirit of the prophet should be subject to the prophet, not the reverse. (1 Cor. 14.32)

13. If after all that you are still not sure, bring the prophecy to the body for discernment; ask your fellowship, or its leaders, to test it.

14. If still in doubt, then pray (as you should have done in the first place anyhow) and ask for the wisdom God promises to give you freely. (James 1.5)

15

The Final Prophetic Vision

REVELATION

Right at the beginning of this volume we noted the longing expressed by Moses in Num. 11.29: 'I wish all the LORD's people were prophets and that the LORD would put his Spirit on them!' And now we have seen how that longing found dramatic fulfilment in Christian times, starting with the day of Pentecost when God poured out his Spirit for all who would receive him.

The Israelite prophets foresaw that day and had some foretaste of its power in their own experience. It is therefore not surprising that it became one of the main focuses of their teaching. In each generation they faced different challenges and so many of their words were addressed to the needs of their own day, but they were all aware that God had a purpose in history stretching far beyond their time. Over the centuries as the picture unfolded, they began to speak of a coming Messiah, a race of prophetic men, a showdown with the powers of evil, re-establishment of Eden-life, and finally a new heaven and new earth.

Since God brought so much to pass through Jesus, Christian prophecy looked back in praise as well as forward in hope, but the ultimate vision of a full restoration of Paradise remained its final focus. And now, with so much already fulfilled, God was ready to unfold the next stages in greater detail. Jesus spoke of them in his day (see Luke 21). Paul also taught concerning them when he wrote about a general resurrection that is to happen in the twinkling of an eye when the trumpet of heaven sounds at the end of time,

219

when death will be done away with, and Jesus will hand over the kingdom to God (1 Cor. 15.20– 28; 50–57; 1 Thes. 4.13–18). He also said that event would be preceded by a time of rebellion led by a 'man of lawlessness' who would vaunt himself against God and with Satan's power perform signs and wonders to lead people astray (2 Thes. 2.1–12). But the most detailed unfolding of the things yet to come is given to us by John in Revelation.

It is generally believed that Revelation was written about 95 AD by the apostle John. That was the view of most of the early fathers of the Church, though some have always questioned it because the language and style are a little different from what we find in the fourth Gospel and John's epistles. The arguments are interesting and detailed, but need not delay us, since it is the message that concerns us here.

John tells us he was granted his revelation while 'on the island of Patmos because of the word of God and the testimony of Jesus' (1.9). His exile there has, since the second century, been associated with a wave of persecution in Domitian's time. Domitian took emperor-worship much more seriously than most of his predecessors; refusal to worship him was regarded as treason. It is important to keep that in mind when reading, because many of the details of John's visions are to be understood in the light of strong tensions between Church and State, the sort of tensions many Christians in different parts of the world still have to live with today. The message of Revelation remains as relevant now as it was in John's day.

The visions are often quite complex, but fortunately their central message can be grasped without overdue attention to the details, fascinating though these may be. John makes free use of the language and imagery of the apocalyptic parts of the Old Testament to describe what he saw, drawing particularly from Ezekiel, Daniel and Zechariah, and so it helps to be familiar first with their writings. But it is important to remember that John saw the whole vision in one day and it was only later, presumably after much thought about its details, that he wrote it down (1.9f). Here we want to catch the full sweep of the message, for if we start by concentrating on the detail we may fail to see the wood for the trees and end with strange interpretations – like many that have been drawn from this book and have plagued the Church down the centuries.

1. THE PROPHETIC WORD TO THE CHURCHES (CHS. 1–3)

John introduces his book as 'the revelation (Greek: *apoka-lupsis*) of Jesus Christ, which God gave him to show his servants what must soon take place', which suggests that what we are about to read is apocalyptic rather than proph-ecy (see pp. 129f). However, John does also call it 'proph-ecy' and in its opening chapters we do hear echoes of the direct confrontation language of the old Israelite prophets.

1.4–19: *John tells of his vision of Jesus.*
John writes to 'the seven churches in the province of Asia'. There were other churches there besides those he names (at Colosse, for example), but many things in Revelation are organised in sevens. It is the number of the week, of cre-ation, and so of totality and completeness. John's book is thus addressed to the whole Church of Christ in Asia, indeed everywhere (v. 4).

Similarly he speaks of 'the seven spirits' of God, meaning the Holy Spirit in his totality, but also in the symbolism of his vision as he relates to each of the (seven) churches individually (v. 4).

He calls Jesus 'the faithful witness'. The Greek word for 'witness' gives us the English 'martyr': Jesus bore witness by his martyrdom, and to know that is encouragement for those facing potential martyrdom now. But equally encour-aging are the facts that he is 'the firstborn from the dead', for that reminds us that we shall rise too, and that he is 'ruler of the kings of the earth', even of the oppressive ones, which means that nothing happens outside his control (v. 5).

God's message, given to strengthen those he loves and

calls to serve him as his priests, is summed up in vv. 7–8: He is coming soon to execute his justice, and the world will know it when he comes, for he is 'the Alpha and the Omega' (the first and last letters of the Greek alphabet, 'the A and the Z', signifying the Beginning and the End of everything), 'who is, and who was, and who is to come, the Almighty'. These titles are used several times throughout the visions to remind the reader who God really is.

Just like some of the Old Testament prophets, John begins with an account of his encounter with the Lord, telling how he received his prophetic message to the churches. The vision reminds us of similar ones seen by Ezekiel and Daniel (Ezek. 1; Dan. 7), but it is alive with fresh symbolism of its own. The prophetic vision is always essentially the same, but it is also always fresh and new.

Particularly significant is the fact that in it Jesus is 'among the lampstands' (the churches). That is where he must be, since the Church is his people and his bride. And that is where he still is, protecting, guiding and encouraging. The message he gave for the churches of Asia he continues to give for our churches today.

Chs. 2–3: The prophetic message to the Church.

When John heard these words, just over sixty years had passed since the birth of the Church, but already it was in

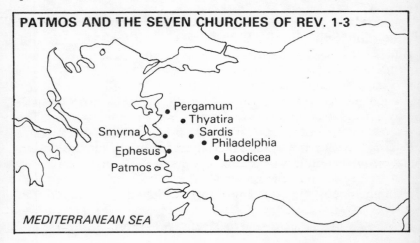

PATMOS AND THE SEVEN CHURCHES OF REV. 1-3

Pergamum
Thyatira
Smyrna Sardis
Ephesus Philadelphia
Patmos Laodicea

MEDITERRANEAN SEA

need of reviving, as the letters themselves clearly show. In every age revival is the business of prophets and their message is always basically the same, calling the Lord's people to repentance and perseverance in faith. The message of the letters is a complete blue-print for personal and church revival in any age.

Ephesus (2.1–7): Early Christian writers tell us Ephesus was where John settled and lived on into old age. The church was clearly strong on good works, perseverance and doctrine, but –

> *You have forsaken your first love. Remember the height from which you have fallen! Repent and do the things you did at first.*

Smyrna (2.8–11): A poor church, yet rich towards God. Smyrna and Philadelphia are the only two churches that faced greater dangers from outside than from within the congregation itself.

> *Do not be afraid . . . Be faithful, even to the point of death.*

Pergamum (2.12–17): Basically faithful, but with some members who are not sound. Pergamum was the main centre of emperor-worship in Asia and so John calls it the place 'where Satan has his throne'.

> *You remain true to my name . . . Nevertheless, I have a few things against you . . . Repent therefore! Otherwise, I will soon come to you.*

Thyatira (2.18–28): A mixed congregation, some standing firm in their faith, others not.

> *You tolerate that woman Jezebel, who misleads my servants . . . unless they repent of her ways . . . Now I say to the rest of you . . . Hold on to what you have.*

Sardis (3.1–6): A church that seems alive, but is mostly dead.

> *Wake up! Strengthen what remains and is about to die . . . Remember what you have received and heard; obey it, and repent.*

Philadelphia (3.7–13): Like Smyrna, weak and facing much opposition, but standing firm and true.

> *I have placed before you an open door that no-one can shut. I know that you have little strength, yet you have kept my word and not denied my name. . . . Hold on to what you have.*

Laodicea (3.14–22): A church that is well-to-do, but riddled with apathy.

> *You are neither cold nor hot. I wish you were either one or the other! . . . Be earnest and repent. Here I am! I stand at the door and knock. If anyone hears my voice and opens the door, I will come in and eat with him, and he with me.*

The spiritual condition of each church is, of course, different. Some are praised more than others, but the message is always the same: Repent and stand firm. The promises attached to each, though expressed in different language, are also basically the same: that those who are faithful will inherit their share in Christ's kingdom.

The letters are addressed to angels, but it must be remembered that John is 'in the Spirit' (1.10), seeing everything from a spiritual perspective. This is prophetic vision, not just letter-writing. What John witnessed is of the same order as what Micaiah witnessed when he saw the LORD sending a spirit with its message to Ahab's prophets (1 Kings 22.19–22) and what Jeremiah experienced when he 'stood in the council of the LORD to see or to hear his word' (Jer. 23.18). John heard the message being given to angels because he too was with the Lord.

The letters to the churches correspond in John's prophetic

book to the revival messages of the Old Testament prophets, the word addressed to the present-day crisis. In the rest of Revelation John tells of his unfolding vision of the future and of the end.

2. THE COURSE OF HISTORY NOW AND TO COME (CHS. 4–11)

To capture the dynamic flow of these visions, they need to be read through without puzzling too long over detail. Try to read as if you were yourself seeing the vision, or as if you were watching a video recording of it, remembering that the action moves on fairly swiftly.

Ch. 4: John enters God's throne-room in heaven.

In the temple in Jerusalem Isaiah had a foretaste of what John saw, as did Ezekiel on the plain by the River Kebar (Isa. 6; Ezek. 1), and so his description carries many echoes of theirs, though as always it is full of fresh symbolism and life. Here again we see the throne, the rainbow and the flashes of lightning. Once more we encounter the living creatures, Isaiah's seraphim, Ezekiel's cherubim, and still they sing their eternal 'Holy, holy, holy'. But now we are shown more, for around the throne and the living creatures are twenty-four other thrones with twenty-four elders who bow before God and worship him whenever the living creatures sing. We do not need to identify any of these. John does not do so. But as they lay their crowns before God we are reminded that he is King of kings and Lord of lords, the Almighty.

The door into heaven John saw was an open door. The Jews hung a veil over the entrance to the Most Holy Place in the temple, but Christ's sacrifice has caused 'a new and living way (to be) opened for us through the curtain' into God's presence (Heb. 10.20). And before his throne are seven lamps blazing, the seven spirits of God, which are, as we have already noted, the Holy Spirit himself as he goes out from God to the churches, that is, through this door in heaven opened by Christ's sacrifice. John was not trans-

ported to a place behind closed doors where the churches
and the world are no longer of importance, but to a place
where he can view earth from God's perspective.

Ch. 5: The Lamb receives a scroll from God's hand.

The vision of ch. 4 is of God the Creator, the Eternal, God
of the Old Testament as much as of the New. Now the
vision moves on in time as we watch Christ, the Lamb of
God, approach the throne of heaven.

One key to understanding ch. 5 is to recognise that it is
his death that makes Jesus worthy to take the scroll (v. 9).
John sees the whole of history before the cross telescoped
into a moment of time in vv. 1–4, where he weeps that no-
one was found worthy to open the scroll. But everything
changes when the Lamb 'looking as if it had been slain'
approaches the throne. At that moment heaven erupts in
praise and John becomes aware of more life around him
than he noticed before – thousands upon thousands of
angels, and every creature in heaven and on earth and under
the earth and on the sea, all praising the Lamb. The effects
of Christ's death are comprehensive.

A second key to unlocking this chapter, and the next, is
to realise that the scroll is the record of history, not just of
names, dates and events, but of the full sweep of history
and God's great purposes in it. And the first message is that
a new phase in its outworking began with the crucifixion –
hence the 'Amen' of the living creatures.

Ch. 6: The Lamb begins to open the seals on the scroll.

As the Lamb opens the seals we are shown some fairly
horrifying scenes. Rather than thinking of a historical progression, it is better to view these as samples of what happens regularly on earth, as though we were turning the
pages of a daily newspaper or switching from one news
programme to another on television. And what we are
shown through the visionary-symbolism is first: (1) war, (2)
civil war, (3) famine, and (4) death, affecting a fourth of
the earth (v. 8).

Then follow two longer and more detailed scenes, with
more sense of progression about them. First we see (5)

persecution, with the martyrs crying out, 'How long?' Then we are shown (6) an earthquake that puts terror in the hearts of men, the first rumblings of the day of 'the wrath of the Lamb'. But the end is not yet – that only comes with the opening of the seventh seal. Earthquakes and such attendant terrors are in our world today. In them God shows he is not deaf to the prayers of the martyr-church, but is already expressing his wrath in history.

These accounts of the horrors that ravage our earth are fairly factual. We are told little about their theological significance at this stage, but later we learn that God allows and causes such things to stir men to repentance.

Ch. 7: John is granted refreshing views of heaven again.

Opening the seventh seal must signal the end, for it is the last on the scroll, but if it were opened directly, we might feel God's only purpose is to terrify and destroy. On the contrary it is to redeem. An angel therefore calls a halt and John is shown the redeemed. First there are the 144,000 of Israel (the number signifies completeness, the full number of their tribes, 12 x 12 x 1,000), but he only heard their number. What he saw when he looked was 'a great multitude that no-one could count, from every nation, tribe, people and language', all robed in white, praising God and the Lamb along with the angels, the elders and the living creatures. The only ones his attention was specially drawn to were the martyrs, already enjoying Paradisal bliss.

On that note the chapter ends. John needed an encouraging interlude before facing what comes next, as we also do. There is a limit to the amount of horror we can take without a break. John's attention is repeatedly drawn away from earth back to heaven in this way throughout the book, but that is just how God regularly strengthens his saints with times of refreshing from heaven.

Chs. 8–9: The seventh seal and the sounding of seven trumpets.

The silence following the opening of the last seal is virtually impossible to interpret. It may simply signify a pause for us to catch our breath, or a passing without comment over a stretch of historical time, but it does create a sense of suspense and anticipation as the revelation of the end is withheld for the moment. More must first be unfolded, for we have not yet been sufficiently prepared to understand it. If it came now we would miss its full significance.

The vision moves almost directly to another series of seven, seven angels blowing seven trumpets. These are preceded by a sudden intensification of prayer, but an angel dramatically hurls the censer used to accompany the prayer to earth amid rumblings of wrath. The trumpets will sound God's final answer to the prayers of the martyrs (6.9f) and their fellow saints (cp. 5.8). The censer will be needed no more.

Jesus and Paul both said angelic trumpets would herald the end (Matt. 24.31; 1 Thes. 4.16). As the trumpets sound, we still watch the unfolding of history, just as when the seals were opened, but there is a greater sense of end-time urgency about what we are now shown. History has moved on. These are now truly the last days. And the impact of wrath is more widespread. A third of everything is affected: (1) parts of the earth become desert, (2) sea turns to blood and fish die, (3) fresh-water springs and rivers become undrinkable, (4) a third of the sky is darkened. Whatever John thought of all that, we cannot help but think today about the effects of pollution on our environment. However, it is the symbolism that is most striking, for here we find clear echoes of the plagues that were God's ultimatum to Egypt. The trumpets now sound forth God's ultimatum to earth.

Before the fifth trumpet sounds our thoughts are dramatically interrupted by an eagle screeching 'Woe! Woe! Woe!' in mid-heaven, warning the inhabitants of earth about the urgency of the times. The woes are sounded again just before the sixth and seventh trumpets.

The fifth trumpet (5) heralds the unleashing of monstrous locust-scorpion-like creatures with limited power to kill and torture, but significantly 'their faces resembled human faces' (9.7), for they represent the hellish brutality with which men treat each other. This is not a vision of persecution against the Church (v. 4), but of man's inhumanity to man. The sixth trumpet (6) unveils world war with armies so large John cannot estimate their size but has to be told it (9.16). These two visions reveal times of terrible warfare with vast, frightening armies quite unlike anything known in John's own times.

Then finally we are told why God allows such things. Just as Amos had seen so long before, they should stir men to repentance, but as in his day, so still men will not heed the lesson (9.20f; cp. Amos 4).

Chs. 10–11: Christian prophetic witness before the end.

Just as with the opening of the seals, John is granted an interlude before the seventh trumpet sounds. There is, how-ever, a different feel here, a greater sense of urgency. This time he is not taken to heaven, but to the Church to be shown the power of its prophetic witness in the last days. These are now the last hours of history, the last opportunity to preach the gospel before the end comes, and what John sees is a dramatic upsurge of end-time prophetic witnessing.

It is in this period before the end that we live today. We already know the suffering, the pollution and the inhu-manity of the first six seals and trumpets, but with God's saints and martyrs we pray and long for the seventh to be fulfilled. At the start we were told that time is near (1.3); now we are reminded of its nearness again (10.6). The challenge to John, and to us, is therefore to receive God's prophetic word ourselves and take it to our fellow men now.

Our Church is God's prophetic voice for the last days. That was symbolised for John in his vision when a voice bade him eat a 'little scroll' (as distinct from the large scroll the Lamb holds) and go, prophesy. The experience was virtually identical with Ezekiel's when he was given his scroll of prophecy to eat (Ezek. 2.9 – 3.3). And again the message is sweet for the faithful, but bitter for the world.

However, just like some of the Israelite prophets, so also some of the Christian witnesses will suffer persecution and death at the hands of cruel men (11.1–10), but God will not abandon them and they will be raised up to be with him in heaven.

In reading this passage we are more conscious than ever of the symbolic nature of John's language. Measuring the temple is an image used in Ezek. 40–41 (cp. Zech. 2.1–5) and represents protection for the Lord's people. The 42 months, or 1,260 days, or three and a half days are the 'time, times and half a time' of Dan. 12.7 (= three and a half years), signifying symbolically, not mathematically, the duration of these last times before the end. The two olive trees are found in Zech. 4 and symbolise the Messianic anointing of Jesus that Christians share. The lampstands are the symbols of the churches we have already seen in John's visions (1.20). The fact that there are only two here and not seven, as in ch. 1, indicates that this kind of witness by martyrdom will only ever be the calling of a proportion of Christians.

With the martyrdom of the witnesses and their resurrection we already begin to hear the rumblings of the end (11.13) and after a final warning woe (v. 14) the seventh trumpet sounds. Thereupon we hear again the praises of heaven, this time rejoicing because the hour has now come (vv. 15–18), and we see God's wrath flashing in the sanctuary in heaven (v. 19). This is more than we were shown at the opening of the seventh seal, but it is still only a preliminary viewing and again the vision is withdrawn without our discovering its outworking. There is again more we need to learn first.

3. THE BUILD-UP TO THE LAST BATTLE (CHS. 12–19)

The further we progress, the more the tension mounts. The fury of earth and hell becomes more furious and the urgency of the call of the Church and of heaven becomes more urgent, until eventually all that is left is final confrontation. But before going through another series of seven, we are first shown something of the spiritual activity that lies behind the present process of history. John is, as it were, allowed to look behind the scenes and see the deeper spiritual dynamic of all that happens and will happen in our world.

Ch. 12: Satan is thrown out of heaven and now vents his fury on earth.

Earth has its history, but so also does heaven, and the two are closely interrelated. Satan in Old Testament times, even though he had fallen from grace, still had access to heaven (cp. Job 1.6; 2.1). 'Satan' is not a name, but a title used of the devil (Hebrew *ho-satan* means 'the accuser'), describing his activity of bringing accusations against men. One day a woman (the People of God, the Bride) gave birth to a child (Jesus) against whom he could bring no accusation. He tried to destroy him at birth, but in vain, and the day that child 'was snatched up to God and to his throne' the archangel Michael and his angels drove Satan and his angels out of heaven completely, having overcome him 'by the blood of the Lamb' (v. 11). And now 'filled with fury, because he knows that his time is short' (v. 12), he roams the earth seeking vengeance against the woman and the rest of her offspring (the Church and its members), but without much success, for they are protected against him.

Ch. 13: Satan summons the power of the state to his help.

In frustration at his impotence Satan, who has been portrayed as an enormous red dragon (12.3), now takes his stance 'on the shore of the sea' (13.1). To this point the sea has been tranquil in the vision, looking 'like a sea of glass, clear as crystal', delusively attractive as it stretched out before God's throne (4.6). But it was only tranquil because God ruled over it (cp. Ps. 93.3f; Prov. 8.28f). It is in fact a reservoir of monstrous creatures (Ps. 74.13f; Isa. 27.1), it is a barrier the redeemed must pass to enter their rest (Rev.15.2f), and in the end it will be no more (21.1). Daniel had seen monstrous beasts symbolising oppressive empires rise out of it (Dan. 7), and now John sees another, one with ten horns and seven heads bearing blasphemous names. The dragon invests it with his power (v.2). It has a pseudo-Messianic aspect, seeming to have been fatally wounded, though not really, and men follow it as though it were their saviour (vv. 3–4). But its words and actions tell all, for it blasphemes God and persecutes his saints (vv. 5–10).

The beast from the sea is imperial Rome – and every other imperial power that has opposed God's people ever since. It has an assistant, a beast from the earth, which also has a quasi-Messianic stamp, seeming in some ways like a lamb and also having a fatal wound that never was fatal, even performing miraculous signs to deceive men (vv. 11–14). But its function is that of a police force, by any means to enforce worship of the imperial beast (vv. 15–17). It has a number, 666, that, however pretentious and however often repeated, clearly falls short of God's perfect 'seven'.

Ch. 14: John is shown the forces of heaven ranged against the beast.

Heaven is not meantime inactive. John is shown the Lamb accompanied by '144,000 who had his name and his Father's name written on their foreheads', in contrast with the blasphemous names on the beast's. The thunder of heaven grumbles in the background, but with them there is a sense of tranquility as they play their harps and sing their new song. They are Christ's army ready for battle, with no deceit in their mouths, again unlike the beast. V. 4 does not imply that they are celibate. The allusion is to an Old Testament regulation that soldiers in war-time must keep themselves from women (Deut. 23.9f; 1 Sam. 21.5; 2 Sam. 11.11). God's army is consecrated and at its station.

But before any battle can be engaged, the gospel must still be proclaimed and men must be given a final opportunity to repent. Hence John sees three angels in succession fly out with last minute invitations and warnings (vv. 6–12). The warnings are frightening, but John is reassured that blessing awaits the faithful (v. 13).

Then at last he sees the harvest of earth begin. This is not the last battle, but the final reaping before it, when Christ swings his sickle and gathers in the faithful. There is a great sense of urgency in this part of the vision, for those that are not gathered in this harvest face a later, dreadful harvest, when men will be gathered like grapes and trampled in the great winepress of God's wrath.

Chs. 15–16: *The seven angels with the seven bowls of God's wrath.*

This series of seven is the last. The end is approaching and the time has passed for looking into the scroll of history or hearing the heraldic trumpets. It is time for the outpouring of God's wrath, and this time there will be no interlude before the seventh bowl is poured out, for the hour of God's wrath has fully come.

Satan had stood on the earthward shore of the sea when he summoned the beast to his aid. We are now shown the heavenward shore, and there we see the redeemed who have crossed it in the final exodus, like the Israelites after they had crossed the Red Sea, singing their song of salvation, 'the song of Moses the servant of God and the song of the Lamb' (15.1–4; Exod. 15).

When the seventh trumpet sounded, heaven's tabernacle was laid open for the outpouring of God's wrath (11.19), and now out of it come seven angels with the bowls of his wrath for that outpouring (15.5–8).

If the earlier sevens bore some resemblance to events and conditions in the world as we know it, this seven bears little. The effects of the plagues are total this time, not just affecting a quarter or a third of the earth like the earlier ones. However, it is not all mankind that is afflicted by them, but only those 'who had the mark of the beast and worshipped his image' (16.2), who 'have shed the blood of your saints' (v. 6). What we witness is the beginning of God's judgment on the empire of the beast (vv. 5–7) and the run-up to the last battle (v. 16). First come four plagues afflicting the citizens of the beast's empire (vv. 1–9), then one dethroning him and plunging his kingdom into darkness (vv. 10f), a sixth releasing demonic powers to run rampant in his kingdom and prepare the way for a massive invasion (vv. 12–16), and finally one that shakes the earth and causes the collapse of his capital city, Babylon (vv. 17–21).

The vision of a cosmic battle at the end of history is found in Ezek. 38–39 and Zech. 14, but the name Armageddon ('Mount Megiddo') is only used here. The plain of Megiddo was the scene of many battles in Old Testament times and Zechariah spoke of weeping there (Zech. 12.11), but what-

ever the derivation, like other names in John's vision, it is
a symbol, and we should not try to locate it on a map, any
more than we should think literalistically about identifying
Babylon. It is also a name used symbolically, this time based
on the bitter memory of Babylon's destruction of Jerusalem
in 587 BC.

Ch. 17: The beast's identity is revealed.

The earlier series of seven were all general surveys that had
to be filled out with closer study. So too here, after being
shown the broad sweep of the end, John is given a closer
view of what it involves.

First he is shown a lurid whore riding a monster. The
vision is utterly disgusting, but she was bedecked in finery
and many found her seductively attractive (vv. 1–6). Even
John stared at her in amazement until an angel interrupted
to explain the symbolism (vv. 6–18). The identification of
the woman with Rome, which was built on seven hills, is
manifest (v. 9), though the identification of its seven kings
and ten kings is not so clear (vv. 9–12).

While this vision clearly applied to Rome in John's day,
it continues to apply to any oppressive state that vaunts
itself against God. The state may often seem to have a
power beyond that exercised by God, but ultimately such
appearance is proved mere delusion as the beast is found
to be one who 'once was, now is not, and will come up out
of the Abyss and go to his destruction', that is, in contrast
with God who 'was, and is, and is to come' (v. 8; cp. 4.8).
The beast's true nature is also revealed in the end when it
turns against the one that rides it (vv. 15–18).

Ch. 18: The spectacle of Babylon's fall.

The last call we heard from the angels of heaven was a call
for repentance (14.6–11). Now even at this final moment the
same call goes out once more: 'Fallen! Fallen is Babylon . . .
Come out of her, my people.' (vv. 2,4) But instead of
wholesale repentance, we see kings shocked at the sudden-
ness of her fall (vv. 9f), and merchants and seamen lament-
ing the loss of their rich trading markets (vv. 11–20). As if
to silence their self-pitying, ungodly noise, an angel dramati-

cally hurls a large millstone into the sea and pronounces Babylon's final demise (vv. 21–24).

Ch. 19: The victory song and victory procession of heaven.

In the end the last battle has proved to be no battle at all. God simply spoke from heaven: 'It is done!' (16.17), and so it was. This is the first time God actually speaks himself in John's vision, but that was how God created in the beginning and that is how he acts in the end. Heaven's armies never had to engage the enemy. Like Jehoshaphat's troops (2 Chron. 20.21f), they simply sang while God did it all (14.2f; 15.3f). And the songs they sang were all songs of victory (19.1–8).

The contrast between the Lamb, who comes riding on his white horse called Faithful and True and the whore who came riding on an ugly beast is most striking. Christ's robe is dipped in blood because of his crucifixion, but his followers all wear pure white robes washed in his blood (cp. 7.14). And he rules, not by seduction, but simply and directly by the sharp word that comes from his mouth, for his name is the Word of God (vv. 11–16).

However, as after any battle, there are mopping-up operations to be done. Already the vultures gather over the corpse-strewn battle-field, but the enemy commanders are still at large. John therefore sees the beast from the sea and the false prophet (the beast from the earth) thrown into a fiery lake of burning sulphur, while the rest of their troops are left to the birds (vv. 17–21).

4. THE TIME OF THE END AND THE END OF TIME (CHS. 20–22)

The ultimate goal of God's purposes is the restoration of Paradise, to which the overthrow of earth's empire is only the prelude. John is now shown God's rule established on earth and then the restoration of that Eden-life he had created in the beginning.

Ch. 20: The Millennium and the Last Judgment.

In this chapter we have the only mention in the Bible of what is commonly referred to as 'the Millennium', the thousand-year rule of Christ on earth before the final end of all things. Presumably the figure, like every other figure in the book, is symbolic, but however we interpret it, the drift of the vision is clear. The battle is over, and just as any battle is followed by assertion of the victor's rule over the territory he has conquered, so now Christ, having won back the earth from the devil, has him bound and imprisoned, while he, with the help of his martyr-army, establishes his rule and peace throughout his conquered territory (vv. 1–6).

However, as Ezekiel foresaw, even that would not be the end, for Satan would get loose again and rouse the hoards of Gog and Magog ('Gog, of the land of Magog' in Ezek. 38.2), but the outcome of that will be the final end of Satan himself (vv. 7–10).

Then comes the great last judgment. Before it takes place earth and sky simply vanish. All that is left is 'a great white throne and him who was seated on it', before whom stand all men that have ever lived 'and books were opened'. Daniel saw something of this scene (Dan. 7.9f), but now there is a difference, for as well as the books containing the records of men's deeds, there is another book called 'the book of life', described elsewhere as 'the Lamb's book of life' (21.27; cp. 13.8), since it contains the names of those that are Christ's. In the final analysis being in his book is the only thing that secures salvation.

Ch. 21: The new heaven and new earth, and the new Jerusalem.

With the last judgment 'the last enemy' (1 Cor. 15.26) is removed. There is now no beast, no Satan, no Gog, no death, none of their supporters or spiritual ancilliaries, and finally no sea (v. 1). Now at last is the time for God to make all things new.

The new Jerusalem comes 'prepared as a bride', for it is not a city of bricks and mortar, but the Church of God, the bride of Christ, made of 'living stones' (1 Pet. 2.5). As the voice from the throne itself says, 'the dwelling of God is with men' (v. 3). Now we see all the promises of Scripture fully come to pass. The curse of death, mourning, crying and pain that was consequent on Adam's fall is removed, and God ministers healing to his people (v. 4), granting the thirsty to drink freely 'from the spring of the water of life' (v. 6).

Just as Ezekiel was conducted round the temple in his last vision, so John is shown the Holy City, 'the bride, the wife of the Lamb' (vv. 9f). Architecturally it is a peculiar city, being in the shape of a cube, as high as it is broad and long, about 1,400 miles each way (v. 16), entirely made and bedecked with precious stones and metals (vv. 18–21).

Again we need to look at the symbolism to get the message. The Most Holy Place in the temple in Jerusalem was also cube-shaped (1 Kings 6.20), and as in John's city, the glory of God resided there (v. 11; cp. 1 Kings 8.10f; Ezek. 43.5). The new Jerusalem is in fact not a city as we think of cities, but the inner sanctuary of heaven itself. That is why John 'did not see a temple in the city', its only temple being 'the Lord God Almighty and the Lamb' themselves (v. 22). As the death of Christ opened the way into the Most Holy Place (see on ch. 4), so in the end it is there that 'those whose names are written in the Lamb's book of life' will be, right in the presence of the glory of God himself, where there is no more need for sun or moon or any other light (vv. 22–27).

Ch. 22: Paradise restored.

As John is shown the city more closely, he sees what Ezekiel saw before him, that it has all the marks of the Garden of Eden in its original goodness, with its river of the water of life and its tree of life with eternal food and healing leaves (vv. 1–2; Ezek. 47.1–12), and the curse of the fall fully removed (v. 3). But the end of all things is not just a place. Rather it is a person, God himself, and his servants 'will see his face' (vv. 3–4), for he himself is 'the End,' just as he was 'the Beginning' (21.6).

The rest of the book (22.7–21) reminds us of the urgency of the vision. God's Spirit and the bride (the Church) invite us to come now and take of the free gift of the water of life God already offers us in Christ. John himself prayed, 'Amen. Come, Lord Jesus.' Let us join him in that prayer as we rejoice in the wonderful things the Lord has prepared for those who love him.

PART SEVEN

CONCLUSION

17

Christian Prophecy since New Testament Times

The New Testament Church was manifestly charismatic/prophetic, but the letters in Rev. 2–3 suggest that some of the Spirit's fire was already burning low by the end of the first century. Charismatic gifts continued in use in the second, though increasingly among a minority. Towards the end of that century, Ireneus, Bishop of Lyons, even referred to the charismatics he knew as Christ's 'true disciples', the 'spiritual' Christians (*Against Heresies* II.32.4 and V.6.1; both these passages are quoted by Eusebius in his *Ecclesiastical History* V.7.3– 6). However, the gifts were still recognised as from God.

Distinguishing between true and false prophecy continued to be a problem. *The Didache*, a little handbook on morals and church practice from the early second century, has a section (ch. 11) devoted to the subject. It demands high respect for the true prophet and suggests he will be recognised by the degree that his character and way of life reflect those of the Lord, particularly with regard to money.

Another early church manual, *The Shepherd* by Hermas, also from the early second century, has a whole chapter (the eleventh Mandate) on true and false prophecy. Like *The Didache*, it bids us observe the prophet's way of life, but it also points out that the difference will be obvious from the prophet's behaviour before the assembled church at prayer. As in 1 Cor. 14, it speaks of prophecy as a gift for the body that operates in the context of congregational worship. There the false prophet will be exposed as the body discerns his emptiness.

One of the earliest and most striking instances of extra-Biblical Christian prophecy relates to the fall of Jerusalem in 70 AD. When the Romans took and sacked the city, there were apparently no Christians left in it. No doubt mindful of Jesus' own prophecies about the coming destruction of Jerusalem (Luke 21), but also commanded by a fresh prophecy, they had removed to a small town called Pella in Transjordan before the Jewish revolt started in 66. There they established the new headquarters of the Jewish Christian church in Palestine (Eusebius, *Ecclesiastical History* III.5.3).

In the second half of the second century there was a charismatic revival that swept through Asia Minor and affected places as far away as North Africa and Gaul (France). Either it ran into excess, as some historians tell us it did, or else the Church as a whole was no longer able to understand prophetic endowment well enough to receive it, but by the end of the century it had been condemned by the bishops and was driven from the Church. This movement was known by a variety of names, the most common being Montanism and Phrygianism, after its founder, a prophet called Montanus, and its place of origin, in Phrygia. Its condemnation heralded the birth of a new theology about the gifts of the Spirit, namely that they were given to the apostles to help them launch the Church, but that once it was well established they were no longer needed and so were withdrawn. Any such gifts today must therefore be counterfeit. This kind of thinking is commonly found today in certain evangelical and catholic circles, but it is not Biblical and is based on nothing but presupposition.

By the end of the third century we find some Christians writing as if they were no longer aware of the exercise of the gifts in the churches, though others still make occasional reference to them. To all intents and purposes Christianity had ceased to be charismatic. And so it has continued, with momentary interruptions when small groups or movements have briefly rediscovered the power of Pentecost, that is, until this century in which we have witnessed a phenomenal outburst of prophetic revival that has now embraced about a quarter or a third of all Christians.

Our 'Drama of Salvation' entered its fifth and final act when Jesus came on to the stage of world history, but that act is not yet over. The vision of its end has indeed been revealed and history is manifestly moving towards it. We may not be able to understand all that happens in our world today, but this much is clear, that God's prophetic word and his Spirit are as active as ever, and that again he is doing something new. And he never acts dramatically without first revealing his secret to his servants the prophets. We live in exciting times, but this is also a day when prophetical men need to discern his purposes afresh!

> *Therefore keep watch, because you do not know on what day your Lord will come. Even so, when you see these things happening, you know that the kingdom of God is near.*

(Matt.24.42 & Luke 21.31)

Chronology

The dates given to Biblical events here are often approximations, some of them open to a great deal of debate.

In the Old Testament, for example, some prefer to date the exodus in the fifteenth century, or place Joel in pre-exilic times. Dates for the kings of Israel and Judah are notoriously difficult to pin down.

In the New Testament there are also many problems. There are several views about dating Jesus' birth, the crucifixion can be placed any time between 29 and 33 AD, dates for Paul's life are subject to a lot of discussion, and so forth, but the discrepancies seldom amount to more than two or three years.

The dates used here are widely accepted ones and, despite the uncertainties, they provide a convenient framework for tracing the Bible stories. Fortunately, precise dating of Biblical events seldom affects our appreciation of spiritual truths much.

The dates given to extra-Biblical events are also generally open to discussion. Different scholars use different systems for the history of the second millennium BC, though the discrepancies are seldom much more than 10 or 20 years either way. Dating becomes more precise the nearer we approach Christian times, though plenty of uncertainties remain.

THE SECOND MILLENNIUM BC

.	PALESTINE	EGYPT	MESOPOTAMIA
3000		26–25th c.: The Pyramids	Sumerian City States 2360–2180: Empire of Akkad
2000	The Patriarchs		Fall of Ur 1950 Rise of City States: Mari, Babylon, etc. Emergence of Assyria
1720	Hebrews go down to Egypt	Hyksos ('Foreign Kings') come to power.	
1570		Hyksos expelled	Ascendancy of Assyria
1400		1400–1350: Amarna Period	
1290		1290–24: Rameses II	
	The Exodus The Conquest		
1224	The Judges Philistines settle	1224–11 Merniptah – battles with Sea Peoples 1183–52 Rameses III – battles with Sea Peoples	[Fall of the Hittite Empire]
1100	Fall of Shiloh Samuel	End of Egyptian Empire	Period of weakness
1050	Saul		in
1010	David		Mesopotamia

THE DIVIDED KINGDOM

	JUDAH	ISRAEL	INTERNATIONAL
970	Solomon		
931	Rehoboam 931–14 Abijah 914–11 Asa 911–870	Jeroboam I 931–10	
900		Nadab 910–09 Baasha 909–886	Expansion of Assyria begins
	Jehoshaphat 870–48	Elah 886–85 Omri 885–74 Ahab 874–53 *Elijah* Ahaziah 853–52	Assyrian advance halted at Qarqar 853
850	Jehoram 848–41 Ahaziah 841 (Athaliah 841–35) Joash 835–796	Jehoram 852–41 *Elisha* Jehu 841–14	Jehu pays tribute to Shalmaneser III 841
800	Amaziah 796–67 Uzziah 767–42	Jehoahaz 814–798 Jehoash 798–82 Jeroboam II 782–53 *Amos* Zechariah 753–52 Shallum 752	
750	*Isaiah* Jotham 742–35 *Micah* Ahaz 735–15	Menahem 752–42 *Hosea* Pekahiah 742–40 Pekah 740–32 Hoshea 732–22 _____722	Tiglath-pileser III takes Damascus 732 Sargon II deports the people of Samaria 722
700	Hezekiah 715–687 Manasseh 687–42		Sennacherib beseiges Jerusalem 701
650	Amon 642–40 Josiah 640–09 *Jeremiah* *Zephaniah* *Nahum* *Habakkuk*		Rise of Babylon Fall of Nineveh 612

| 600 | Jehoahaz 609
Jehoiakim
  609–597

Jehoiachin 597

Zedekiah 597–87
  Ezekiel
  _____587 | | Nebuchadnezzar
takes
Jerusalem 597 |
| 550 | *Obadiah*
Isaiah 40–55 | | |

THE POST-EXILIC PERIOD

	PALESTINE	INTERNATIONAL
	THE PERSIAN PERIOD	
539		Cyrus takes Babylon
538		Cyrus' Edict allows exiles to return
537	Exiles start to return and Sheshbazzar is made Governor	
535(?)	Zerubbabel is appointed Governor	
520–15	The Temple is rebuilt ***Haggai & Zechariah***	
522–486		Darius I
486–465	*Joel* ?	Xerxes I
465–424	*Malachi*	Artaxerxes I
458	Ezra arrives with more exiles	
445	Nehemiah is made Governor	
423		Xerxes II
423–404		Darius II
404–358		Artaxerxes II
	THE GREEK PERIOD	
336–323		Alexander the Great conquers and establishes his Greek Empire
323		After his death, the Empire is divided between his generals

	Palestine is taken under the rule of the Egyptian Ptolemies	
200	The Seleucids take Palestine	
		Antiochus IV Epiphanes (175–63)
168	The Temple is profaned and the Maccabean Revolt begins	
164	The Temple is rededicated and Judas Maccabeus establishes the Hasmonean Dynasty	

	THE ROMAN PERIOD	
63	Pompey takes Jerusalem	
39–4	Herod the Great rules Palestine	
27		Augustus Emperor (– 14 AD)
5	Birth of Jesus Christ	
4	Palestine divided between Herod's sons: Archelaus (Judea & Samaria), Herod Antipas (Galilee & Perea) Philip (Iturea & Traconitis)	

THE EARLY CHURCH

	BIBLICAL		IMPERIAL
27	Jesus begins his ministry	14–37	Tiberius Emperor
30/31	The Crucifixion	26–36	Pilate Procurator of Judea
35	Paul's Conversion		
38	Paul visits Jerusalem	37–41	Gaius (Caligula) Emperor
38–45	Paul in Syria and Cilicia	41–54	Claudius Emperor
43	Herod's Persecution (Ac. 12)	41–44	Herod Agrippa I, King of Judea
45	Paul & Barnabas in Antioch		

	BIBLICAL		IMPERIAL
45–46	Famine relief taken to Jerusalem		
46–47	First Missionary Journey		
48	Jerusalem Conference *Galatians?*		
48–51	Second Missionary Journey *1 & 2 Thessalonians*	49	Claudius expels Jews from Rome
51–53	Paul back in Antioch	51–52	Gallio Proconsul of Achaia
	Galatians?	52–60	Felix Procurator of Judea
53–59	Third Missionary Journey *1 & 2 Corinthians* *Romans*	53–90	Agrippa II, King of Northern Palestine
		54–68	Nero Emperor
59	Paul arrested in Jerusalem		
59–61	Paul held at Caesarea		
61	Paul sails for Rome	60–62	Festus Procurator of Judea
62–64	Paul held in Rome *Philippians* *Colossians* *Philemon* *Ephesians*		
64–67	Paul freed & goes to Spain? *Mark's Gospel* Paul returns to Asia? *1 & 2 Timothy* and *Titus*	64	Neronian persecution
67	Paul & Peter martyred in Rome? Jerusalem Church moves to Pella *Matthew* and *Luke-Acts?*		
70	Fall of Jerusalem	70–79	Vespasian Emperor
74	Fall of Masada		
		81–96	Domitian Emperor
95	*Revelation* Clement of Rome's letters *To the Corinthians*	95	Domitian's persecution
95+	*John's Gospel* and *Epistles*		

Glossary and Index

(REFERENCES TO MAPS ARE IN ITALICS)

People

Places

Theological & Historical Titles & Themes

Summary Outline and Reading Guide

The following pages serve a double purpose:
1. They show at a glance the contents of the main Biblical books covered in this volume.
2. They divide these books up in such a way that reading them can be spread evenly over a period of about six months.

As you read your Bible, keep your mind open to hear what the Holy Spirit has to tell you. Allow him to speak to you personally through its pages.

Watch carefully for what God does and says, and for how the men of Old and New Testament times respond to him, because that is what the Way of the Spirit is all about.

And don't forget to keep asking yourself what lessons you should be learning from their experience, so that you can apply them to your own life as a Christian.

(The reading scheme outlined here forms the basis of the home study course advertised on p. 270.)

Week 1

The Birth of Prophecy in Israel
Gen. 12: God's word of promise revealed to Abraham.
Exod. 20: God's word of command revealed to Moses.
Deut. 30: Disobedience and the possibility of repentance.
Josh. 24: Faith in God's word is vindicated.
Judg. 2.1 – 3.6: Spiral of decline and deliverance.
Judg. 19–21: Plunge into anarchy.
Deut. 18.14–22: The prophets' vocation.
Num. 22–24: A prophet of the nations.

Week 2

Israel's First Prophetic Movement and Revival (1 Samuel)
Chs. 1–2: Samuel's infancy and youth.
Chs. 3–4: His call to be a prophet and the fall of Shiloh.
Chs. 7–8: Revival breaks out.
Chs. 9–10: Israel is given a prophet-king.
Chs: 11–12: Saul's coronation and first faith challenge.
Chs. 15–16; 19.18–24: Samuel, Saul, David, the prophets and the Spirit.
2 Sam. 7 & 11–12: God's promise to David and his rebuke.

Week 3

Elijah, Elisha and the Sons of the Prophets (1 Kings 17 – 2 Kings 13)
1 Kings 11.26–40; 12.21–24; 13.1–10; 14.1–18; 16.1–7: Elijah's
  forerunners in the tenth century.
1 Kings 17–19: Elijah and the start of a second wave of revival.
1 Kings 20–21; 2 Kings 1: The prophetic voice increases and grows in
  confidence.
2 Kings 2–5: Elisha and the 'Sons of the Prophets'.
2 Kings 6–8: Elisha's charismatic ministry continues.
2 Kings 9–10; 13.10–21: The overthrow of Baalism and the end of Elisha's
  ministry.
1 Kings 13 & 22: The problem of true and false prophecy.

Week 4

Warnings of Approaching Judgment (Amos and Hosea)
Amos 1–2: Judgment on the nations and on Israel.
Amos 3–5: Look at your record and repent!
Amos 6–8: The relentlessness of coming judgment.
Amos 9: The judgment and beyond.
Hos. 1–3: Hosea's prophetic marriage.
Hos. 4: The main reasons for God's disgust.
Hos. 5–7: An extended plea for repentance.

Week 5

God's Anger and his Compassion (Hosea and Micah)
Hos. 8–10: The consequences Israel can expect as the result of her sin.
Hos. 11: A Father's love for his son.
Hos. 12–14: A final plea for repentance.
Mic. 1: God's judgment on Samaria and Jerusalem.
Mic. 2–3: Greedy leaders and false prophets.
Mic. 4–5: 'Now' and 'in the last days'.
Mic. 6–7 God's compassion and Israel's ingratitude.

Week 6

The Challenge of Holiness and Faith (Isaiah 1–12)
Chs. 1–2: Seek justice.
3.1 – 4.1 & Ch. 5: God's verdict on Jerusalem.
Ch. 6: The Holy One of Israel and the Holy Remnant.
Chs. 7–8: Faith in a crisis.
Chs. 9.8 – 10.34: Assyria and Jerusalem.
Chs. 4.2–6; 9.1–7; 11.1–9: The Age of Messiah (cp. 32.1–8).
Ch. 12: In that day you will praise the LORD.

Week 7

The Whole World as God's Kingdom (Isaiah 13–27)
13.1 – 14.23: Against Babylon.
14.24 – 16.13: Against Assyria, Philistia and Moab.
Chs. 17–18: Against Damascus and Cush.
Chs. 19–21: Against Egypt, Cush, Babylon, Edom and Arabia.
Chs. 22–23: Concerning Jerusalem and Tyre.
Chs. 24–25: On the day of God's end-time visitation.
Chs. 26–27: The final gathering of God's people.

Week 8

The Testing of Faith in a Crisis (Isaiah 28–39)
Chs. 28–29: Woe to the city of David.
Chs. 30–31: Trust in the LORD alone.
Chs. 32–33: The coming of God's new kingdom.
Chs. 34–35: Judgment and redemption.
Chs. 36–37: The deliverance of Jerusalem.
Chs. 38–39: And the Davidic King – did he learn faith?

Week 9

A Call for Repentance and a Change of Heart (Jeremiah 1–13)
Ch. 1: Jeremiah is called to be a prophet.
Chs. 2–4: Return to the LORD.
Chs. 5–6: Take heed before it is too late.
Chs. 7 & 26: Jeremiah's 'Temple Sermon': Your religion is corrupt and will not save you.
Chs. 8–10: No-one repents of his wickedness.
11.1 – 12.4: Jeremiah begins to learn the cost of prophetic ministry.
12.5 – 13.27: The LORD sends him back to prophesying.

Week 10

Confrontations (Jeremiah 14–29)
Chs. 14–15: Jeremiah's second experience of persecution.
Chs. 16–17: God spells out the challenge to Jeremiah.
Ch. 18: At the potter's house.
Chs. 19–20: In the stocks.
21.1 – 23.8: On the future of the David's line.
23.9 – 25.38: On false prophetic views about the future.
Chs. 26–27: Jeremiah's prophetic word on trial.
Chs. 28–29: Prophet against prophet.

Week 11

Jeremiah's Passion and Near-Martyrdom (Jeremiah 30–52)
Chs. 30–31: Visions of restoration and the future beyond.
Chs. 32–33: Promises of restoration.
Ch. 34: Jerusalem's faithlessness even at the end.
Chs. 35–36: How will Zedekiah respond to the prophetic word?
Chs. 37–39: The prophetic word is rejected and Jerusalem falls.
40.1 – 41.15: Gedeliah's community at Mizpah.
41.16 – 44.30: Jeremiah in Egypt.
Ch. 45: A disciple's lot!

Week 12

God's Plan for Israel and the Nations (Zephaniah, Nahum, Obadiah, Habakkuk)
Zeph. 1.1 – 2.3: The day of the LORD is near.
Zeph. 2.4 – 3.20: Judgment and beyond.
Nah. 1: His way is in the whirlwind and the storm.
Nah. 2–3: The judgment on Nineveh.
Obadiah: As you have done, it will be done to you.
Hab. 1–2: The righteous will live by his faith.
Hab. 3: Yet I will rejoice in the LORD.

Week 13

God's Glory and Jerusalem's Faithlessness (Ezekiel 1–16)
Ch. 1: Ezekiel's vision of the Glory of God.
Chs. 2–3: Ezekiel receives his call.
Chs. 4–7: Dramatic prophecies of Jerusalem's fate.
Chs. 8–9: Idolatry in the temple.
Chs. 10–11: God's Glory leaves Jerusalem.
Ch. 12: Ezekiel dramatically prophesies the exile.
Chs. 13–14: He condemns false prophets and calls the elders to repent.
Chs. 15–16: Jerusalem is a useless vine, an unfaithful bride.

Week 14

God's Judgment on Jerusalem and the Nations (Ezekiel 17–32)
Chs. 17–18: The LORD's planting and individual responsibility.
Chs. 19–20: A lament and a historical survey.
Ch. 21: Babylon is to be the instrument of God's judgment.
Chs. 22–3: The totality of Jerusalem's sin; Oholah and Oholibah.
Ch. 24: The turning point.
Chs. 25–28: Prophecies concerning foreign nations.
Chs. 29–32: More prophecies concerning foreign nations.

Week 15

The Restored Community and the New Jerusalem (Ezekiel 33–48)
Ch. 33: Ezekiel's new appointment and the fall of Jerusalem.
Chs. 34–35: God's purpose to shepherd and protect his people.
Chs. 36–37: The LORD's plans for Israel's future.
Chs. 38–39: The LORD's plan for the future of the nations.
Chs. 40–42: The plan of the new temple.
Chs. 43–46: The temple springs to life.
Chs. 47–48: The overflow from the temple into the land.

Week 16

Preparing the Way for the Lord (Isaiah 40–55)
Chs. 40–41: Comfort my people! Say, 'Here is your God!'
Chs. 42–43: Israel is to be a light to the nations.
Chs. 44–45: I am the LORD, and I say Jerusalem will be rebuilt.
Chs. 46–47: I am the LORD and there is no god besides me.
Chs. 48–50: From now on I tell you new things.
Chs. 51–52: Awake! Depart! Proclaim, 'Your God reigns!'
52.13 – 53.12: The LORD's Servant.
Chs. 54–55: Zion's Future Glory.

Week 17

Restoring Vision and Purpose (Haggai and Zechariah)
Haggai: Work, for I am with you.
Zech. 1–2: First to third visions of restoration.
Zech. 3–4: Fourth and fifth visions.
Zech. 5–6: Sixth to ninth visions.
Zech. 7–8: A call to live in repentance and the vision of blessing.
Zech. 9–11: The times of Messiah.
Zech. 12–14: The times of the end.

Week 18

Final Preparation for the LORD's Coming (Isaiah 56–66, Joel, Malachi)
Isa. 56–59: The prophet calls for repentance again.
Isa. 60–62: He reaffirms the vision of Zion's future glory.
Isa. 63–64: He prays for God to come and fulfil the vision.
Isa. 65–66: God answers that the punishment will give way to glory.
Joel: I will pour out my Spirit.
Mal. 1.1 – 2.16: Why do you break faith?
Mal. 2.17 – 4.6: Suddenly the LORD will come.

Week 19

Jesus and the Rebirth of Prophecy (Luke 1–12)
Chs. 1–2: First stirrings of the prophetic Spirit.
Chs. 3–4: Jesus is attested as a prophet of the Lord.
Chs. 5–6: Forming the team and first teaching.
Ch. 7: Is he a prophet? 'Are you the one?'
Chs. 8–9: Ministry training and revelation.
Ch. 10: The ways of Kingdom mission.
Ch. 11: The ways of the Spirit, of sin and of religion.
Ch. 12: Right attitudes for the last days.

Week 20

The Challenge and Culmination of the Prophet's Ministry (Luke 13–24)
Ch. 13: Repent or perish.
Chs. 14–15: Care for the poor, love the lost.
Chs. 16–17: The day has arrived, come now with repentance and faith.
Chs. 18–19: To Jericho and then to Jerusalem.
Chs. 20–21: Jesus' final challenge.
Chs. 22–23: The Prophet's last hours.
Ch. 24: Final preparation of the prophet team.

Week 21

Growth of the Christian Prophetic Movement (Acts and Corinthians)
Acts 2 & 19.1–7: 'I will pour out my Spirit and they will prophesy.'
Acts 3–4: Peter and John's miracle and their boldness.
Acts 6–7: Stephen's dynamic witness and martyrdom.
Acts 8–9: Philip, Paul and Peter.
Acts 10–11: Peter with Cornelius and Barnabas at Antioch.
1 Cor. 2 and 2 Cor. 3: The general prophetic endowment.
1 Cor. 12–14: The gift of prophecy.

Week 22

The Final Prophetic Vision of History Now and to Come (Revelation 1–11)
Ch. 1: John tells of his vision of Jesus.
Chs. 2–3: The prophetic message to the Church.
Ch. 4: John enters God's throne-room in Heaven.
Ch. 5: The Lamb receives a scroll from God's hand.
Ch. 6: The Lamb begins to open the seals on the scroll.
Ch. 7: John is granted refreshing views of heaven again.
Chs. 8–9: The seventh seal and the sounding of seven trumpets.
Chs. 10–11: Christian prophetic witness before the end.

Week 23

The Last Battle and the End (Revelation 12–22)
Chs. 12–13: Satan is thrown out of heaven and summons the beast.
Ch. 14: John is shown the forces of heaven ranged against the beast.
Chs. 15–16: The seven angels with the seven bowls of God's wrath.
Ch. 17: The beast's identity is revealed.
Chs. 18–19: Babylon's fall and the victory procession of heaven.
Ch. 20: The Millennium and the last judgment.
Chs. 21–22: The new heaven and new earth, and the new Jerusalem.

Tapes and Work Sheets

A Bible Reading Course for Home Study

THE WAY OF THE SPIRIT

A Bible Reading Course

Part 3: HEIRS OF THE PROPHETS

The present book can be used as the working manual for a complete six-month home study course suitable for use by groups or individuals.

The additional materials available are: a folder of weekly work sheets and a set of six tapes, each with four 20-minute talks relating to the week's reading. Assistance by correspondence can also be arranged if required.

For details of this and other courses, please write to: The Way of the Spirit, Roffey Place Christian Training Centre, Faygate, Horsham, West Sussex RH12 4SA.

Also available
Booklets explaining the Holy Spirit dynamic in various aspects of faith and parts of the Bible.
Write for details.